Innovation in Real Places

Innovation in Real Places

Strategies for Prosperity in an Unforgiving World

DAN BREZNITZ

OXFORD
UNIVERSITY PRESS

OXFORD
UNIVERSITY PRESS

Oxford University Press is a department of the University of Oxford. It furthers
the University's objective of excellence in research, scholarship, and education
by publishing worldwide. Oxford is a registered trade mark of Oxford University
Press in the UK and certain other countries.

Published in the United States of America by Oxford University Press
198 Madison Avenue, New York, NY 10016, United States of America.

© Oxford University Press 2021

First issued as an Oxford University Press paperback, 2023

Library of Congress Cataloging-in-Publication Data
Names: Breznitz, Dan, author.
Title: Innovation in real places : strategies for prosperity in an
unforgiving world / Dan Breznitz.
Description: New York, NY : Oxford University Press, [2021] |
Includes bibliographical references and index. |
Identifiers: LCCN 2020050294 (print) | LCCN 2020050295 (ebook) |
ISBN 9780197508114 (hardback) | ISBN 9780197695173 (paperback) |
ISBN 9780197508138 (epub) | ISBN 9780197508145
Subjects: LCSH: Technological innovations—Economic aspects. |
Technological innovations—Government policy. |
Industrial capacity—Economic aspects. | Industrial policy. |
Community development. | Economic development. | Globalization.
Classification: LCC HC79.T4 B695 2021 (print) | LCC HC79.T4 (ebook) |
DDC 338.9—dc23
LC record available at https://lccn.loc.gov/2020050294
LC ebook record available at https://lccn.loc.gov/2020050295

DOI: 10.1093/oso/9780197508114.001.0001

Paperback printed by Marquis, Canada

To Shiri: two kids, three decades, four continents, and I still dream of you.

Contents

Acknowledgments

This book took me the longest to write, by far. This experience also taught me a very valuable lesson: it is one thing to conduct research and write it for scientists, and a completely different task to explain what it means to daily life. As a result, I developed a whole new appreciation for scholars who not only try to think about the implications of their research, but also go on to write about them in a way everyone can relate to.

This book is also a diary of a very long journey of studying, researching, and being involved in the development of, and experimentation in, innovation policies. This was not a journey I took alone. Accordingly, this book could not have been written without the many friends who shared this road with me. Many a time they had to save me from getting lost; always, though, they shared with me insights and beautiful examples of human ingenuity I would have never known otherwise.

Standing tall among them are Amos Zehavi, who literally traveled with me over three continents and also shared the very painful experience of being PhD students together so many years ago that we both find it difficult to count them. Further, after all of that, he very patiently waited for me to (finally, with great delay) finish this book, so we can also finish our joint one. Michael Murphree, who started as my student, turned into an employee and then back to being my student, before transitioning into a partner in crime, all the while being an amazing friend. Without you I would have never gotten to know China and walked so many of its alleys. John Zysman, who for no apparent good reason took me under his wing at Berkeley when, as a young stressed-out freshly minted PhD, I spent a year in what he calls the Junior College on the peninsula. Since those early days of 2006, we have worked so closely together on so many projects that I lost count. Martin Kenney, with whom I have been constantly sharing ideas as they evolve and form in our minds. Darius Ornston, a friend, a colleague, and a shy genius, with whom I have been writing what I think are some of my best papers (the same ones he probably views as, at best, reasonable drafts). Zak Taylor, who, like Amos, should be thanked, if only because he still talks to me even after knowing me since we were all PhD students, but much more so for our valuable and constant brainstorming, and the fact that he somehow kept me sane in Atlanta. Aldo Geuna, for friendship, arranging the opportunity to spend first a year and then many more months throughout the years in Turin, and many intellectual endeavors since. Giulio Buciuni, for showing me the amazing stories of innovation in northeastern Italy, and for far too many craft beers (yes Giulio, unlike coffee, red wine, whiskey, and Armagnac, there is such a thing as too many beers). Gilles Rabin has opened my eyes to the many facets of innovation in France and Europe, giving me companionship along the road. Thanks to you, my friend, I now go and explore the main public transportation terminals in every city I visit around the world. In Finland, Petri Rouvinen gave me a crash course in Finnish innovation and economic policies, while introducing me to everyone, everywhere. Serving with you on the committee to evaluate the Finnish Innovation System was one of the most valued educational and public service experiences of my life. More importantly, however, was your help in fulfilling my childhood dream, and hooking my children up to the best stories in the world—the Moomins.

In the fair city of Atlanta, Georgia Tech has been a wonderful home for eight years, shaping me as a scholar and letting me wonder wider and wilder than many other universities would allow young assistant professors. I will forever be grateful to William Long and Diana Hicks for their instrumental role in bringing me there, and the many friends in the Sam Nunn School and the School of Public Policy who made it a home for the first five years. Special thanks are owed to Kirk Bowman, who taught me how to think outside the box. I'm looking forward to many more opportunities to do so together in all of the Americas, and to Brian Woodall, Sy Goodman, Adam Stulberg, and Michael Best for making us feel at home and making the Sam Nunn School such an interesting place to be. Doug Noonan, Hans Klein, John Walsh, Phil Shapira (in both Atlanta and Manchester, UK), Aaron Levine, and last, out-smiling them all, Paul Baker did the same in the School of Public Policy, demonstrating that friendly intellectual competition does wonders for everybody involved.

Jerry and Marie Thursby hold a special place of honor, together with the strategy group they built and ran at the Scheller College of Business at Georgia Tech. The intellectual vibrancy and camaraderie I enjoyed during my three years there were second to none. I still miss our weekly seminars. If you ever get bored with retirement, you are always welcome to come to Toronto for a week, a month, or a few years. In the strategy groups, having daily discussions with Matt Higgins, Alex Oettl, Marco Ceccagnoli, and

Annamaria Conti defiantly shaped my thinking. Just as important were the interactions with PhD students in all three schools, especially Vincenzo Palermo. Stu Graham should be thanked for giving me his office while he was seconded as the very first Chief Economist of the US Patent Office. Last, but certainly not least, having Chris Forman around the corner to work with was an immense pleasure, which continues even after we both moved North.

Georgia Tech is also a magical place for the many activities it does in economic development throughout the state, led by truly exceptional people. The amount of help in developing, and experimenting with what can only be called whacky innovation policy ideas is a unique experience I am not sure many other assistant professors have anywhere else in the world. Standing tall among them are Robert Lann, Stephen Fleming, and Greg Laudeman. Being able to call Stephen Cross a friend, mentor, and my VP Research all at the same time was both a true honor and enormous help. I will forever be in debt to Georgia Tech and its people; it is a blessing to call so many of them friends.

Janice Stein and Joe Wong are both good friends and scholars, but here they should be thanked for orchestrating our move to Toronto. Once we arrived, Ron Levi, Mark Manger, Randall Hansen, Sarah Namer, and the magical Margaret McKone helped us feel at home. At the Munk School, the thrill of working together with David Wolfe in expanding and co-directing the Innovation Policy Lab (IPL) has been a true intellectual joy. David's leadership of The Social Sciences and Humanities Research Council (SSHRC) collaborative project on creating digital opportunities served as the best platform one can have as an introduction to and embeddedness into Canadian public policy. At the IPL I had the unique fortune to meet Peter Warrian, who soon became a friend on the road both physically and intellectually in multiple continents of soil and spirit. Co-directing the IPL also allowed me to get back in touch with another former MITer, Dan Munro, who has since made sure I consider ethics when I think about innovation and growth. The members of the IPL, including our post-docs throughout the years, helped me to transit the focus of my research to explore more deeply the societal outcomes of innovation. Steven Samford not only turned into a partner for the road, but into a good friend as well. All my post-docs from now on will have to live in your shadow. Kristen Pue was a star PhD student and an invaluable research assistant. Nicolas Conserva did heroic work on the history of Cleveland. Alix Jansen and Prashant Rayaprolu did the same on the question of workers and skills, with Prashant being sent as an advance scout every time I had a new idea. In the final stages, as I was gasping without breath, Reuben Aboye calmly stepped in and masterfully took all the dispersed data collected, arranged it, and ... suddenly it made sense. Also, once in Canada, interactions with The Centre for International Governance Innovation (CIGI), under the tutelage of my friend Rohinton P. Medhora, kept me engaged, enraged, and sharp on the issues of innovation and growth. The third part of this book owes a lot to those interactions.

As I transitioned to thinking more and more about distribution and innovation, and not just growth and profits, my dear friend and mentor Peter Cowhey at UC San Diego asked me to join him in organizing an eye-opening project on innovation and production in the United States. We could not have done it without the Connect Innovation Institute under the leadership of the late Duane Roth and the very much alive and active Mary Walshock. Here I had the immeasurable opportunity to work together with Susan Helper, William Lazonick, Erica Fuchs, Josh Whitford, Elisabeth Reynolds, and Jenny Kuan, and to collaborate in disseminating our findings with Mark Muro, Howard Wial, and Bruce Katz. Luckily for me, at the exact same time my main mentor and dear friend at MIT, Suzanne Berger, was also working on the same issues. Thus, I just sat at the perfect structural hole gobbling up knowledge for two years. Thanks to Suzanne, I was also introduced to William Bonvillian, who urged me to continue with this line of work whenever I faltered.

All of this came together when the impressive, resolute, and tenacious Rachel Parker convinced me to organize a scholarly network to think about the questions of innovation, equity, and the future of prosperity, and apply to the Canadian Institute for Advanced Research (CIFAR)'s global competition. Feeling emboldened with Susan Helper and Amos Zehavi at my side, we did. After which the (far smarter than I) fellows and advisers of the Innovation, Equity and the Future of Prosperity (IEP) network became the perfect invisible college.

Some of the most important people for this book, many of them now friends, work in numerous innovation agencies and development banks across the world. Without them this book would never have been written, and my life would have been a pale, uninteresting shadow of itself. Many of them prefer to stay anonymous, but of those that do not, special thanks are owed to Yevgeny Kuznetsov at the World Bank; Alexander Lehmann at the European Bank for Reconstruction and Development (now at Bruegel); Claudia Suaznabar, Pablo Angelelli, and Facundo Luna of the Inter-American

Development Bank; and Kirsten Bound and Alex Glennie of Nesta, UK. In Chile, Pablo Catalan was a friend and a wise guide, in both Concepción and Santiago, and the people of Corporación de Fomento de la Producción de Chile (CORFO) and its many programs were a constant source of information and ideas. In Panama, Victor Sánchez of SENACYT has become our wise and gentle friend, protector, and partner in designing innovation policies. Here also, Julio Escobar, Eli Faskha, and the people of CAPTEC formed an amazing team of friends, thinkers, and doers to work with. Taiwan is filled with friends; of them, Otto Lin was especially helpful (also in Hong Kong and China). In Argentina, Miguel Lengyel was instrumental in introducing me to doing innovation policies in times of (repeated) national turmoil. In China, there are hundreds of people to thank, the most courageous of whom has been Xielin Liu of the Chinese Academy of Science. In Poland, my friend Andrzej Sławiński was the perfect host, and under his directorship the research unit of the national bank was a home away from home. In Canada, the list of amazing civil servants I need to thank is too long to fit in one book; it is also not clear to me that they wish their names to appear in this book. Hence for all of you in the Ontario, Newfoundland, and Labrador, Alberta, Quebec, and the federal public and civil service (IRAP included), especially CL and BK, keep on doing what you know should be done.

One of the most important experiences in helping me formulate this book was the advanced experimental and experiential MGA course I co-taught with different international innovation agencies at the Munk School. Over five years we immersed ourselves in the strategic concerns of some of those organizations, working with their directors on devising new policies on issues they always wanted to touch, but never had the time. In Ireland, Seán Coughlan, being the amazing person he is, agreed to make himself and the remarkable organization he co-founded, Social Entrepreneurs Ireland, be the first guinea pig for me and my MGA students. In Mexico, Ruy Cervantes, and the team of the Ministry of Science Technology and Innovation, proved invaluable as we expanded on this approach. In Israel, our partner was the Office of the Chief Scientist, just as it restructured itself during our three years of joint work in the Israeli Innovation Authority. Here Uri Gabai was our guardian angel, with Sagi Dagan playing the sage mentor and Aharon, the IIA's CEO, welcoming us in. Uri was also partner to many voyages to different countries, always trusting (one does wonder why) that he really should come with me to this out-of-the-way-place to interact with local innovation policymakers. The openness of those innovation agencies to working with

my students, and the impact the students' work had on those agencies policies, demonstrated the amazing potential of human resourcefulness. They
also demonstrated how those agencies are ahead of the curve and how fortunate I am to work in the Munk School and the University of Toronto, which
not only allows those educational experiments, but encourages them.

Then there is, and always will be, Cobalt. Seán Fran and Vivian Eyolfson
are the heroes here, when everything else failed, and when the computer just
refused to write this book for me, they took me up north, put me in their
house near Cobalt, and told me not to come back until I finished the first two
chapters. Since then I have found that all roads do lead to Cobalt. You should
go there yourself; there is no place in which to think like the Tri-Towns.
Go to Bass Lake to enjoy a day, or stroll down White Wood Avenue in New
Liskeard, and go for a coffee or board game in Chat Noir, after which have
a bite to eat in the Country Kitchen, and go talk to Tom as you buy the best
steaks and summer sausages in the world at Quality Meats. Just remember
they are Mennonites, so the store is open only on Friday and Saturday. Go to
Mowat Landing, rent a boat, and try to convince Trevor to sell you one of the
last copies of the Tri-City Monopoly edition. If even that does not help, then
rent a canoe and more from Smoothwater on Temagami Lake, and get lost in
crown land wilderness; if you are lucky and determined enough you will be
the only human you will see for two weeks.

There is also a gallant set of special people, without whom this book
would have never been written, since I would not have had the courage to
even start it. Daniel Isenberg was the first to set me down this road, after
reading my first two books and admonishing me for not writing in forms
and forums that can influence public debate. Dan also introduced me to the
marvelous Andrew O'Connell, editor supreme and a friend, who guided me
into the art of translating social science into writing for HBR and the educated public. Without knowing that Andy was on call, always willing to help
when my writing veered off course, I would have never started this book.
William and Weslie Janeway, through many talks, convinced me that there is
a need for such a book. When I dithered with uncertainty when they housed
me in Maine, Weslie just looked at me and said, "Why do you not just call it
the Little Beige Book of Innovation-Based Growth and start writing?" I sat
down and did just that. Also, in New York, David Adler, once he heard that
I was thinking about writing such a book, proved to be a good friend and
fellow traveler down the path of asking how all communities in America can
enjoy prosperity. I am not quite so sure I helped him find the answers he

was looking for, but he certainly helped me find some of the answers I was looking for. At a critical moment in writing this book, Dane Stangler, then still at the Kauffman Foundation, stepped in, told me this book should be written, and arranged the critical support I needed to keep going.

One of the best things that happened after our move to Canada was meeting Jim Balsillie and Neve Peric. Not only did they become good friends and mentors, but even more importantly they made sure that I never forgot the debt to the public that social scientists working in a public university have. This book would have never happened without Jim's constant (and surprisingly gentle) push and encouragement to find my public voice, and Neve's wise counsel on how to do it. May we share many bottles of wine together late into the night, in Paris, Toronto, or anywhere our paths take us my friends!

Dave McBride has been my heroic editor at Oxford University Press; he is everything an author can wish for. The team at OUP, led by Dave's assistant Holly Mitchell, is owed more thanks that there is space to put them. As the book went into production, Liz Davey, Peter Jaskowiak, Kathrin Unger and Bríd Nowlan made sure it was copy-edited, indexed, proofread, and reached production on time, even with me acting as the sand in their well-oiled machine.

I also wish to thank the financial (and moral) support of a number of organizations. First and foremost is the Kauffman Foundation, whose directors of policy research, first Dane and then Jason Wiens, not only supported this book at the most critical early point, but also had more patience then anyone should have as they shepherded me through the extremely long process of writing. At their side, Tammy Flores was my personal saint. The Lupina Foundation supplied much more then financial support and became a partner for the road as I wrote this book. The continued support of the Collegio Carlo Alberto, the Department of Economics and Statistics S. Cognetti de Martiis, and The Compagnia di San Paolo in Turin has been priceless. In Venice it was Università Ca' Foscari and my host Vladi Finotto who supported me for a crucial summer of research. I also gladly acknowledge the financial and scholarly support of the Canadian Friends of Tel Aviv University, where thanks for going over and above the call of duty are owed to Jonathan Hausman, the Brookfield Institute, the Munk School, and the Munk Chair of Innovation Studies.

Last, but certainly not least, thanks and gratitude are owed to my children Mika and Tom, not only for reminding me daily why I was writing this, but also for supporting me in doing this even when it meant that I was off to a random far-away part of the world. Best were the times when you joined me in those travels. Mika was also a diligent editor of parts of this book. Shiri, my wife and partner for the regular and scholarly world, this book is dedicated to you; as I said before, you are my dream.

Introduction

"Tell me something about yourself and the country you came from,"
said the Scarecrow, when she had finished her dinner. So she told
him all about Kansas, and how gray everything was there, and how
the cyclone had carried her to this queer Land of Oz.

The Scarecrow listened carefully, and said, "I cannot understand
why you should wish to leave this beautiful country and go back to
the dry, gray place you call Kansas."

"That is because you have no brains" answered the girl. "No
matter how dreary and gray our homes are, we people of flesh and
blood would rather live there than in any other country, be it ever so
beautiful. There is no place like home."

The Scarecrow sighed.

"Of course I cannot understand it," he said. "If your heads were
stuffed with straw, like mine, you would probably all live in the beautiful places, and then Kansas would have no people at all. It is fortunate for Kansas that you have brains."

—L. Frank Baum, *The Wonderful Wizard of Oz*

It took me too many years to write this book.

In the end I left everything and went up north to hide near a small lake
to disconnect from the world and start writing. I found myself near Cobalt,
Ontario, at a site that, coincidentally, reinforced my motivation for writing
about innovation and growth.

The discovery of rich silver deposits in 1903 created Cobalt overnight and
set off a mining boom. Between 1905 and 1914, millions of people—more
than the entire population of Canada at the time—traveled by train to Cobalt.
The town became ultra-rich. At its peak, Cobalt had several theaters and
some of the world's most impressive murals. Cobalt was, literally, Canada's
economy. But it all ended as quickly as it had started. Today Cobalt has barely

1,100 inhabitants, one grocery store, one pub, and one diner. The train does not stop in Cobalt anymore.

The mining rush affected more than just the town of Cobalt, though. It also transformed another small, sleepy Ontario town: Toronto. The silver boom needed sophisticated venture financing, a stock market, and a trading center, all of which took root on the Lake Ontario shore 300 miles to the south. The silver of Cobalt built Toronto's financial hub of Bay Street. That is the difference between a growth bubble based on the newest shiny thing and sustained development based on innovation and knowledge. Those who live by the bubble die by it; those who create knowledge have a chance to continue to prosper. Mining has moved on from Cobalt, but Toronto is still a global center for sophisticated financing.[1]

So the friendly, kind, smart people around Cobalt, as well as the abandoned mineshafts that dot the scenery of lakes, cliffs, and forests, formed an evocative backdrop as I wrote. They were a constant reminder of the risks of misguided development, and of the hope that underlies my efforts.

As I have watched communities struggle to generate sustained development through innovation-based growth, I have become convinced that it is my obligation, as a scholar who bridges economics and politics, to assemble the latest knowledge in the most accessible form possible so that it can be widely appreciated. This task became more urgent with the current COVID-19-induced economic crisis. We have a unique opportunity and an urgent need to rekindle sustained economic growth, as numerous communities are desperately looking for ways to gain sustained prosperity. My hope is that people from all walks of life—anyone who cares about their community—will use this book to gain a pragmatic understanding of the nature of innovation and growth. My dream is that this understanding will translate into better, more-far-reaching decisions, and, ultimately, that my own children will have a better future.

Where This Book Will Take You

This book is a journey—across history, countries, businesses, and into research, both mine and that of my colleagues. It is structured to provide answers to crucial questions about innovation-based growth: Which development path is best? How can communities follow through on their chosen routes and bring about change? How can public policies and institutions help (or hinder) communities reach the hoped-for results? How do crises such as COVID-19 and the recent political upheavals factor into the equation? Do they signal a moment of opportunity in which old battle lines are disrupted and fresh thinking can gain ground?

What this book does *not* do is offer cookbook-style recipes for growth. Such books do exist, of course. They purport to show how to create high-technology clusters wherever and whenever you want, if you just follow their five simple steps. These books are of questionable value. Apart from the impracticality of trying to follow simple steps in today's highly complex economic environment, the main problem with these books is that they rely on generally accepted views of innovation, which contain a number of myths.

One is that an eagerly ambitious region outside the established start-up hubs might have a reasonable shot at combining high-concept tech ideas with venture capital (VC) to become the "next Silicon Valley." Another is that beyond trying to become the next Silicon Valley, the growth choices are extremely limited. Both of these myths stem from an even more pervasive misconception: that innovation equals high-tech industries, new businesses, and/or new gadgets.

Innovation is not just the invention of new shiny things. If it was, it would have a feeble effect on economic growth and welfare. We should care about innovation, because it is the *only* way to ensure sustained long-term economic and human-welfare growth, not because it is new or cool.

So what is innovation?

Innovation is the complete process of taking new ideas and devising new or improved products and services. It comes in all stages from the first vision, design, development, production, sale, and usage, to the after-sale aspects of products and services. The true impact of innovation was not in the invention of the internal combustion engine, nor even the invention of the first automobile. The true impact of innovation is represented by the continuous stream of implementation of large and small inventions to make the car a better and cheaper product, to improve the way it is produced, and to continuously find ingenious ways to sell, market, and service cars. If innovation was invention, there would be no continued progress and growth in welfare. For example, without innovation, there would be no smartphones, since a phone would still be a very large wooden box with a rotating dial, and it would take about a minute to even attempt a call.

In technical terms, invention is the process of coming up with a truly novel idea, while innovation is the process of using ideas to offer new or improved products and services at the same factor cost. This is the reason why the most effective innovation agency in the world in the last half century, the Israeli Office of the Chief Scientist (now the Israel Innovation Authority, or IIA), had one clear and simple core mission statement: the maximization of private-sector R&D activities.

However, we now live in the world of fake news and misconceptions, and too many people and organizations make too much money by selling myths about innovation. We are going to find that the purveyors of these myths—the religious believers of techno-fetishism—have a feeble understanding of the big picture of global production and innovation. For example, they have not noticed—or will not tell you—that there is a significant obstacle to creating the next VC hub in Oklahoma or Ohio or Bouches-du-Rhone in France or Emilia-Romagna in Italy: namely, the overwhelming power of the *real* hubs, which siphon up vast amounts of talent and money.

The misconception-mongers also seem unaware of the research showing that promoting VC-backed high-tech startups can end up *widening* the gulf between rich and poor, and that a region can therefore waste a lot of time, money, and energy trying to improve its economic health by shopping for high-calorie, low-protein, and low-fiber start-ups. Those start-ups might indeed make their founders and funders rich, but they will not supply the wider employment and growth benefits that the regions seek. In todays' world of globally fragmented production and dominating high-tech clusters, not all boats are raised when high-tech start-ups succeed.

And as development efforts along these lines falter, citizens, funders, and elected officials become frustrated. Lack of growth sets off waves of gloom and depression. Weaknesses in demand and supply spur each other to ever-lower lows. Workers drop out of the job market. Hope that the future will be better for their children is lost, people call their elected officials bad names, and demagogic candidates with divisive, unproductive ideas find it easier and easier to seize people's imaginations. This dynamic is particularly problematic with regards to innovation. This is because innovation always has both winners and losers. Accordingly, as Mark Zachary Taylor has demonstrated in his excellent book *The Politics of Innovation*, societies that ensure that innovation's positive benefits are widely distributed, while its negative impacts are contained, continue to innovate and grow. On the other hand, those that do not do this fade into cycles of stagnation and poverty—even societies that once ruled the world.[2]

There Is More Than One Road to Rome

As we will see, the greatest opportunities for growth lie in communities' recognizing their own advantages, then fostering forms of specialized innovation that rely on those advantages.

The opportunities include raising the growth trajectories of existing small and medium-size enterprises, figuring out specific sets of activities within the global production networks that dominate our world, and attracting start-ups that are outside of information technologies and biotech, in fields as diverse as agro-tech and textiles.

At the same time, communities must encourage the development of public institutions to provide critical support, including fostering sources of what is known as "patient" capital, a set of "shared" assets that provide unique competitive advantages, and collaborative public spaces, where isolated businesses and individuals find ways to become part of cohesive ecosystems. Certain areas of the globe have become production powerhouses by following this approach.

We should also remember and be proud of what we, humanity, have achieved in the last few decades. Since the 1980s, as part of globalization, more people have been lifted out abject poverty then any time before, infant mortality is decreasing, and life expectancy is on the rise. Further, human welfare and the choices we have as consumers have never been so high, affordable, and rich. A smart girl in Africa, with a computer and an Internet connection, can take some of the best courses at the best universities. If for me, born in Jerusalem in 1970, MIT was a distant dream of a fabulous place that existed over the rainbow—a palace of knowledge I was finally allowed to join twenty-seven years later, and only by physically moving to Cambridge, Massachusetts—for hundreds of millions today it is just another website they use to get a great education while staying in their homes, tightly woven in their communities.

Overall, humanity has never had it so good.

I am aware, of course, that people live in well-defined communities, and that while they might cheer for other communities, their main concern is for their own. The good people of Alabama might very well feel proud about the innovations and economic achievements of New York City and Silicon Valley, and hardworking Manitobans might be brimming with delight over Toronto's growing stature in the world, and both might share a deep delight in the amazing wealth that has accompanied the rise of hundreds of millions of people out of poverty in China and India. Nevertheless, their actions and their disposition toward the future are firmly anchored in what happens in Manitoba and Alabama, perhaps even specifically in Dauphin or Huntsville.

Therefore, while this book is intended to appeal to people seeking a broad understanding of what makes the innovation-based world go round, it also focuses on micro-level behavior. It argues that the growth policy that truly matters to people will not be decided in Brussels, Beijing, or Washington, but on the ground, by people from both the public and private sectors who work together daily to ensure that their communities prosper. This book views the world from, and sympathizes with, the perspective of communities, looking at both the issues they face and the tools at their disposal.

The opportunities are long-term—I will be up front about that. In this book I do not put forth any solutions that could come to fruition next month or even next year. But the solutions are real and practical, and they can have a big impact. After all, economic growth is the goose that lays the golden eggs. When the economy is growing, people feel confident that their quality of life, as well as their children's quality of life, will improve, and consequently they make choices that lead to increases in both demand and supply, which in turn brings further growth. People's faith in government and business rises, and would-be demagogues remain at bay.

Cynicism Can Be Beautiful

Throughout this journey I will also provide a few other need-to-know economic details that can help in maximizing the chances of creating innovation-based growth.

These include the ugly facts about our broken intellectual-property (IP) system, which shows no signs of getting any less ugly or any less broken as countries and deep-pocketed interest groups squabble over patent rules, copyrights, trademarks, technology standards, trade secrets, and trade deals. In fact, this book will show how local leaders, working to benefit their communities, can strategize to "game" the IP system. It will also show how to utilize other gaps between economists' "efficient market" assumptions and the messy realities of human-made regulations. Purists and moralists may accuse me of being cynical in showing how growth can be optimized in specific contexts. As an academic, shouldn't I be illuminating the path toward a generalizable economic utopia where all of humanity can finally sit next to the campfire holding hands and singing Kumbaya?

My response comes back to my sense of obligation. Social science has accumulated a great deal of knowledge about economic growth. Academics, especially those of us working in public universities, have a duty to make this knowledge available to people seeking to understand the economic workings of the world. We also have a duty to offer tools that people of action can use to improve lives—even if that sometimes entails advising them to take advantage of flaws in the economic system.

As a hopeful cynic, I would also argue that putting the best minds to work figuring out the flaws is the best way to optimize complex systems. As a cynical political economist, I would also remark that there is nothing like a dosage of competition to shake comfortable oligopolies out of their stranglehold on power.

PART I
THE STATE OF INNOVATION

1

The New Globalization of Innovation

> The Scarecrow sat in the big throne and the others stood respect-
> fully before him. "We are not so unlucky," said the new ruler, "for
> this Palace and the Emerald City belong to us, and we can do just as
> we please. When I remember that a short time ago I was up on a pole
> in a farmer's cornfield, and that now I am the ruler of this beautiful
> City, I am quite satisfied with my lot."
>
> —L. Frank Baum, *The Wonderful Wizard of Oz*

Last spring I went with my children to buy new bicycles. We entered the store
to buy a product whose design, shape, and mechanics were finalized over a
hundred years ago. There is a diamond-shaped (or fancier but, in effect, still
diamond-shaped) frame, two wheels, pedals attached to a gear-controlled,
chain-operated power transmission system, and brakes. What innovation
can happen here? And why should anyone care?[1]

The answers are simple and powerful: a lot of innovation, and we should
care, because those innovations allowed two companies, one Japanese
and one Taiwanese, to completely transform the global bicycle industry,
enlarging the market by making bicycles a much more appealing and con-
venient transportation solution for all sections of society, and moving production, profits, and jobs to their local communities in Taiwan and Japan;
and away from Europe and the United States. That is the reason why innovation matters, and why we must not equate it only with the creation of new
"high" tech industries.

Look carefully at your bikes. The gears bear the name Shimano, and you
might not realize it, but if your bikes are both strong and light, chances
are that your frame (and maybe even the bike brand) is made by Giant
Manufacturing Company. Shimano is a Japanese company from Sakai City
in Osaka; Giant is a Taiwanese company based in Taichung. Neither of those
cities comes to mind as innovation superpowers, and yet both companies

innovated their way to global domination of the bicycle industry, each one of them coming at it from a completely different stage of production.

Further, as the COVID-19 crisis has powerfully demonstrated, Taiwan's and Japan's mastery of what this book will term the *third-stage innovation model* meant that they were much more resilient, and able to supply all their medical personal protection equipment (PPE) when needed, while America, with its mighty Silicon Valley stage 1 innovation model, needed to beg, coerce, and bribe its way to even the most simple products, such as N95 Masks and alcogel (hand sanitizer).

If there is something truly new in our supposedly new global economy, it is the global fragmentation of production. As production of goods and services fragments, and vertically integrated production—a system in which a product is manufactured from basic materials to a final product in one location—comes crashing down, new entry points for innovation-based growth have been opening in old and new industries—but only for places who know how to exploit them.

Shimano, founded in 1921, built upon an opening in the global bicycle component market following the upsurge in bicycle sales after the oil crisis of the 1970s. Since then it has focused on intense incremental innovation in the gear and power transmission systems, allowing it to dominate the global marketplace for bicycle components. Do not believe me, though. Simply go to a store and try to buy a bike without any Shimano components. I wish you luck. It is almost as difficult as buying a computer with no Intel or a mobile phone without Qualcomm or Samsung components.[2]

This is a lesson worth learning: when an industry moves to globally fragmented production, positions of power can be gained by innovating in key components and systems. You do not need to produce and innovate the complete product in order to enjoy the highest profit share of the final sale. Ask HP or Dell whether it is them or Samsung and Intel that enjoys the best profit margins when someone buys Dell or HP computers.[3]

Giant came to its market domination position in a different way, a path that shows the importance of public leadership to successful innovation-based growth. Giant was established in 1972 as a small bicycle manufacturer by a group of ten friends, led by King Liu, who had metalworking experience, and Tony Lo, who had international business experience. Giant's first breakthrough came when the leading American bicycle producer and seller of the time, Schwinn, started to use it as a supplier in 1976. By the 1980s, with Schwinn orders consisting of 75 percent of Giant's production, the company decided to hedge by starting its own bicycle brand, a move that served it well when, in 1985, Schwinn moved production to China (one of a series of questionable business decisions by Schwinn that led to its bankruptcy by 1992). The crisis triggered by Schwinn's decision to cut its ties with Giant also led Giant and the Taiwanese bicycle industry as a whole into a unique innovation trajectory that has been the basis of its growth ever since.[4]

In response to the crisis, Giant embarked on a joint project with Taiwan's premier public research organization, the Industrial Technology Research Institute (ITRI). ITRI, through its newly established Materials Research Laboratories, headed by Dr. Otto Lin—utilizing the same model that allowed it to kick-start and then support the growth of the Taiwanese semiconductor industry from inception to its rise as a global force— organized a series of joint R&D projects from 1985 onward with industry on advanced materials. Those projects allowed Giant to become the global leader in carbon-fiber bicycle frames, which enabled Giant to offer bicycles that were both stronger and lighter. Those lighter and stronger bikes allowed Giant to expand the appeal of bikes, first to women, and then to ignite and lead the global mountain-bike trend. This public-private R&D system continued to develop and become the backbone of the innovation machine that has enabled the Taiwanese bicycle industry to sustain its prosperity for the last four decades. This growth and prosperity—for example, Giant now has annual revenues of US$2 billion—was achieved in difficult and volatile global market conditions, with the American and European industry losing both the innovation lead and market share, and the Chinese and Indian industries becoming the hub for cheap, lower-quality bicycle manufacturing.[5]

What has happened here? Why, once we move to fragmented production, does the calculus of power and innovation change?

Welcome to the Jenga Game of Global Fragmentation

My kids love to play Jenga—I can always tell when they are at it because of the long, tense silence followed by shouts, and the sound of wooden blocks scattering on the floor. I wonder whether Leslie Scott, who developed Jenga from a game her family played in Ghana with wood from a local sawmill, is aware that she created an elegant metaphor for the evolving modern economy. The old production system of vertical integration was a Jenga tower that came tumbling down when companies learned to buy, instead of make, most of their inputs.

Although by then businesses and communities fully recognized that materials and components could be bought abroad more cheaply, they continued to view the corporation as an eternally local entity, with executives on one floor, designers on another, engineers on another, marketers on another, production facilities across the street, and salespeople fanning out in all directions from a central office.[6]

That view was being undermined by three transformations of our current age: the boom in information and communication technologies, aka "digitization"; advances in transportation of people and goods; and the political opening of global trade.

Digitization allowed companies to cut production into small well-defined stages and send precise manufacturing instructions for any component or system to any location on earth that offered an attractive balance of price and quality. Transportation advances, as well as supply-management technologies, made this process seamless and reliable. And the opening of trade and changing politics allowed the global system of production networks to grow and flourish.

Big tech companies weakened the old Jenga tower by outsourcing their manufacturing—Apple products are labeled "designed in California" (partly true) and "assembled in China" (mostly true); what the company does not bother to add is "and manufactured all over the place."

But the biggest blow came from the thousands of companies that realized they no longer needed to co-locate any of their operations. They saw that they could take advantage of cost savings and pockets of expertise by basing factories in China and South America, designers in Taiwan, engineers in Germany, sales in Ireland, and headquarters in New York. Or they could establish dual headquarters, one in London and one in Ohio.[7]

This is the world we are living in now. A world where both new and old American high-technology companies create almost no jobs in the United States, but instead create many millions of jobs elsewhere. A world where old "truisms" about how innovation translates to economic growth, where it happens, and who gains from it, are scattered on the floor like a crumbled Jenga tower. This is a world where having a General Motors (GM) assembly plant is not a recipe for economic growth, but a sure predictor of an economic decline. However, it is a world where companies, such as Giant and Shimano, can have a humble start in little-known places and grow to dominate the world as well as produce thousands of good jobs for their communities.

A world where communities can choose to excel in multiple forms of innovation. Those choices are real, and, hence, each has its own consequence for the community's economic well-being. In order to excel in specific stages, particular capacities need to be perfected, and not others, and this process needs to be done in tandem with global demands and opportunities that their public and private leaders need to understand and react to.

The World in Four Stages

In technical terms, I call the dynamics behind these processes of global production fragmentation "production-stage specialization and capability building," and "production-stage economies of scope and scale."[8]

What do these bland-sounding dynamic processes mean?

Once digitization and transportation technologies developed to make fragmentation—that is, the cutting of production into ever smaller discrete components and stages that can be done anywhere in the world and shipped to anywhere else—feasible, and the political climate changed to allow this to happen, companies started to specialize. We saw it in bikes, but it has been happening everywhere, from information and communication technologies (ICT) to textiles.

"Production-stage specialization" is the process by which product fragmentation leads companies to develop superior capabilities in particular stages or components of the product network. It is here that we can start to understand the strikingly different trajectories of innovation-based growth enjoyed by Israel and Taiwan.[9]

Have you ever heard about pure-play foundries?

Pure-play foundries, such as the Taiwanese TSMC and UMC, are semiconductor companies that specialize solely in chip fabrication, and whose revenues come from fabricating chips according to the designs of their customers. It was the development of these Taiwanese companies and the technologies that made their business model possible that completely changed the global semiconductor industry. The creation of pure-play foundries has allowed companies in places such as Silicon Valley or Israel to hire only high-end R&D engineers focusing solely on developing and designing new chips, knowing that there will be no need for massive capital investment and the hiring of thousands of workers to make them a reality. With TSMC and UMC, at the moment you finish designing the chip and send them the blueprints, their fabrication facilities in Taiwan can start producing it.[10]

Such specialization enables companies to become better and more efficient in this narrow set of activities. It also helps them to acquire specialized innovation capabilities and knowledge that more vertically integrated firms could not achieve. These capabilities, once acquired, enable these firms to excel in innovation around the particular production stages and set of components they focus on, using their superior skills and unique knowledge. Over time, these two related advantages, in skills and innovation capabilities, grant these companies even more advantages vis-à-vis in-house divisions of vertically integrated companies. We observe this process both in high-technology areas, as in the manufacturing of specialized components or chips (such as graphic cards or memory chips) and in the story of Shimano. They demonstrate that the same dynamics occur in all industries, old and new alike.[11]

"Production-stage economies of scale and scope" is the process by which, once a specific product fragments into discrete stages, suppliers in each stage, by pooling the demand of many customers, create economies of scope and scale that in-house manufacturing divisions cannot. This is the latest manifestation of the logic of economics of scope and scale, which make contract-manufacturing organizations (CMO) the silent kings that underpin global production. The reason is that economies of scope and scale enable CMOs to become more efficient and innovative in production, which allows them to profitably operate on margins that are significantly lower than those achieved by in-house manufacturing divisions. This in turn allows them to further lower their prices while offering the same or even higher-quality products, further speeding the trend toward outsourcing of this stage's manufacturing activities.[12]

We see this process in industries as high-tech as ICT and bio-pharma. This is why Foxconn produces all of Apple's new products, as well as those of practically every ICT and electronic brand-name company whose product you think you just bought. Foxconn (and other CMOs) relies on the Chinese ICT industry's unique abilities in ultra-mass-flexible production—the capacity to produce an array of products in the same place and on the same production lines, constantly changing between them, and ramping production up and down as needed. These abilities have made China into a critically important part of the global ICT industry.[13]

However, this is also the case in low-tech industries such as textiles and apparel. You probably never heard about William and Victor Fung, but you wear their clothes, even if you are completely unaware of that fact. The same goes for your shoes. Take your shoes out of the closet, look at the most expensive brands and tell yourself loudly and proudly: "I own Stella International

Holding Limited shoes." I know it is so much more ego-lifting to say you owe Rockport, ECCO, Givenchy, or Prada, but you owe the truth to yourself.

The same is true for services. Much of India's rapid economic growth is based on its rise to prominence as a software and outsourced-services hub. An example of well-honed expertise in services development is the Indian IT-consulting industry. Tata, Wipro, and HCL have become, by far, the most efficient such firms in the world, basing their competitive position on unique capabilities and tools they developed in project management. In essence these companies developed four critical capabilities: (1) system analysis—the ability to take the ambiguous reality and transform it into a well-defined system of routines (algorithms) that can then be programmed; (2) ever-expanding and improved libraries of reusable code that can be recombined to deliver reliable software solutions to almost every imaginable programming task; (3) project management techniques that enable the programming teams to increase from a few people to several thousand and back down again efficiently and rapidly as needs change; and (4) training programs that create an efficient labor force where workers share the same knowledge and language and can work together on multiple projects without long lead times.[14]

As a consequence, when you buy high-end audio systems or cars, or use online banking, you are the proud user of Indian software, and when you call the support center, you enjoy their services again, even if you speak to a person sitting in North America or Europe.

We live in a world where the production of *both* goods and services is now typically fragmented into stages and carried out in different locations. The fragmentation trend shows no signs of slowing—in fact, it is accelerating, owing to a number of factors that complicate the production landscape. The first of these is what my friend John Zysman calls the algorithmic transformation of services, or rapid reproduction, which itself is a consequence of digitization. Every service that can be routinized into an algorithm can be programmed, and companies can then reproduce it repeatedly without spatial limitations at almost zero cost (think about the history of filling personal annual tax statements: human help, to software product, to online service). This is now coupled with cloud computing, which in essence transforms what were once expensive resources (computing power and data storage) into an ever more cheaply available utility. This combination makes the economics of global fragmentation of services ever more appealing, especially with the rise of new software platforms. These, as has been forcefully shown by Martin Kenney and John Zysman, now transform employment relationships into yet one more thing that can be sold and bought whenever, wherever, and for whatever period of service, at a relentlessly decreasing price.[15]

Welcome to the "sharing" economy.

In developed countries, jobs that not long ago seemed to be secured for life can now easily be done better somewhere else in the world by either software or a human-software combination. Newspaper and media outlets everywhere compete with one another in talking excitingly about driverless cars, warehouse robots, and delivery drones. It only goes to show that most people never run a business. Drivers and warehouses' "order fulfillment associates" are cheap and exist everywhere.

On the other hand, lawyers, business/research analysts, fund managers, and bankers (especially investment bankers) are expensive. Worse, they all demand the same pay structure and bonuses, as if they are all-stars. By so doing they make themselves prime targets for my friends who develop smart(ish) software systems (to call the machine-learning techniques, such as deep learning, that we currently have *artificial intelligence* is unbelievably hubristic and an affront to the word *intelligence*), especially my very-well-financed friends who develop a mix of smart systems with the deployment of really smart(er) and cheap(er) humans in India and elsewhere in the world. I trust that in time my friends will make sure that those professions will no longer bring millions home. I am also willing to boldly predict that there will be many (maybe more than ever before) jobs in the transportation and delivery business, even if they might not be the ones where a driver sits behind the wheel.[16]

Further complicating matters is the rise of the Internet of Things—the diffusion of digital technology with full connectivity into practically every physical item—and what is sometimes called "Industry 4.0," additive manufacturing, or 3D printing. Whatever term you use, the concept of rapid, inexpensive, computerized fabrication shakes the logic of what should be done by whom, where, and from what materials.

However, it is the impact of fragmentation on innovation-based growth that is critical for us to understand.

The Jenga Tower of Innovation

With the collapse of the Jenga tower of vertically integrated production, another parallel tower crumbled—that of innovation. Strangely enough, it seems that news of this has yet to reach policymakers, politicians, and business leaders worldwide. Everyone still wants to become the new Silicon Valley, but is that really the production stage communities should aspire to if they want widely shared innovation-based economic growth?

Several years ago, I published a short piece in the *Harvard Business Review* that became one of the journal's most read and translated into foreign languages. I still get media calls to discuss it. Its title is "Why Germany Dominates the U.S. in Innovation."[17]

We will talk more about the mystical and misplaced allure of becoming a "Silicon-Hyphen," but the reason Germans' enjoy more, and vastly wider, innovation-based prosperity then the Silicon Valley–led United States has to do with the fact that they never fell into what Michael Murphree and I term the *techno-fetishism* of novelty. Instead, Germany built one of the world's best innovation systems for second-generation innovation. Germany does not focus on new industries based on new inventions; instead, it infuses innovation into established industries. Just think about your kitchen and garage—how much of these spaces do you want fill with German products, such as things made by Miele, Bosch, BMW, and Porsche?[18]

In the same way that production has fragmented, so has innovation. The reason this happened is because in order to excel in each stage of production, you need very different innovational capabilities, and very different ecosystems that support them. Others might disagree with my particular definition of each production stage, but almost all would agree that there are four main ones. We will look at each in turn.

However, as you go through this section, keep in mind the region or regions that you know and love. Think about where those regions, and the industries within them, fit into the innovation stages—and where they might fit in the future.

Stage 1: Novelty

You know this stage. It has colonized the imaginations of entrepreneurs, corporate leaders, policymakers, and politicians worldwide. This is the stage that transforms new-to-the-world inventions into useful innovations. This is what Silicon Valley and Israel embody, what New York City wants to be, and what allowed Cleveland to become one of the richest cities on earth only a few generations ago. New technologies, pioneered by new companies and financed by new forms of investment, create whole new industries that produce a lot of wealth for their funders, financiers, and hopefully their communities.

But there is much more to novelty than this. Venture capital–backed tech start-ups constitute just part of the picture. In fact, one of start-ups' pernicious effects is their tendency to obscure other areas of novel innovation. Techno-fetishism leads people to obsess about dazzling, amazing, capital-absorbing start-ups like Jawbone (fitness trackers), Powa Technologies (mobile payments), Quirky (industrial design), Rdio (music streaming), and Secret (a secrets-sharing app), all of which, by the way, had their moment as the flavor of the month and then melted away.

Apart from those that are start-up based, there are a couple of forms of novel innovation that once were highly promising options for regions and communities but which went out of fashion as perception of their potential seemed to wane (incorrectly). Then there is one form that offers significant potential but is often overlooked. First, though, I will discuss the two well-known forms that have lost their public luster.

One involves fundamental system innovation, such as what Thomas Edison did with electricity. In Edison's day, system innovation was fairly straightforward and a real possibility (though it may not have seemed so at the time). An individual entrepreneur could envision an entire delivery network, and then, with ingenuity and funds, make it happen. Today, such radical system shifts are vastly more complicated. For example, bringing about the vaunted green-energy revolution, a present-day example of system innovation, would require the development, commercialization, and diffusion of many suites of complementary technologies throughout society, as succinctly demonstrated by Mark Huberty's work on energy systems' transformation. The innovative agent in these cases is often a government forcing significant changes. Usually, a big governmental push is needed. It is here that what Mariana Mazzucato called the "entrepreneurial state" is at its most conspicuous (although, as we shall see, it is important in all stages of innovation).[19]

Another variant of novel innovation comes from established but highly entrepreneurial companies driving change. Traditionally, these firms needed to be embedded within what are known as "communities of innovation," which has made this innovation type "sticky" to specific places in specific eras, to use Ann Markusen's famous term. Germany, for example, was a hive of invention in Diesel's time, and so were Lyon, France, and Turin, Italy. The current craze about trying to compete for R&D centers of multinational corporations (MNCs) around the world is evidence of the attraction this model has for policymakers and politicians alike. Those MNCs' subsidiaries deliver the most coveted political currency: photo-ops and hyped media coverage, usually following a specific template, such as "Company X announces the opening of a dedicated R&D center in our Region/City/Country, Y jobs to be created." This singular ability to generate such headlines seems to drive Irish, Canadian, and most states of the United States to gleeful policy excesses, costing their taxpayers billions of dollars.[20]

While this might have led to innovation-based growth in the past, in the current world of fragmented global production, those R&D centers have a mostly negative impact on the local innovation ecosystem. Wages (and other perks) go up beyond the ability of local companies to compete; inequality jumps, since almost only R&D engineers are hired; social fragmentation increases, since most workers develop intense collaboration with other people within their firms around the world, and have very little time to get involved with the local high-tech community; and the innovative fruits of the R&D centers are transformed to the MNCs' HQs and then outsourced around the world without ever creating jobs for the non-engineers (who end up paying most of the tax benefits awarded to those MNCs).[21]

Israel is a case in point. My students and I have been working with the Israeli Innovation Agency for several years since 2015. In each year, at least one of the projects was to develop a strategy to limit the negative externalities of having over 300 MNCs' ICT R&D centers in Israel, especially figuring out policies that might lead them to hire more non-engineers in the country.

I fully agree, it is a wonderful problem to have. As a policymaker I will gladly have it!

However, before you embark down the road of innovation-by-FDI (foreign direct investment), you should remember that the rapid flocking of MNCs to Israel happened in parallel with the growth of Israel as a globally critical novel-innovation hub in the ICT industry. It was not the MNCs that made Israel innovative, although they might have helped once the growth was already set. What is clear, though, is that today the MNCs amplify the inequality impacts of the particular novel-innovation economic growth model of Israel.[22]

The novel-innovation form that offers significant potential but is often overlooked consists of companies that are well beyond the start-up stage and now need support and guidance as they aim for greater growth. Call them *tech teens*.

The typical tech teen is five to fifteen years old, and is already selling products or services, which means it has a positive cash flow and it pays taxes. It employs anywhere from five to one hundred people so that it can carry out the many specialized tasks required of businesses. It might have been funded by venture capital, or it might not, but from a financial standpoint it is stuck in what is technically called a suboptimal Nash equilibrium—meaning that it is in constant survival mode, with the founders working crazy hours, hustling for customers, and scrambling to make payroll. If only those founders had access to resources (such as capital and new equipment), they could implement multiple ideas for product development that they already have customers for.

Tech teens are at the blind spot of both private markets and public policies. Stop for a moment and think about all the innovation policies you are aware of. They are focused on either not-yet-in-existence or just-created companies (accelerators, incubators, VC polices), or on the very big companies (let us subsidize a shiny Amazon/Intel/Alphabet/Cisco/Huawei/Tata/Samsung facility). There is very little offered to technology firms older than five years that are not already perceived to be on the road to becoming the next global behemoth within another three.

From the point of view of VCs (venture capitalists), these companies are problematic—and VCs are problematic for them. These companies can offer significant revenue and job creation growth on an annual basis for a long period of time, assuming they can get the needed capital. However, they cannot offer dreams to be marketed to bleary-eyed herd investors on NASDAQ that would allow those companies to be sold at a valuation of over 1,000 percent within five years. Further, for the owners, it makes no sense to give a very large stake of their company in the hope of a later financial exit. They are not searching for financial exits; they have a positive-cash-flow business in search of more growth. They might be able to use debt, if only there were financial institutions with the deep expertise in technologies that would allow them to profitably invest while offering reasonable interest rates. But we no longer have them—our financial regulations made sure that banks such as "Chemical" and "Mechanics" would become "J.P. Morgan Chase."

Why should we care?

The reason we should care is that these companies are the backbone of your local technology industry, whether you are aware of it or not. They are deeply embedded in the community (in the next chapter we will talk about the vacuuming power of the hubs); they aim at sustained growth, not just doing a Cheshire Cat's appearance as they run toward a financial exit; they hire local people (and not just transplant people from other locations to fill their new subsidiary); they hire people for all functions of the firm (not just R&D); they pay taxes (good luck trying to recoup those millions of dollars of taxpayers' money you gave all those MNCs); and they are active positive citizens of the community.

When I was at Georgia Tech, my colleagues and I took a cursory look and found a few thousand such tech teens in the Atlanta area alone. We have found the same in Toronto. Do all of them have bright prospects? Definitely not. A rough guess might be that 2 percent of tech teens are great, and maybe 10 percent are good enough to merit an opportunity to scale-up to the next level. Moving up to the next level usually means expanding R&D functions or rethinking marketing and sales, as well as getting a chance to take a breath, look around, obtain some high-quality mentoring, and plan a coherent growth strategy.

My friend Dan Isenberg has been spearheading the Scale-Up movement. Research by him and his coauthors shows that certain tech teens, if given the opportunity, are capable of growing at annual rates of 20 to 60 percent for a decade. Even if the pool is just a few hundred companies that can be moved to a trajectory of hiring just ten or more employees a year, per year, for a decade, they still constitute a huge opportunity for investors and communities. Remember, ten multiplied by a few hundred equals a few thousand. Now multiple that by ten. In the second part of the book we will visit the former steel city of Hamilton, Ontario, to see how it is experimenting with different modes of new technology companies' formation and growth.[23]

The realization that tech teens are the local community's best economic growth resource is increasing, and in chapters 5 and 6 we will develop frameworks that help enable the development of context-specific policies that can turn this potential into reality.

Stage 2: Design, prototype development, and production engineering

When today's corporations come up with product ideas that seem worth developing but are still too vague to put into production, they often hand them off to other companies that specialize in design, prototype development, or production engineering. The same happens when they know what the products should be, but do not quite have the capabilities to design them, prototype them, and engineer them to production.

These design, product development, and production engineering companies operate in all industries and at all levels. You can find them in very high-end novel product design—for example the US-based IDEO is helping customers develop first-to-the-world-products. You can find them in established high-tech products such as laptops, where the Taiwanese company Quanta Computers is helping customers to design and then produce their latest laptops. And you can find them in very traditional industries, such as high-end luxury women's shoes, where the top global brand names go to the tiny region of Riviera del Brenta just above Venice in northeastern Italy to work with specialized contractors who have the knowledge, skills, and capabilities needed in order to figure out how to design, prototype, and engineer the production of their new footwear.

These firms may in turn rely on various suppliers, sub-suppliers, prototypers, and assemblers (today's tech products, for example, typically contain thousands of components and subsystems) to turn a concept into a working product. Design and production-engineering companies are expert at making components work together and fit within the ever-shrinking confines of the latest gadgets.

Taiwanese companies excel at stage 2 in ICT. Taiwan has become a rich, highly innovative, and successful democratic society by becoming the global hub for stage 2 in electronics and semiconductors. There is almost no electronic product devised in Silicon Valley, Tel Aviv, or elsewhere that does not need Taiwanese innovation and knowledge of design, prototyping, and engineering for production as it moves from blueprints to a physical reality. In that process, high-paying jobs for Taiwanese from all skill levels have been created and sustained.[24]

In Italy, amid the destruction of multiple industries and regions, a few locales have managed to thrive and excel. These are the regions that transformed themselves into global stage 2 hubs in their respective industries. We will delve into Brenta's critical role in the production of the world's most luxurious women's shoes in depth in Part II of this book. Instead, let us travel a few valleys northeast to Alto Livenza. For years this area has been one of the centers of the Italian furniture industry, and as such it was one of Italy's celebrated industrial clusters. However, with the advent of globalization and low-cost competition from China, Alto Livenza was on the verge of destruction. Indeed, many of the other once shining star-clusters of Italian furniture, such as Matera-Bari, which until only a decade ago was the place from which the world's elites bought their fashionable leather sofas and couches, have tumbled down. But instead of dying, Alto Livenza transformed itself into a second-stage innovation- hub. As Giulio Buciuni and I have detailed, if you want to build a high-end boutique hotel and you need to design, prototype, and then rapidly produce unique rooms for the most demanding customers, you will come here to find solutions. If you have unique designs for chairs, tables, or lamps that are such intricate works of art that no one in the world knows how to translate them into a manufacturable product, this is the place you will come to to make it happen. As a matter of fact, if you are a leading American design company, such as Herman Miller, and you are not quite sure that you can come up with enough new designs on your own, Alto Livenza companies will provide you with the designs you lack. If you ever happen to be in New York City, go to the Museum of Modern Art (MoMA) and check out how many of the pieces in their permanent collection originated in Alto Livenza.[25]

In the process, similarly to Taiwan, multiple jobs have been created and sustained for people with different sets of skills. The economic fruits of innovation tend to raise more boats for locales who specialize in stage 2 innovation.

Stage 3: Second-generation product and component innovation

In this stage, firms improve, expand, and redefine a product or its critical components, either by applying incremental and process innovation, or by recombining and expanding its use and utility. This stage, incorrectly seen by some as only that of "fast following" or "incremental" innovation, is often the unsung and despised hero of economic growth. Fascination with novelty obscures this stage's importance. However, we should stop for a moment and think: Was it the invention of the internal combustion engine that changed our lives, or the millions of engineering hours spent every year in constantly improving cars? Was it the invention of the transistor that changed our lives? That of the CPU? Or has it been the relentless application of innovation to improve them, which allowed Gordon Moore, one of Intel's cofounders, to predict in a 1965 paper (what has later become known as Moore's law) that the density of transistors (rough equivalent of computing power) in integrated circuits would double every 18 to 24 months. This relentless innovation, paralleled by similar improvements in memory, data communication speed, and the efficiency of software algorithm, is the only reason that we can dream today about the AI revolution. Without enabling this transformation of computing power, AI would be prohibitively expensive to even experiment with.[26]

In your pocket today is yesterday's supercomputer, equipped with the computing power that a decade ago only military personal would be allowed to use. Today, you call it your smartphone. Speaking of your smartphone, chances are that you probably wonder if the one you bought only a few months ago is not already too old and slow, and hence whether you should change it to a new improved model.

Firms working at this stage specialize in how to make existing products and technologies better, more reliable, and more appealing to wider groups of users. Chances are that if you love cars, you have taken a close look at the German and Japanese automobile industry. Audi, Toyota, Volkswagen, Honda, BMW, Daimler-Mercedes-Benz, and Porsche are the undisputed leaders of second-generation innovation. This stage includes innovation in the underlying components and constituent elements of products in integrating technological advances for example screen technology, microprocessor design, semiconductor-production technology, car engine technology, and material science—or the machine tools that are needed to produce them. Indeed, Germany is a world leader in machine tool innovation, and many of the products pouring in from China are made in China using German machines. This is part of the reason why Germany is one of the few Western economies that has always had a positive trade balance with China, with or without engaging in trade wars.[27]

Remember the bicycle company Giant? This is exactly the way it rose to world dominance. The Taiwanese company reframed what bicycles are and who uses them by developing carbon-fiber frames, and as a result became, literally, the giant of the industry. The profits Samsung accrues from every iPhone sold are second only to Apple's because of Samsung's relentless innovation in memory chips and touchscreens. Wipro, Infosys, and Tata Consultancy Services reshaped and rule the global market of software services by constantly innovating in software project-development techniques and developing their ever-expanding libraries of software components that can be quickly tailored to their customers' needs.

Let us delve into that supercomputer in your pocket. You might have heard about the rapid rise of the Chinese smartphone industry. As a matter of fact, you probably have (or will have) one of their phones. The story of how the area Michael Murphree and I call Dong-Zhen (straddling the cities of Dongguan and Shenzhen) in the Pearl River Delta in southern China became the locale for the new global smartphone brand names is a story of excelling in second-generation innovation, not only by the Chinese companies such as Oppo, Vivo, ZTE, or Huawei, but by a Taiwanese company called MediaTek.[28]

What is the business model of MediaTek?

MediaTek came into existence in 1997, when UMC (United Microelectronics Corporation), Taiwan's very first chip fabrication company, decided to focus on becoming only a pure-play foundry and spun off all its chip design activities. Its home entertainment chipset design unit was spun as MediaTek. Very quickly thereafter, MediaTek found a winning business model: attacking sophisticated home entertainment electronic products controlled by big global brand-name companies, by developing a core chipset (later called "system on chip," or SoC), which would act as the main brain around which smaller and less technically sophisticated companies could build a product and offer it at a significantly lower price. Together with its chipsets and system on chips, MediaTek offers reference design and extensive technical assistance. MediaTek quickly honed this business model, first in CDs and then DVDs, later moving to mobile phones and then to smartphones and tablets.[29]

Effectively, MediaTek platformized and commoditized first the mobile phones, and then smartphones, which allow start-ups, many of them Chinese, to quickly offer their own smartphones by innovating around the core supplied by MediaTek. These start-ups could focus on design, user interface, and other features without having to deal with hardcore mobile communication R&D. The first impact was the rise of a low-quality (the so-called pirate, or "*shanzhai*") mobile phone industry in Dong-Zhen. Later, as these small shops gained experience, the successful ones moved to develop and offer smartphones that are as slick and as sophisticated as those offered by Apple and Samsung. Indeed, since the Chinese government did not allow Google to use the extremely limiting and aggressive (later to be found illegal on antitrust grounds by the EU commission) licensing of Android it has been using in Europe and the United States, Chinese companies also innovated in tailoring Android. This significantly increased Android's utility to their users, and at the same time allowed Chinese companies to develop mobile operation system software skills. Those are the same software development skills that stagnated in the West, where Google and Apple, have been using their market power to squash any attempt to develop to develop them by other companies. In the process of completely transforming these industries, MediaTek has also become one of the world's most successful IC design companies, shipping to the tune of one and a half *billion* units a year.[30]

Stage 4: Production and assembly

This stage involves innovation around the creation of the physical incarnation of a product that has been fully defined and designed. The innovation expertise here involves, first, figuring out how to profitably produce ever more complex products from tens, sometimes hundreds, of thousands of components developed by multiple companies around the world, and second, figuring out how to systemize production using constantly changing materials.

China's Pearl River Delta region, next to Hong Kong, is often derided as an example of faceless, brandless, utterly commoditized manufacturing, whose advantage comes solely from cheap labor and whose future is in doubt as wages rise. However, the truth is that excelling in production and assembly requires a high degree of innovation. Companies must be able to produce, within a short period of time, arrays of extremely sophisticated products, such as tablet computers, smartphones, or e-book readers. In the case of software, they must be able to quickly supply corporate-scale software systems to spec. Furthermore, at a moment's notice, these companies must be able to ramp up production to millions of units or fully abort it. In doing so they incur significant costs, not to mention risk, and they must get by on extremely low margins.[31]

This is a feat of innovative ability that few, if any, American and European companies are capable of performing today—or in fact were *ever* capable of. Even in the glory days of Ford and Bethlehem Steel, at best American companies optimized very long (millions of units) runs of very few standardized products (Model T anyone?), employing up to 100,000 workers in the same complex. Foxconn, to give just one example, employs 250,000 in its biggest facilities in China, where it produces tens, sometimes hundreds, of different products for multiple brand-name companies, and each of those products consists of thousands of components produced by hundreds of suppliers. Furthermore, Foxconn accomplishes this feat in parallel and for short to medium runs, with the ability to ramp production up and down, and change what is produced in each line within a day.[32]

The amount of innovation that is needed to excel in this stage is second to none. It is not glitzy, and does not inspire awestruck media coverage, but it produces sustainable economic growth and jobs for millions of people, and arguably more welfare to humanity then most Silicon Valley start-ups will ever produce.

Most innovation-based growth today happens within one of these innovation stages. A few regions of the world have become home to more than one stage, but this is rare; in most instances, regions focus on just one innovation stage.

Choice

What does this means for regions seeking innovation-based growth? It means that there is a choice to be made: which innovation stage to specialize in.

At the beginning of this chapter, I asked you to keep in mind the region that you know and love the best. Now that we have looked at each of the stages, where does your region fit? What kind of innovation-based growth currently predominates there? If you could have your choice, which stage should the region focus on?

This is not a simple choice. As you might imagine, it is determined in part by considerations about which stage would be most advantageous—what would be the return on a second-generation-innovation focus, for example? The choice is also shaped by what is practicable, given a region's strengths, resources, and challenges. For instance, what financial resources could the region draw on, or create, to support innovative businesses?

But there is a deeper consideration that should be addressed first: What kind of society does the region want to have—and, therefore, what kind of jobs does it hope to create? Most communities never ask themselves this question, and as a result end up choosing one of two deeply flawed development paths.

2

The Silicon Peaches

> Oz, left to himself, smiled to think of his success in giving the
> Scarecrow and the Tin Woodman and the Lion exactly what they
> thought they wanted. "How can I help being a humbug," he said,
> "when all these people make me do things that everybody knows
> can't be done?"
>
> —L. Frank Baum, *The Wonderful Wizard of Oz*

The story of global industrialization is a tale of bursts of intense innovative
energy that transformed regions for a while—sometimes years, sometimes
decades—then quieted or burned out. Britain had Birmingham, Belgium its
metal works, Switzerland its chemical companies, and Turin, Italy, spawned
what seemed back then an endless number of automobile, food, and telecommunication start-ups. Across the Atlantic, in the United States, Cleveland,
Ohio, became the country's innovation hub.

The foundations of Cleveland's growth were laid out in the first half of the
nineteenth century and strengthened after the American Civil War. Its geographical proximity to the Erie Canal and the Great Lakes enabled Cleveland
to become a hub for the extraction and movement of natural resources to the
Atlantic regions. These opportunities attracted New England investors, who
brought capital and technologies to the processing and transportation of natural resources, which spurred the creation of local start-ups, the most famous
of them being Rockefeller's Standard Oil. Patents issued in the 1880s demonstrate how the growth of this sector triggered the creation of local expertise,
which started an endogenous process of technological upgrading of the local
industry away from the production of commodities to the manufacturing
of more complex iron, chemical, and steel products. Related industries such
as machine tools, electrical machineries, and chemicals also began to develop. While in the 1870s Cuyahoga County ranked twenty-second among

US manufacturing centers, in 1900 the county had become the sixth-largest manufacturing area of the country.[1]

In the 1870s–1920s period, Cleveland developed and reproduced a set of institutions that fostered extensive industrial growth and innovation across a variety of sectors. Networks of inventors and investors emerged and carried out two main tasks. First, they provided a venue to gather information and vet new technological ideas for venture investments. The entrepreneurial opportunities vetted in these contexts were not necessarily related to the same industry, and thus the second main task of these networks was enabling the channeling of venture funding to emerging sectors, which were often developed by graduates of the local technical schools, and then channeling the profits back to the investors. Thus, those networks fulfilled a similar function to those of modern-day venture capitalists (VCs), but unlike VCs, who successfully operate in only two sectors—information and communication technologies (ICT) and bio-tech—Cleveland's networks operated across multiple sectors. These networks coalesced many times around local companies, which not only acted as economic agents, but also as hubs that fostered innovation across sectors.[2]

The Brush Electric Company illustrates the functioning of those mechanisms at its best. Charles F. Brush secured the support of the Telegraph Supply and Manufacturing Company to develop and market his dynamo for electric lighting. In 1879 this technology was used for public lighting in Cleveland, and its success led to the establishment of the Brush Electric Company, which electrified public lighting across the United States. The conspicuous financial returns of this success story had the effect of encouraging investments in other local inventions, while also giving Charles Brush and his associates a reputation that allowed them to raise and channel funding for other emerging ventures. This led to the Brush Electric Company becoming an innovation hub by connecting people seeking investment opportunities and inventors eager to pitch their ideas. This mechanism allowed inventors to establish start-ups and spinoffs to commercialize their ideas with the backing of larger firms. As a result, Cleveland gained a strong technological leadership between 1870 and 1920, and it became attractive for nonlocal inventors, too, for example Western Union's founder, Jeptha Wade. Some of the successful stories that emerged out the Brush Electric Company network included the reorganization of the Boulton Carbon Company into the National Carbon Company (later Union Carbide), the Lincoln Electric Company, and the design of batteries by Elmer Sperry, and gasoline cars by

Alexander Winton. The Brush Company was not an isolated case of an innovation hub—the White Sewing Machine Company worked in a similar way.[3]

The sophistication of financial networks increased alongside the industrialization of the local economy and the growing need for credit, and it all led to the establishment of the Cleveland Clearinghouse Association (CCA) and the Cleveland Stock Exchange (CSE) in 1899. The importance of innovation to Cleveland in that period is apparent if we look at the CSE in comparison to other US stock exchanges. In 1900 the listings of stock exchanges across the country, including the New York Stock Exchange (NYSE), were dominated by railroad companies. In the case of CSE, however, railroads accounted for only 40 percent in 1900, and only 15 percent in 1910. This relative decline was due to the increasing presence of innovative manufacturing firms such as American Multigraph, Brown Hoisting Machinery, National Carbon, and the White Motor Company, among others. The number and value of stocks sold rose steadily and reached a peak in 1928, while the value of the membership increased from $100 in 1900 to $15,000 in 1929.[4]

The profits of this industrial growth were often channeled by local businessmen to charitable activities, including schools and universities. In 1882 donations allowed the relocation of the Western Reserve University from Hudson to Cleveland, as well as the establishment of the Case School of Applied Science in the same year. The Case School, in particular, supported innovation by providing technical training to local inventors who were its graduates. Case was an enormous success—what we excitingly just rediscovered and call an "entrepreneurial university." For example, one-quarter of its students in the 1910–1912 cohorts obtained at least one patent during their lifetimes. Furthermore, the institute cultivated relations with local entrepreneurs and former graduates. For instance, Case's first president, Cady Staley, met Herbert Dow during his undergraduate years and became a stockholder and member of the board of the Dow Chemical Company from its foundation.[5]

This increased sophistication of finance, research, and human capital led to even higher levels of innovation. Michael Fogarty and his coauthors demonstrated the growing quality of Cleveland's innovations by looking at the increasing number of *important* patents produced by Clevelanders that constituted the technological basis to foster growth within related and unrelated industries. By 1900, Cleveland had the highest rate of important patents per capita. Another measure of Cleveland's success at the turn of the century was the concentration of wealth: in 1892, Cleveland was home to eighty-five millionaires, representing the second-richest Midwest city and the fourth American city overall in terms of bank deposits per capita in 1920.[6]

Nonetheless, Cleveland's success story came to an ugly end, which was almost as rapid as its rise. In the period after the end of World War II, Cleveland's levels of productivity relative to the US average plunged, and so did its population, marking a 60 percent decline. In the years between 1970 and 1987, Cleveland lost 130,000 jobs, while the share of manufacturing employment dropped from 47 to 27 percent. In 1969 the Cuyahoga River caught fire yet again due to excessive pollution, this time leading *Time* magazine to describe it as the river that "oozes rather than flows," and in which a person "does not drown but decays." Many in the United States thought that Cleveland could not decline further.[7]

How wrong they were. Things only got worse, reaching a climax in 1978 with the city defaulting on its debts. Despite the multiple attempts to retrigger its innovation-based growth, as in the case of the strategies and investments devised by local entrepreneurs through the organization Cleveland Tomorrow, Cleveland remains the second-poorest American city after Detroit.[8]

We, of course, no longer have to worry about such stories, because we have come a long way since then. Cities and regions have seen what happened to Cleveland and other regions in the industrial North, and they have smartened up. They have learned from gurus such as Michael Porter and Paul Krugman to prize entrepreneurism and to see the value of business clusters. They have learned from Clay Christensen about the risks and opportunities of disruption. They have tried hard to emulate Silicon Valley—so much so that many of them have taken nicknames suggesting lineal descent.[9]

They call themselves Silicon Beach (Los Angeles), Silicon Hills (Austin, Texas), Silicon Prairie (American Midwest), Silicon Alley (New York), Silicon North (at least five cities in Canada claim that title), Silicon Island (claimed by both Ireland and Taiwan)—even Silicon Wadi (Israel).

Among these Silicon-Hyphens is the Silicon Peach—the Atlanta, Georgia, area. And, to be honest, if any region is worthy of the name, it would seem to be greater Atlanta. In some ways, Atlanta and the San Francisco South Bay area are twins separated at birth: both mercantile centers were situated within agriculturally rich areas (the region now known as Silicon Valley was especially famous for its peaches, incidentally Georgia's official fruit and nickname). In both areas, tech communities grew out of the defense industry, which boomed during and after World War II. In California, the spark was the US government's aeronautics base in Sunnyvale; in Georgia, it was the Bell Aircraft factory.

The "Bell Bomber" plant, built in the cotton-growing town of Marietta, near Atlanta, hired tens of thousands of people to build the B-29 Superfortress. It also helped shape the region's future. After the war, the Georgia Institute of Technology in Atlanta expanded its graduate programs and began metamorphosing into one of the nation's top engineering schools. Like Stanford and Berkeley, Georgia Tech produced grad students who launched technology businesses. In 1951 a group of seven Georgia Tech engineers created a radar-research start-up they called Scientific Atlanta (SA).[10]

Scientific Atlanta's story is a classic start-up tale. The tiny firm quickly expanded into satellite and cable communication and became a multibillion-dollar company. By 1999, SA had grown to 2,800 employees and $1.1 billion in sales. By 2005, with 6,500 employees in seventy countries and $1.9 billion in sales, it was vying with Motorola for global dominance of its market segment and was the largest producer of set-top boxes for cable TV.[11]

Atlanta was also home to MSA, founded in 1963 by five Georgia Tech graduates as a bespoke programming company. By the early 1980s, when it went public, MSA was the largest software applications company in the world.

Even more promising was the fact that in the 1980s, Atlanta's companies were prominent worldwide in the then-burgeoning data communications industry. Digital Communications Associates (DCA) controlled the PC-to-mainframe market with its IRMA product, which was one of the top five best-selling products in the PC industry in the 1980s. Hayes Microcomputer Products topped the modem market. Microstuf led the modem-software market with Crosstalk, a communications program that became the industry standard for modem-to-computer communication.[12]

As the years passed, the area continued to look in certain respects like a start-up hothouse. Atlanta epitomized every factor or theory cited by academics, officials, and business executives as necessary for the growth of new technology companies. Institutions of learning expanded, as did one of the most prominent of America's federal research organizations—the Centers for Disease Control and Prevention (CDC). R&D money poured in, and Atlanta became the fourth-richest US hub in research investment.

The region has one of the youngest and most highly educated "creative" workforces in the country, with a net inflow of twenty-five to thirty-four-year-olds—not surprising given Atlanta's cultural and social attractions, and the fact that Atlanta is one of the biggest music industry clusters in the country. Arts and theater organizations proliferated; the Summer Olympics came to town; the region developed a large and active lesbian, gay, and queer community; and it became famous as the hometown of Martin Luther King Jr. and other prominent African American political and business leaders. Further, the region has had one of the country's largest concentrations of Fortune 500 companies in America.[13]

There was no lack of energy or resources when it came to spin-offs and new ventures: SA cofounder Glen P. Robinson Jr. assumed the role of leader of the local technology industry, enthusiastically promoting business-growth initiatives such as the Advanced Technology Development Center, Georgia Tech's incubator.[14]

There were some real entrepreneurial stars: In 1992, Christopher Klaus, then a student at Georgia Tech, released a freeware program he called Internet Security Scanner. In 1994 he founded Internet Security Systems (ISS) to sell the application. SA veteran Thomas Noonan took the helm as CEO in 1995. In 1996 the company received $3.6 million in its first round of venture capital from Sigma Partners' Boston fund. In 1996 and 1997, the company developed more products, acquired additional venture capital, and opened offices in Belgium, Japan, the United Kingdom, and France. In 1998 ISS became a public company listed on NASDAQ and, using its new financial muscle, acquired several firms in the United States and Europe. By 2004 ISS employed more than 1,200 people in twenty countries, had revenues of $290 million, and saw its technologies used by more than 12,000 organizations.[15]

Other tech start-ups popped up on a regular basis. In 2006, for example, local serial entrepreneur Jeff Haynie joined with Nolan Wright to start Appcelerator. By the time Haynie started Appcelerator, he was a hero of the Atlanta tech community and an outspoken promoter. However, things changed very quickly.

First, like most of Atlanta's start-ups, Appcelerator was funded primarily by VCs from other American cities. In Appcelerator's case, it was a venture capitalist in Menlo Park, California. In other words, its funding did not come from the local area. The reasons for this differ according to who is asked: local VCs took too long to put a deal on the table, did not have enough connections to offer, or cared far more about finance than ideas. The reality is that in most Silicon-Hyphen tech clusters, the local VCs do not invest in most start-ups, and it is not clear whether they even have the expertise or the networks to help the start-ups they do invest in.[16] This time, Haynie had enough, and only two years after its founding, Appcelerator left Atlanta.

Haynie explained this in an open blog to the community he left behind, stating that he believed that by moving the company to Mountain View, California, he could take advantage of every option possible to help the start-up succeed. "Silicon Valley is the heart of where things are happening today," he wrote. Haynie saw Silicon Valley as a place where he could work with partners who had achieved start-up success "over and over again."[17]

Well, you may say, what's the loss of one small start-up in a healthy entrepreneurial landscape? But, in fact, Atlanta's entrepreneurial landscape has been far from healthy.

A Failure to Thrive

Look closely and you will see the details. Several times, Atlanta has been host to the biggest companies in the hottest high-tech market niches. But after becoming industry leaders, they either shriveled or expanded on their own without engendering much collateral local growth.

Atlanta's dominance in the modem market did not last long, for example. At the same time that the Internet was transforming the data-communication industry into a fast-growing market niche, presenting unparalleled opportunities for growth, Atlanta was unable to build on its pioneering success. DCA, Hayes, and Microstuf, as well as SA, went bankrupt or were acquired, and Atlanta lost its leading position while Silicon Valley companies rose to prominence.

The 1990s and 2000s were no different. MSA was unable to change its products and business model to keep pace with the software industry's transformation from mainframe to personal computing, and in 1990 it was acquired for $333 million, slightly above its annual revenues, by Dun & Bradstreet.[18]

The number of large technology companies in Georgia declined by more than half from 2000 to 2006. ISS, for example, was unable to cement its position as a top Internet-security company, and in 2006 it sold itself to IBM for $1.3 billion. SA, so successful during its run, was acquired in 2006 by California-based Cisco Systems for $6.9 billion. The company blended into Cisco and faded away.[19]

Since 2006 the region has failed to create thriving high-tech businesses. No Atlanta start-up has grown large enough to be listed on NASDAQ. As in early twentieth-century Cleveland, the burst of high-tech entrepreneurship had waned.

What happened?

Many of Atlanta's most promising companies have done what Appcelerator did—they have packed up and left. A key factor in Appcelerator's departure was that the start-up was funded not by Atlanta money but by a venture capitalist in Menlo Park, California. This was the last straw that led Jeff Haynie to believe that only by moving the company to California could he take advantage of every option possible to help Appcelerator succeed.[20]

As my research with my former student Mollie Taylor has found, Atlanta has become a "feeder" cluster to Silicon Valley, Boston, and New York, creating promising start-ups only to see them pack up and grow elsewhere. In the many interviews I conducted in Atlanta, I saw that industry leaders were acutely aware of this problem and the challenges it poses for continued growth.[21]

Tech firms need to be embedded in extensive social networks in order to find employees, managers, ideas, and investment. They need to put together teams of creative engineers to design and problem-solve. They need to figure out which markets to target. They need partners willing to invest in the research, as well as others willing to give the new products a try. These demands are met through various kinds of social networks consisting of groups of engineers, designers, investors, vendors, customers, and analysts.[22]

But for companies in Silicon-Hyphens, most of these networks are not physically based in the local community, and not because the community lacks people from these groups. In the tech realm, Atlanta has what social science terms "poor social capital." It has the specialized talent that tech companies need, as well as entrepreneurial role models, and, at least potentially, the best set of customers one can imagine from the Fortune 500 and 1000 companies' club. Yet these elements don't come together in the kinds of social networks that nurture and sustain start-ups. Atlanta has the ingredients to cook a wonderful entrepreneurial ecosystem, but they refuse to be mixed together.

When Mollie Taylor and I analyzed the social network maps of Atlanta's start-ups, the most persistent finding was how each and every company and entrepreneur is isolated from her Atlanta peers. No matter how much we tried to torture the data to make it look more optimistic, Atlanta's entrepreneurs always walked alone.[23]

The reality of the Silicon-Hyphens is stark: in order to be successful, firms located in these areas need to weave themselves into the industrial communities of the more established clusters such as Silicon Valley or Boston. This long-distance embeddedness comes with a cost—a significant negative impact on the development of a coherent industrial community at home. With their limited social resources focused on what they view as critical long-distance relationship with financiers, customers, peers, and key individuals at the dominant clusters, the amount of time and effort management invests in the local community is gravely reduced. Additionally, as they become more embedded within the dominant cluster, promising firms tend to relocate into it. The result is social fragmentation of the industry at the Silicon-Hyphens.

Furthermore, this social fragmentation is self-reinforcing. Operating in an environment where companies lack a strong local community, and already have at their disposal role models for success and institutionalized patterns enabling them to get embedded within the original Silicon Valley, promising new start-ups will look outward for their social-business interactions from their inception. In today's connected world, it is easy—perhaps too easy—for companies to surmount this local deficit by going national or global to tap the networks they need. Atlanta's start-up leaders, designers, marketers, and business developers can use phones, e-mail, travel, and other means to connect with the people who can help, wherever they may be based.

Thus, Appcelerator wove itself, long-distance, into a well-established cluster elsewhere. My research shows that this is a common pattern. Even if they are based in metropolitan areas, many tech companies attach themselves to established clusters, sometimes in California, sometimes in Massachusetts or New York. Managers are left with little time or motivation to invest in their local communities. Instead, they invest in becoming part of far-away and already successful industrial communities. The Appcelerators of this world strengthen the already successful regions and further weaken their own local embeddedness, as well as their hometown social capital.

As companies become more and more deeply embedded in communities far away, the likelihood builds that they will relocate to one of the established hubs. This is reinforced by the VCs. The reality is that venture capital is networked. To make money, VCs weave their invested firms into their own local networks of companies, talent, and capital, no matter where the start-ups began.[24] Investors often move companies to their own home turfs. Guess where three-quarters of all venture capital invested in America goes to? Correct, California, New York, or Massachusetts, with Silicon Valley alone raking in more VC investment then the combined sum of the other four next locales put together. The states of the US Midwest get less than 10 percent of the total, Ohio gets under 1 percent.[25]

The firms that are most prone to moving away are the tech start-ups. Of firms listed in the *Atlanta Business Chronicle*'s list of "Top Venture Capital Deals" from 1999 to2007, 40 percent left within three years of getting their first round of venture-capital investment.[26]

Through this self-reinforcing process, Silicon-Hyphens become *socially fragmented*. In fact, they never really become entrepreneurial ecosystems at all, since their companies' most significant ties are with firms, investors, customers, and peers far away. There is no community back home, just a shared geographical space. The Silicon-Hyphens invest years, billions, and their best efforts only to become the minor league, a place where their own greatest young brains play for the shortest possible time as they aim to prove themselves and move to the majors.

That is why the tech landscape in developed economies consists of a small number of dominant clusters served by a large number of subordinate feeder clusters. The feeder clusters end up specializing in creating new companies whose full economic benefits are enjoyed by—you guessed it—the dominant clusters. It is not necessarily a bad thing to become home to a feeder cluster. Feeder clusters do generate some economic activity. But economic-development resources are limited, and communities need to be aware that even a massive investment in the creation of a hoped-for start-up cluster may yield nothing but a launching pad for companies that ultimately benefit the larger hubs. Worse, in the current version of the global economy we work in, start-ups do not necessarily generate growth in their local community.

You might argue that this is incorrect, and that research has shown that tech start-up creation is now occurring in more hubs around the world. As a matter of fact, in a special survey the *Economist* celebrated this trend and correctly identified the technological causes—the current stabilization of technological platforms—that allow the rapid creation of specific kinds of tech start-ups.[27]

Nonetheless, remember what our goal is: economic growth in our community. If you read these reports and this research closely, you will be filled with unease, since it does not offer answers to the most important questions regarding these tech start-ups: How would these activities translate to economic growth in *specific locales*, and is this movement toward tech start-ups inflation only the latest twist moving us into even more economic inequality? Are we doomed to life in the new gilded age?

I argue that if we wake up to the global reality and change our innovation policies, there is no reason to believe that the future of democratic capitalism is either horrifying levels of inequality or depressing economic stagnation. Nonetheless, unless we develop a new understanding of how innovation and entrepreneurship translate into sustained economic growth in different ways in different places, we will be doomed to one of these two options.

If there is one new thing in "globalization," it is the new system of fragmented global production of goods and services. Great innovations and entrepreneurship *always* translate to growth and job creation. However, in the current global economy, growth and job creation do not necessarily occur at the place of innovation. For example, if you compile the employment and wage figures, and you are Danish, Irish, or Swiss, you will be delighted to discover that the latest American biotech boom means an amazing future filled with good jobs for your middle classes. Too bad for Americans that their elected officials' policy failures mean that many of the good people of the United States will not share in that future—a future fully paid for by their tax dollars.

So let us dispel the vision of glory in the Silicon-Hyphen dream and figure out what is really going on globally—what changed in the way in which innovation translates to growth and distribution. To do so we have to understand how goods and services are now being globally produced, what innovation is, how different kinds of innovation translate to growth and jobs, and whether what the *Economist*'s report presents as the latest stage of development—the growth of platforms that allow rapid creation of new ventures on top of them—is indeed new.

The easiest question to answer is the last: Are platforms and new tech start-ups hubs in the global industrial fringes a new phenomenon? The answer is no. If we go back to former generations of transformative high-tech and look at the places that were at the fringes back then, we will find incredible new hubs of innovation in cities (just like Shenzhen, China, today) that were barely a village a generation before. For example, if during 1910 we took a stroll in downtown Turin, then a humble town that had just turned into "the capital" for the newly unified Italy, we would see scores of start-ups playing in the latest high-technology sector: cars. Many of these car manufacturers, such as Diatto and Chiribiri, were the leading lights of innovation in that period, even if today we only remember Fiat, Lancia, and Abarth.[28]

The reason this has happened? The platform technologies for cars were stabilized enough that it was technically and financially feasible to open a tech start-up, literally in one's garage. Within a few decades, however, the platform and industry moved on, to the point where you need many millions of dollars and hundreds of engineers to open a globally competitive start-up.

Technology always changes the economic equilibrium. Furthermore, technology and innovation are most effective in what Josef Schumpeter called "creative destruction" (and if you care about growth, you should remember the *destruction* half of the term, instead of focusing solely on the *creative* part) precisely when companies and policymakers think they "got it." That is the reason why innovation is the main engine of economic growth and why economic theories based on static equilibrium and price competition proved so bad at explaining our dynamic and evolving reality. Thus, celebrating the current moment of the ICT revolution as the new growth paradigm is wrong.[29]

However, before we go on to explore the inner working of innovation and economic growth in our world of globally fragmented production, let us first explore a few more caveats about VC-funded tech start-up cluster creation as a strategy for growth.

3

Start-Ups Are Everywhere!
(but the Growth Statistics)

"I am the Guardian of the Gates, and since you demand to see the Great Oz I must take you to his Palace. But first you must put on the spectacles."

"Why?" asked Dorothy.

"Because if you did not wear spectacles the brightness and glory of the Emerald City would blind you. Even those who live in the City must wear spectacles night and day. They are all locked on, for Oz so ordered it when the City was first built, and I have the only key that will unlock them."

He opened the big box, and Dorothy saw that it was filled with spectacles of every size and shape. All of them had green glasses in them. The Guardian of the Gates found a pair that would just fit Dorothy and put them over her eyes. There were two golden bands fastened to them that passed around the back of her head, where they were locked together by a little key that was at the end of a chain the Guardian of the Gates wore around his neck. When they were on, Dorothy could not take them off had she wished, but of course she did not wish to be blinded by the glare of the Emerald City, so she said nothing.

—L. Frank Baum, *The Wonderful Wizard of Oz*

You might still be unconvinced. There are, you might argue, many places that still managed to make themselves into dominant high-tech hubs. Look at Israel or San Diego.

I fully agree—there is still a chance of becoming a very successful Silicon-Hyphen, slim as it is. But, imagine that you are successful? Is this what you should aspire to for your community? If we take a few steps back, we can see that there is an even bigger problem with the dream of hosting VC-backed start-ups, filled with glorified initial public offerings (IPOs) on NASDAQ, and multibillion-dollar financial exits such as Google: the very effects of venture capital itself on your model of growth.

If you read popular press accounts (many of which are actively promoted by VCs), you might think that VCs are social innovators devoted to the common good and the growth of their communities. The prominent venture capitalist Vinod Khosla once said in an interview that he found it "distasteful" when investors "are more focused on the deal, on the big payoff," than on a pure desire to create something new. A lot of regions have come to believe this mythmaking, which is why they tend to have a starry-eyed view of venture capital. But studies show that regions can never be sure of benefiting from these investors' success; only Wall Street can.[1]

A perfect example comes from the contrast between two Canadian companies: Research in Motion (RIM), now BlackBerry Limited, and Shopify. RIM, the most spectacularly successful private ICT company in Canadian history, made its mark with the BlackBerry, first a two-way pager and then a global smartphone brand. Throughout its early growth its co-CEOs refused to accept VC funds, instead utilizing every government, debt, and local institutional investor they could apply for. Further, when finally doing its IPO, RIM was led mostly by Canadian underwriters.[2]

Shopify, an e-commerce company that is the current flagship of Canada's high-tech industry, took the more stereotypical start-up route of seeking VC funding through Series A, B, and C, investments in which investors came to own greater and greater proportions of the company. By the time it was ready for its IPO, 53.68 percent of its stock was owned by VCs, with another 7.49 percent owned by private equity. Fully 42.15 percent of the stock was owned by American investment entities. Similarly, most of its underwriters were American.[3]

Not very surprisingly, when the two companies were first listed on the Stock Exchange, the massive financial profits unleashed helped two different countries. Most of the financial profits from RIM's IPO were gained by Canadian investors and the company's founders and employees. In the case of Shopify, most of the gains, both on the day of IPO and in the weeks that followed (as stocks allocated to American entities by the underwriters were quickly sold to Canadians for an extra profit), flowed to Shopify's American investors, especially to Wall Street's insiders' club.

With RIM, where no VCs were involved, the local innovation success generated financial flows coming from Wall Street to Waterloo. In the case of Shopify, where American VCs took the lead, the success of an Ottawa company generated a significant transfer of capital from Canada to Wall Street.

From the point of view of the local communities and the tax dollars spent by their policy leaders in the hope of securing a future of innovation-based growth, it is quite clear which road is the one to be taken. Tragically, it is almost always the road not taken.

The Silicon-Hyphens idolize venture capital.

The best VCs are the some of the world's savviest and most cold-blooded businesspeople. Their business model is simple: they buy cheap companies and sell them at a premium, preferably more than a 1,000 percent premium, in a time frame of five years. They do not aim to secure growth and employment for all. They are focused on one thing only: securing big and fast financial exits. As one of the most successful Israeli VCs once confided to me, "IPOs on NASDAQ are a pain in the neck." It's an "unbelievable hassle before I get my profits and can distribute them to my investors. I so much prefer to sell my companies to bigger companies. I get out the money cleanly and quickly, and I can focus on the next deal. I only do IPOs because the best entrepreneurs dream about IPOs and if you develop a reputation that you only do M&As, they will never work with you."[4]

For the best VCs the current situation of Unicorns—that is, private companies valued at one billion or more USD without ever needing to have profits (sometimes even revenues)—is paradise on earth. The shrewdest VCs manage to secure profits in excess of 1,000 percent by selling small parts of their Unicorn's equity at ever more ridiculous valuations to other (less sophisticated) private investors. Those secondary investors hope to do the same by selling their equity at even more stupid prices to even less sophisticated investors (at which point the truly smart VCs sell their remaining equity and try not to laugh as they run to the bank).[5]

Sadly, Hyman Minsky, the economist that mainstream economists prefer to forget when the world is not in the midst of a global financial crisis, is going to be found correct yet again. Capitalism is prone to massive investment bubbles, especially when profits are high and interest rates are low.[6]

We must understand that this is EXACTLY what VCs should do. VCs are trusted with very large sums of money by their investors. They are tasked by those investors to make them more money, not help local economic growth or improve Mother Earth. I will personally pull my money within seconds out of any VC fund if I even suspect that the VCs are not 100 percent focused on making me more money.

The question for communities is whether the effects of the VC-based innovation growth model are ones they are willing to "enjoy."

You might argue that I am contradicting myself. Am I not the scholar who gained his first fame from his analysis and celebration of Israel's rapid-innovation-based growth? Am I not the scholar who together with my colleagues Chris Forman and Wen Wen showed that VCs are instrumental in ushering in new technological paradigms?[7] Indeed I am and I did, which is precisely why I know that the VC effect can be seen on a large scale in Israel, which is, by far, the most impressive miracle of innovation-based growth the world has seen in the past half a century.

In 1968, Israel's industrial sector had a total of just 886 R&D workers with any academic education (introductory courses in major North American universities often seat up to twice that number of students in one classroom). Business-sector R&D investment stood at 1 percent, which was the lowest in the OECD at the time. Moreover, from 1978 to 1986, Israel suffered raging inflation of 109,187 percent (yes, over *one hundred thousand percent*). The name of the currency bears the scars of this period: the country now uses the new Israeli shekel—the "plain" shekel survived for less than five years after it was introduced to replace the rapidly becoming-worthless lira, the currency Israel established when it gained independence.[8]

Yet by the end of the 1990s, Israel had moved to the top of the global league in business R&D investment intensity, number of high-tech companies listed on NASDAQ (in absolute terms second only to the United States and China, in per-capita terms unparalleled), and level of VC dollars invested. These factors have fueled Israel's impressive economic growth over the last twenty years. Israel has fully embraced the nickname given to it by Dan Senor and Saul Singer—"start-up nation."[9]

This is a true economic miracle. It allowed the Israeli economy to join the ranks of the OECD (a club of the world's rich developed countries), and without it Israel would suffer existential economic crises.

Yet during these years of unparalleled innovation-based growth, the rest of the economy enjoyed *no* positive spillovers. Productivity (and with it wages) in all other sectors of the economy declined or remained stagnant. The high-tech boom focused exclusively on financial exits—rarely on growing companies that would employ large numbers of non-engineers. In the case of Israel, the VC-inequality effect operates on steroids. Over

95 percent of the VC capital invested in Israeli firms is foreign, and when the financial exits occur all that money and profit leaves the Israeli economy and goes back to the foreign bank accounts they came from. Thus, the boom has been completely divorced from the rest of the economy. In effect, Israel has really become a start-up nation—or, more aptly a VC-nation—where a very small slice of the population, the extremely high-skilled and those born rich, is allocated lottery tickets in the form of stakes in the start-up economy, and the vast majority of Israelis find themselves forever running on a treadmill to nowhere.[10]

Israel has become two economies sharing one physical space. The results, in terms of inequality, could not be more striking: Israel went from being the second-most-egalitarian society in the West to the second-most-unequal one. Recent OECD studies show that while the country's high-tech entrepreneurs and financiers (and the celebrity chefs they love to frequent) have gained almost unbelievable wealth, every fifth household in Israel now "enjoys" being under the poverty line. To Israeli taxpayers and the society at large, the main gift of innovation-based growth has been levels of inequality that are comparable to those of Mexico and Turkey.[11]

Why does the VC-based start-up-to-financial-exit model lead to such outcomes?

For that we must understand how the VC model works. VC funds are usually organized as partnerships between general partners (GPs) and limited partners (LPs) for a duration of up to ten years. GPs are the individuals who make the investment choices, impose active management, and are involved in the companies in which the fund invests. They are the ones whose profession is being a venture capitalist, and the ones commonly referred to as VCs. LPs are institutional investors or wealthy individuals, who passively invest in a VC fund.[12]

In order to understand VCs' investment behavior, it is important to grasp how they make their money. VCs have two sources of revenue. First, every year the fund takes a management fee, usually 2–3 percent of the fund's total investment capital. Although this can be lucrative for the VCs, the more significant payout is the second source: the gains from a financial exit of their invested companies, either by IPO or by being acquired by another company (mergers and acquisitions, or M&A). At that point, the VCs distribute the proceeds between themselves and the LPs, with VCs retaining around 20 percent of the profits. For the VCs to be able to secure investment for their next fund, they need to show current and prospective LPs that, after taking all costs and risks into account, their fund's rate of return on investment (RoI) is more attractive than other investments.[13]

Accordingly, VCs aim to invest in firms that they predict (or, more correctly, hope and pray) will achieve a financial exit two orders of magnitude above the firm's valuation at the time of that investment within three to five years. These constraints lead even the best VCs to refer to a rule of thumb known as "one in ten." Under this rule, a VC needs at least one in ten of her investments to be a "home run"—an investment that generates not only enough profits to cover the other nine but also enough to ensure an RoI to the LPs high enough to justify follow-up investment in the next fund. If this sounds to you like running a casino using other peoples' money, you are correct.[14]

Another fact of the VC business model, hardly spoken about in polite circles, is that VCs also act as intermediaries between their invested firms and the financial markets, and hence are always very keen to offer whatever the current technological flavor of the month is on Wall Street. Indeed, as Chris Forman, Wen Wen, and I conducted our research, one of our interviewees (a founder and a CEO of a successful software company) offered a candid view of the intimate role of VCs as Wall Street's salespersons:

> Good VCs do not invest without knowing where the exit would come from, so they will constantly think about what will help them get good valuations in terms of future exits—which means that they are thinking about what new technologies will be hot. In effect the VC-investment-bankers connection is much stronger and intimate than the VC-portfolio company.[15]

Last but not least, it is important to remember that there is a huge variance between the best VCs and all the rest. The best VCs are extremely successful and have a critical coordinating role in ushering in new technologies. The rest of the VCs operate with a herd mentality, following the lead of the best VCs, and as a result are truly professional at losing other peoples' money while making a fortune for themselves. As a matter of fact, unless you can invest in the top 1 percent of the VC funds, you are better off buying index funds (or if you truly like to play the casino, go to the blackjack tables or even the roulette; as long as you pick either black or red you are still better off than investing in most VC funds).[16]

The economist and highly successful VC William H. Janeway provided an insightful analysis of this system in his book *Doing Capitalism in the Innovation Economy*. Following Hyman Minsky's theory of investment bubbles, he argued that bubbles are a necessary condition for the innovation economy (and the VC model). The reason is that you need a speculative bubble to allow the channeling of massive resources into unproven technologies, which, while ensuring that most investors lose their money, enables transformative changes to the economy. We can see the positive long-term effects of, in his terminology, "productive bubbles" all along the history of the Industrial Revolution, from the railroad system to the Internet backbone. Since new technology is unproven and uncertain, you need massive experimentation in order to solve two inherent issues: (1) figuring out how to make it work in a way that is economically useful, and (2) figuring out the business models that allow firms to make money using it. For that reason, we need a thousand failures to have one success.[17]

For that exact same reason, when played full tilt, even when successful, the VC-based financial model transforms places from communities into insiders-versus-outsiders war zones. Think for a moment about Silicon Valley, where, if you work for a technology company you have a fabulous salary, amazing perks, and an allocation of stock options (aka lottery tickets). However, if you do not, you can consider yourself lucky if you can afford to sleep in your own car.

Further, who is allowed to play the VC-financed start-up game in Silicon Valley?

Correct! The graduates of Stanford, Berkeley, MIT, and other elite universities. In short, the already fabulously well-off and those who won the lottery of life through no fault of their own.

All of this, without even taking into account that VCs manage to make money and have positive impact in terms of technological development in *only two sectors*: ICT and biotech—sectors that might, or might not, be the sectors you think your own community can excel in. VC is just one, very narrowly successful, solution to the inherent problem of channeling capital into new technologies and new firms. It is high time that we start to see some innovation in the business of financing innovation.[18]

On the macroeconomic level, the VC-fueled ICT and biotech revolution make sense as an economic growth strategy. Nonetheless, as a leader of a region, city, or county, you should stop for a moment and think: "Do I really think that my $100 million or even $500 million investment in a VC fund would ensure that I get access to the top one percent of VC talent?"

And even if you do, is the future you envision for your community that of extreme inequality? If not, then it might be time we start to understand how the global economy works, and what alternatives it offers us for innovation-based development.

4

Making America Great Again?

Thereafter he walked very carefully, with his eyes on the road, and when he saw a tiny ant toiling by he would step over it, so as not to harm it. The Tin Woodman knew very well he had no heart, and therefore he took great care never to be cruel or unkind to anything.

"You people with hearts," he said, "have something to guide you, and need never do wrong; but I have no heart, and so I must be very careful."

—L. Frank Baum, *The Wonderful Wizard of Oz*

A driving tour through some parts of the industrial North during autumn, when the leaves are turning orange and red, can be a beautiful way to spend a weekend—and a good way to get a sense of how manufacturing's flow and ebb has transformed the economy. If you are in the United States, try the cities and towns of northern Ohio, say, or Pennsylvania, or New York State, or New England. The foliage is gorgeous, and so are many of the buildings.

You will notice that in many of these places, the business district is bisected by a river, and along it are some of the classiest-looking assisted-living institutions, condo developments, and arts centers you have ever seen: enormous brick buildings in the Federal style, some of them hundreds of meters long, with orderly tiers of windows, in many cases dominated by a clock tower or—most telling of all—a smokestack.

Not all of these buildings have been renovated, of course. Many remain empty, feeding local tales about coyotes, ghosts, and bygone prosperity. Whether repurposed or decrepit, they are the remains of the manufacturing companies that powered the economy for a century and a half—the textile weavers, watchmakers, brass-tubing rollers, weapons assemblers, and engine builders that needed so many employees for their labor-intensive factories that they routinely built neighborhoods of single-, two-, and three-family wood-frame homes nearby so workers drawn from all over the region could live nearby and walk to work, lunch pails in hand. These were usually built well out of sight of the hills where the owners and executives lived in their multiroom mansions.

The industrial buildings are also a reminder of the all-in-one philosophy that once dominated manufacturing, the venerated vertically integrated production system. A paradigm of this thinking was the Ford Motor Company. Henry Ford dreamed of owning, operating, and coordinating every part and every stage of automobile construction. At the height of Henry Ford's reign, the company owned 700,000 acres of forest, iron mines, and limestone quarries in northern Michigan, Minnesota, and Wisconsin. He also owned mines covering thousands of acres in the coal-rich land in Kentucky, West Virginia, and Pennsylvania. As if this was not enough, there was also a fully owned and operated rubber plantation in Brazil. The pinnacle of this empire was his plant on the Rouge River in Dearborn, Michigan, where all those raw materials were shipped to (using Ford-owned boats and rail), in order to produce complete automobiles from scratch. All of this was, of course, powered by the company-owned power plant. "The Rouge" as it was known, was the optimum of the "ore to car" production paradigm.[1]

In Bethlehem, Pennsylvania, Bethlehem Steel did something similar. As it was doing so, the company also impacted the ways we think and manage work to this day.[2]

Donald Trump, the forty-fifth president of the United State, has touted his business education at the Wharton Business School in the University of Pennsylvania, calling the school "the best business school in the world" on his TV show *The Apprentice*.[3] Wharton is named after Joseph Wharton, the cofounder of Bethlehem Steel, who established it in 1881 as the world's first collegiate school of business.[4]

However, probably a greater and more lasting impact is remembered by only a few. As Bethlehem was growing, it experienced difficulties in efficiently managing integrated steel production on a large scale. As a result, in 1898 it hired a young mechanical engineer by the name of Frederick Winslow Taylor. The result of this experience would later lead Taylor to publish *The Principles of Scientific Management*. In this book Taylor laid down his theory of managing humans (also known as labor) by breaking work into the simplest feasible tasks, which are then timed to ensure maximum efficiency. Labor, in this view, need not think—only management need do so. Labor just follows established procedures and is then supervised relentlessly by constant surveillance. This theory of management, nicknamed Taylorism, still has its proponents, including Amazon, which employs it almost dogmatically to manage and optimize its warehouses. Incidentally, while Taylor is celebrated by business schools and management consultants as the founder of both industrial engineering and modern management consultancy, he made his fortune as an innovator. He had more than a hundred patents to his name. The most lucrative of which was the Taylor-White process of treating tungsten steel, developed together with Maunsel White during the time he was working at Bethlehem.[5]

I still have vivid recollections of Bethlehem Steel and the Fordist mode of production. A year before Bethlehem Steel finally filed for bankruptcy in 2001, my then professors at MIT, Michael Piore and Richard Lester, took me with them to site visits of innovating manufacturers in Lehigh Valley, Pennsylvania. As part of this tour we were taken to the old country club, where when the, old, white and male, gentlemen entered, they were announced by their title at, and the years working for, Bethlehem Steel.

There are very few people today who would envision a return to Fordism. Things changed very drastically from the days when business leaders thought that the smart and most competitive strategy would be to own, control, and coordinate every material and every part of production. After World War II we moved quickly from the world of the Rouge to the world of international production, where Japan and South Korea rose to prominence and US integrated-production corporations declined. Soon Japan and South Korea were joined by other Asian "tigers," and supply chains started to weave themselves around the world.

As those changes came to be, the businesses and policymakers of the rich countries changed their focus. They aimed at bringing about a new tech-oriented era of manufacturing, in which companies would source materials and components from all over the world to make super-high-end products that would be constantly improved and redesigned—thus leaving any potential foreign competitors in the dust. These products would command high premiums, which would more than cover the relatively high labor costs of North American and European workers. By the early 1990s, US manufacturing excelled at generating clusters of producers of such items. Two such clusters were centered in Elk Grove, California, and Colorado Springs, Colorado, which grew so rapidly that they soon were seen as heirs to the great, bygone American factory centers.[6]

The year 1992 was especially good for both clusters. In Elk Grove, which is located a few miles down State Route 99 from Sacramento, Apple opened a plant that employed 1,500 people to make circuit boards and desktop computers seven days a week. The facility became the centerpiece of the Sacramento region's successful campaign to lure high-tech companies away from San Francisco Bay. By the mid-1990s, many people considered Sacramento to be the new computer-manufacturing capital of the United States.[7]

At the same time, Apple was putting the final touches on a state-of-the-art, 360,000-square-foot facility in Colorado Springs that would go on to produce more than a million PowerBook and desktop computers each year.[8]

Both regions were congratulating themselves on getting it right: they had acknowledged and adapted to the changed realities of global sourcing, and they had attracted the world's brightest high-tech company to be a manufacturing anchor. Other producers were flocking in. Regional officials savored the heady smell of what appeared to be long-term economic growth.

Too bad the world was still changing, and at an even faster pace.

In 1996 Apple once again demonstrated its pioneering spirit and sold its Colorado facility to a contract-manufacturing organization, or CMO, known as SCI Systems. This was the start of a very quick process by which Apple shifted the manufacturing of all its products to other companies, many of them overseas. Currently, Apple's main manufacturing-services supplier is Foxconn, part of the Taiwanese multinational company Hon Hai Precision Industry, the world's biggest electronics contract manufacturer. Foxconn employs about one million people, most of them in China.[9]

Sacramento and Colorado Springs soon lost all of their major manufacturing as other companies followed the same path. Today American ICT companies do not even bother to open their own factories. Cisco and HP's products, the Amazon Alexa, and Google Home products are all made by CMOs.

Elk Grove and Colorado Springs had done a commendable job of catching a moment, but the moment had passed. They then felt all too clearly how quickly companies can move once they detect the availability of cheaper alternatives, whether in labor, materials, or some other input factor. They saw how rapidly a cluster's supporting companies can collapse, leaving a legacy of bitterness.

Experiences like those have led many economists to forcefully reject the dream of bringing back manufacturing to developed countries like the United States, even in its modern-day, less-inclusive forms. When asked directly about what it would take to rekindle the rusting Bethlehem Steel plant in Pennsylvania, the economist Paul Krugman forcefully argued that "[t]here's no way to bring back all those steel plants and steel jobs, even if we stopped all imports. . . . So this is all a fantasy."[10]

Even more telling is the late Steve Jobs answer to then President Obama's question: "What would it take to bring back Apple's advanced manufacturing jobs to the United States?"

"Those jobs aren't coming back" answered Jobs.[11]

That unequivocal rejection, widely embraced by many development officials, has helped drive more and more regions toward the bright shiny object of VC–backed tech start-ups. But as we saw in previous chapters, the hunt for start-ups and venture capital can be both fruitless and, ultimately, self-defeating economically.

So what is a region to do?

The real problem lies with the framing of the options. Many economists would have regions believe that they face a simple, binary set of choices—"bringing back manufacturing," in the pattern of Sacramento or Colorado Springs, and/or chasing after VC-funded tech start-ups. When I ask people—even knowledgeable policymakers—what innovation might look like *outside* those options, I get a blank stare.

This poor framing of the options stems from an incomplete understanding of the landscape of business processes. Communities have forgotten that there are many types of innovation, and many of these types can lead to growth. The term "innovation" applies to *any* action that allows an enterprise to offer better products or services at current or lower costs. Growth can stem from incremental change as well as from improvements anywhere along the value chain, from ideation to production to consumption—even to the post-user phase. Communities overlook the reality that incremental and process innovations have been the real heroes of innovation-based growth.[12]

Hiding in plain sight within the world's rapidly changing production terrain are numerous innovation-based growth opportunities that have nothing to do with—and are much better than—trying to create Internet, biotech, nanotech, quantumtech, fintech, next-massive-tech, bubble-tech start-ups, or lure science-based manufacturing industries.

Regions have multifaceted options for fostering innovation-based growth, generating jobs, and making those jobs stick. The community and business leaders of Sacramento and Colorado Springs fell victim to the lulling idea that once you have brought a big manufacturing center to a region by encouraging a specific company, the development work is done. They failed to understand how dangerous it can be to place big bets on specific companies instead of on a set of capabilities. They did not see that regions need to learn to create sustainable growth by making significant, targeted investments in creating a unique offering around a particular stage of innovation production; that regions—not just companies—need to become innovative about production. Sacramento and Colorado Springs were unable to persuade Apple and the other companies that continuing to maintain operations in these clusters would have provided a competitive advantage.

Manufacturing, more properly called *physical production*, is a viable option. Indeed, it is the core of stages 3 (second-generation product and component innovation) and 4 (production and assembly), and the reason why they produce more good jobs for a wider variety of skills. Nonetheless, the regions that succeed in them are not the regions that build new GM factories, but the regions that developed the ability to constantly innovate in those stages. As a matter of fact, it was only recently that Apple tried to prove Steve Jobs wrong and bring manufacturing back to the United States. This time Apple opened its assembly factory in Austin, Texas, but only to find that after years of neglect there is no longer an ecosystem of innovative-production in the United States, even in a high-tech center such as Austin. Not only did Apple find it very difficult to find the right skills, such tooling engineers, but it could not even source the right screws.[13]

As other regions, away from California, Colorado, and Texas, understood that the focus is not companies but the skills and institutions to excel in stages 3 and 4, the world's biggest corporations are lining up and pushing each other to send more work and orders their way. Shenzhen, China, and North Carolina, USA, are attractive for ICT and biotech production, respectively, not because they are cheapest or offer multibillion investment incentives, but because they offer a unique set of skills and ecosystems.

The reality of our new global system is that communities prosper by developing a specific set of innovation capacities and capabilities, not by paying large amount of taxpayers' money for companies to locate an isolated activity. To succeed you need to put the old adage—if you build it they will come—on its head. The reality is that if you have what they need, they will come and build it. For each stage of innovation there is a need for a specialized set of innovational capabilities, and for those to be created and sustained, a very different ecosystem is required. Look at the world's most successful innovation-based locales, situated in widely diverse countries from the United States to Germany, Korea, Japan, Finland, Israel, Taiwan, Denmark,

China, Singapore, and India. These regions are not cookies coming from the same cutter. As a matter of fact, even in China, three regions all working in broadly the same stage of production—Shenzhen, Beijing, and Shanghai—are as different from one another as they are from foreign regions.[14]

Communities that want to succeed need to stop thinking about specific technologies and industries. Indeed, they need to stop thinking about science or even R&D. Instead they need to start thinking about innovation: what are the specific capabilities that would allow them to excel in innovation in a particular stage, and how they are going about growing and sustaining them? Companies come and go, seeking that rarest of all resources: knowledge and the ability to transform it to useful products and services.

It's time we learn how to go about building our new Jenga towers in a world of fragmented production.

PART II
INNOVATION AND PROSPERITY

5

Four Are Better Than One—But First, Let Us Plan It Strategically

"Can't you give me brains?" asked the Scarecrow.

"You don't need them. You are learning something every day. A baby has brains, but it doesn't know much. Experience is the only thing that brings knowledge, and the longer you are on earth the more experience you are sure to get."

"That may all be true," said the Scarecrow, "but I shall be very unhappy unless you give me brains."

The false Wizard looked at him carefully.

"Well," he said with a sigh, "I'm not much of a magician, as I said; but if you will come to me tomorrow morning, I will stuff your head with brains. I cannot tell you how to use them, however; you must find that out for yourself."

"Oh, thank you—thank you!" cried the Scarecrow. "I'll find a way to use them, never fear!"

—L. Frank Baum, *The Wonderful Wizard of Oz*

Now that we have seen how thoroughly the world has changed, the question for regions seeking innovation-based growth is this: Is it possible to devise an analytical framework that will allow regions to systematically develop a context-specific policy for their community? The answer to this question is yes. The framework consists of identifying and supporting what I call agents of innovation—firms and individuals—and understanding the available models for success and how they apply in the different stages of globally fragmented innovation.

The elements of the framework will unfold over the next three chapters. To get there, let us look first at a tragic, morbidly fascinating innovation paradox: Canada.

Canada has everything that academics and consultants alike argue is needed to excel in innovation. It has extremely high levels of education, with students constantly scoring well on international tests from kindergarten through university. Public investment in R&D is 0.8 percent of GDP, which is the highest among English-speaking countries. Canada has maintained significant investment in science, with three universities ranked in the world top's fifty (Israel, Finland, Ireland, and Taiwan combined have zero), which translates to an impressive outpouring of high-impact scientific publications—more than 2,500 scientific papers per million inhabitants annually. Further, many important technologies, in fields as diverse as materials science, robotics, agriculture, energy, artificial intelligence, web search, vaccination, telecommunication, and media, originated in Canada.[1]

Yet once we turn our gaze away from invention and look at innovation, the trends go in the opposite direction. Private-business R&D expenditures took the opposite trend to the public ones and have been continuously shrinking, dropping to a steady level of below 1 percent of GDP. This figure makes Canada one of the worst performers in the OECD. Not surprisingly, with this level of business R&D investment, patents and other forms of IPR have followed the same downward trend, and labor productivity is stagnant and abysmal. The most damning statistic of all is that since 2007, the more the Canadian government has invested taxpayers' money in trying to spur innovation, the less Canadian private businesses have done so. Canada easily wins the wooden-spoon award for the worst innovation policy among all developed economies.[2]

The reason: Canadian politicians and policymakers have always confused innovation with invention.

Innovation is not invention, nor is it research. Indeed, it is not even R&D. Innovation is, pure and simple, any activity along the process of taking new ideas and devising new or improved products and services and putting them in the market. It comes in all stages of innovation specialization, from the first vision to design, development, production, sale, usage, and after-sale of products and services. This definition should also immediately tell you who the agents of innovation are: firms and individuals. The rest of the players in and around innovation, even the world's most amazing research universities, are at best enablers, and at worst a distraction. Indeed, although the Times Higher Education Survey ranks Oxford and Cambridge as the world's top two universities, looking at the UK's economy one would be hard-pressed to find any discernible positive effects on innovation coming from this amazing achievement.[3]

Canada is the most striking example of how people from all venues of life can consistently refuse to learn the most basic economic lesson: If you want success in innovation, focus on its agents. Having a higher-education policy is a wonderful thing; having S&T and research policy should also be celebrated; having intellectual-property policy is a true blessing. Nevertheless, these elements are *not* to be confused with innovation policy. Further, a "strategic" industrial policy that focuses on "high-tech sectors" is also *not* an innovation policy.

The logic of innovation policy is fundamentally different from industrial policy. Often it is the very opposite. To have an industrial policy, you need to know the industry, the customers, the products, and the business models. Taking those into account, you can devise "strategic" policies to build competitive advantage. Innovation policy starts with the assumption that you have no clue what the industry, products, customers, and business models involved in innovation would look like. If you *do* know what all these aspects of innovation look like, I highly recommend that you quit your current job and use this knowledge to become a billionaire. Innovation policy achieves success if the agents it creates and stimulates go on to disrupt business as usual in innovative—hence currently unknown—ways.[4]

Accordingly, innovation policy's aim is to:

1. Equip the agents of innovation—companies and individuals—with the capacities they need in order to excel.
2. Develop, support, and sustain the economic ecosystem that innovators need in order to thrive.
3. Find the most effective ways to stimulate said agents to innovate and grow their businesses. While it would be truly wonderful, for multiple reasons, to have the most highly educated science, technology, engineering, and medical workforce in the world, if the individuals in that workforce don't engage in innovation, then all your investment in skills and education is for naught.

This is the first part of the framework that communities can use to devise policy on fostering innovation-based growth—understanding how to identify and support agents of innovation. But there is substantially more to it than that. Communities also need to ask: What models do we have to succeed in innovation? And do they look different for the four stages of globally fragmented innovation?

As we have already seen, it is very clear that different stages of innovation necessitate diverse innovational capacities, and that for each stage, developing, sustaining, and utilizing those capacities requires a different ecosystem. To start our foray into systematically analyzing the needed capacities and ecosystems, let us introduce a few concepts.

Growth Models

The theoretical concept of "growth models" was first developed by my friend John Zysman. Growth models are defined as what it takes for firms at given specific periods to compete in markets, create value, and generate jobs. Thus, growth models are different at different periods and for different stages of innovation. This is an evolutionary process, and, accordingly, a growth model also refers to the needed evolution in the roles governments must play in kindling, sustaining, and supporting innovation. In our joint work, John and I have shown how utilizing the growth-model perspective focuses attention on two dimensions of innovation: the growth *tasks* and possibilities that apply to firms and locations at given moments in the global economy, and the institutional and political *capacities* required to address the problems. A significant advantage of this approach is that it considers at its core the institutions and political arrangements that create the ability to address tasks.[5]

Thus, the notion of growth models immediately leads us to think about the differences in firms' strategies in each stage, how those strategies lead to different tasks, and the varied capacities that are needed. As the focus of attention in this book is the individual locale, we also need to pay attention to what, in several collaborative works with Peter Cowhey, Giulio Buciuni, and Michael Murphree, I came to call the *four fundamentals*, and how they differ in the different stages of innovation.[6]

The Four Fundamentals

1. *Flows of local–global knowledge, demand, and input.* Since we live in a world of fragmented production, continuous success requires a region to establish and institutionalize modes of ensuring constant

bidirectional flows of these three critical components. That means institutionalizing the modes in which the local interacts with the global and the global interacts with the local. In technical terms, the literature on this topic discusses the interaction between "local buzz" and "global pipelines." It also talks about "strategic coupling"—the ways in which local firms interact and become critical parts, controlling key sets of activities, within the fragmented global production networks. These activities represent key strategic decisions for firms. As we shall see, different modes of strategic coupling are more or less compatible with building and sustaining the capacities that are needed in different stages of innovation.[7]

2. *The supply and creation of public and semi-public goods.* Innovation, by its very essence, is a collective endeavor that requires an array of public and semi-public goods, from the supply of specialized skills, be they craftspeople or R&D engineers; to shared assets, such as testing facilities, trade shows, or specialized prototyping-to-production facilities; to what I call collaborative-public spaces, the socioeconomic places where an industry moves from sharing knowledge to becoming an industrial community.[8]

3. *A local ecosystem that reinforces the firm-level benefits* of the previous two fundamentals and allows access to critical resources, such as finance or legal services, that fit the business models and the local stage of innovation specialization. In time, the elements of the ecosystem support one another as the locale develops in a specific innovation-based-growth trajectory. For example, as we have already established, having an American-like venture-capital industry is complementary to having a start-up-led stage 1 local industry. The supply of venture capital stimulates specific business models, which require certain skills and the involvement of certain financial and legal institutions, including an intimate coupling with Wall Street and NASDAQ; the start-ups' significant financial exits further feed this particular cycle of growth.

4. *Co-evolution of the previous three fundamentals* and the role of public policy as the locale grows and excels. One of the classic mistakes of policymaking is the assumption that what works in one time and one place will always work across time and space. This is the real meaning of rigidity: the inability to change your behavior as the environment around you changes. As my friends Andrew Schrank and Michael Piore have shown, this built-in legal and structural rigidity is what led the

once-innovative US regulatory regime down the drain, while allowing seemingly old-fashioned French/Spanish regulators to sustain flexibility and co-evolve with the industry they regulate. Let us think about it for a moment: Should we assume that the role of government will be the same when you have no innovation-based industry and when you lead the world in both industrial R&D investment ratio and VC investment and IPOs on NASDAQ per capita? Would we truly expect programs that at one point supported bicycle manufacturers to be as helpful when those companies lead the world in materials science? Innovation policy is always an evolutionary process. Different market failures become more acute as industry cycles change both locally and globally. To stay effective, policies need to be able to evolve with those changes.[9]

These four fundamentals are a crucial element of the framework for understanding how to foster innovation-based growth. Let us now take those four fundamentals and see how they help us to understand cases, across stages and spaces, of locales working in multiple industries. For reasons that will become apparent later, we'll go in reverse order, starting with *stage 4: production and assembly*.

The Transformation of Shenzhen

Regions excelling in stage 4 of innovation specialization are the best innovators when it comes to the production of goods and services—that is, the final creation and assembly of fully defined-and-designed-elsewhere products and services. The elements of innovation expertise in this stage are: first, figuring out how to profitably produce ever-more-complex products from tens, sometimes hundreds, of thousands of components developed by multiple companies around the world; second, figuring out how to systemize production using constantly changing materials; and third, managing wide fluctuations in demand, moving within days from several workers to multiple hundreds of thousands of workers. Success requires creating and sustaining an ecosystem that allows companies to excel in those three elements.

In some cases, the advantages of stage 4 ecosystems have given rise to globally dominating firms. To understand the power of these ecosystems, let us look at China. The rise of China to global dominance cannot be explained without the rise of Shenzhen and its surrounding cities and townships at the tip of the Pearl River Delta, adjacent to Hong Kong. If you read the popular press or follow the academic literature, you might be led to believe that the real challenge to the rest of the already wealthy world is the immense power of Chinese science and R&D, emanating from prestigious research universities and institutions such as Tsinghua, Beijing, Fudan, and Jia Tong Universities, as well as the Chinese Academy of Science. This would then lead you to look with admiring eyes to Beijing and Shanghai.[10]

That would be a mistake. If we care about innovation, we should always focus on its agents. Once you draw up the list of the Chinese companies that have truly become global competitors—such as Huawei, Tencent, Oppo, and ZTE in ICT; DJI in drones; or BYD in batteries and electric cars—you realize that they are all from the greater Shenzhen area. While Shenzhen now features in surveys of leading outlets such as the *Economist* as a fountain of production innovation, it still has no prominent universities or research institutes. Furthermore, as recently as 2011, when Michael Murphree and I were interviewing prominent Chinese business and research leaders and mentioned that we were researching innovation in Shenzhen, a typical reaction was laughter, followed by: "Shenzhen? Shenzhen is nothing but a manufacturing center, not a place to do R&D." This was also the conclusion of multiple academic researchers throughout the 2000s. Following this reasoning, after the 2008 global financial crisis erupted, academics and pundits alike declared the death of Shenzhen, predicting that companies would leave the area in a quest for ever-lower labor costs.[11]

Instead, Shenzhen not only continues to thrive, proudly branding itself as the "production capital of China," but has also become the darling of every academic and pundit (sometimes the same ones who had just declared its imminent destruction), featuring as the "new innovation hub" in multiple surveys. Reading those new admiring reports, one might wonder what exactly Shenzhen is, and what kind of innovation we are talking about, since there has never been any cutting-edge scientific R&D conducted in Shenzhen.

The story of the transformation of Shenzhen starts in 1979, when China decided to open up to the West and experiment with adding capitalistic features to its economic system. The Chinese central state leadership was looking for places remote from anything of importance, so that if the experiments failed they could be shut down without political consequences. Shenzhen was chosen as one of five Special Economic Zones (SEZ), and a fortified wall with heavily armed checkpoints was built around it to ensure that nothing of this dangerous capitalistic experiment could leak into China without approval. At that time Shenzhen was a series of villages and fishing communities along the Hong Kong border. The entire land area of Shenzhen Municipality (2,020 square kilometers) had a population of 314,100. Some 80 percent of residents worked as fishermen or farmers. Less than 20 percent of the GDP came from industry of any kind, and the entire area had only eight kilometers of paved roads. More interestingly for those who dream about innovation, there were only *two engineers* in the whole of Shenzhen, and of course no centers of higher education or research.[12]

Once the SEZ project was initiated, however, Shenzhen quickly became the richest city per capita in China. By 2017, per capita income in Shenzhen had reached 100,173 RMB, 1.5 times the national average. Between 1980 and 1986, the economy grew at an average of 44 percent, and from 1987 to 1995, GDP grew 29 percent annually on average. By 2017, Shenzhen already had a GDP of 2.249 trillion RMB ($96.65 billion USD), and by 2015 the population had reached 11.275 million. As the SEZ developed, manufacturing moved out from the three SEZ districts directly adjacent to the Hong Kong border and spread to the Bao'an and Longgang districts outside the SEZ barrier fence and along the Shenzhen-Dongguan-Guangzhou corridor.[13]

Thus, Shenzhen was built from the simplest production activities upward. It became what it is today—the world's most successful and fastest-growing innovation-based region—by mastering the art of assembly and production for the world's best multinational corporations (MNCs) in multiple industries, and, in doing so, developing its innovation capacities. To understand what it takes to be a successful stage 4 locale, let us look at the rise and evolution of its mobile phone industry.[14]

Production of mobile phones in Shenzhen and neighboring Dongguan began in the mid-1990s and accelerated in the 2000s. Since the 2008 financial crisis, the manufacturing sector has faced substantial challenges. Labor costs have risen rapidly. Many mobile-phone multinationals have closed their facilities: Nokia's plant closed in 2015 and Samsung shifted most phone production to Vietnam. Firms contracting with MNCs have seen orders reduced by up to 90 percent. Nonetheless, mobile-phone production remains robust and its sophistication is only growing, with Huawei, ZTE, Oppo, and Vivo becoming leading global brands, and Foxconn ensuring that the latest iPhones are produced in Shenzhen.[15]

This resilience is built on the comprehensive local production chain. Unlike the situation in Texas, described in chapter 4, where Apple found it difficult to source things as simple as screws or assemble more than four qualified production engineers in one room, in Shenzhen up to 90 percent of all components and parts needed to produce a smartphone can be sourced locally, and experienced high-quality production engineers can be found literally on every street corner. The growth of the local production chain has been a private and public policy goal that has been constantly upgraded in the last two decades through meeting sophisticated overseas clients' demands; relentless focus on incremental and production innovation; and reliance on local government support to create, enhance, and sustain public goods and the ecosystem as a whole.

Mobile-phone production requires the integration of thousands of components from hundreds of suppliers, amassing and assembling components in a single location with extremely tight deadlines and very low error tolerances. Smartphones utilize technologies from multiple sectors, including wireless communications (digital signals processing chips, receivers, antennae), computers (CPUs, PCBs), materials science (screens, cases, glue), and software. Final assemblers or brand manufacturers draw upon subsystem suppliers (motherboards, screens, batteries, power supplies) working for multiple clients. Subsystem suppliers rely on an even larger network of electronic, metal, and plastic components producers making discrete, often commoditized, parts. The highest single value-added components are the integrated circuits from specialized firms such as the American company Qualcomm and the Taiwanese company MediaTek, whose rise to prominence was discussed in chapter 1, or memory, where the Korean behemoth Samsung controls the global market. It is the growth and development, since 1979, of the sophisticated local production networks and innovational capacities that allows Shenzhen to continue to excel.[16]

The electronics industry was one of the first to start when the SEZ was established in 1979. The first participants were Hong Kong's electronics firms, which opened assembly plants. In the late 1980s, Taiwanese firms followed suit, which proved critical, since the Taiwanese manufacturers demanded that their sub-suppliers relocate with them. A key company has been Delta, a maker of power supplies and one of Apple's core suppliers, which mandated that three hundred of its Taiwanese suppliers co-locate in Dongguan. In the 2000s demand began exceeding these relocated firms' capacity. Individual entrepreneurs, some of them former line workers eager to seize opportunities, established independent component suppliers and contract manufacturers that could pick up overflow orders. Thus, the local ecosystem became more resilient and developed an even greater innovative capacity in production and assembly. By the mid-2000s, mobile phone manufacturers could source almost any electronics component from producers within a travel radius of three hours. The region had developed a complete electronics production chain of multinational and domestic firms.[17]

This was the specific intention of local government officials, who came to see the completion and perfection of this production chain as central to their regional competitiveness strategy. As a top official remarked:

> It is not policy per se that makes companies wish to invest here. Rather the location for investment is determined by the production chain and supplier network. Our region has a nearly complete computer production system which means investors want to set up here. The suppliers and customers for component manufacturers are close. This is why we focus on ensuring that the complete production chain exists and is sustained here.

When Michael Murphree and I conducted interviews with small, large, and foreign factory owners, they all agreed, and interestingly used almost the same words in 2007 and in 2017. An entrepreneur we first interviewed in 2007 bluntly told us:

> I chose to come here because this industry's production base is here. The providers are all located here. If I had my company in Beijing, then I would have needed to ship all the parts from here to Beijing. Since all the parts are manufactured here, it is a great advantage for my company to be here. For example, even if in the morning I realize that I am missing critical parts, I just call my friends and within a few minutes these parts are sent and delivered to me.

In 2017, when we interviewed a leading multinational, the manager described his decision to locate in Shenzhen:

> Whatever you want to make, you can find the parts immediately in this area. If our factory was in Vietnam, the components would not be there. This would be bad for a firm like ours. General production might be able to go to

Southeast Asia, but for production R&D and new product manufacturing, this is the best place to be. The chain is complete.

Utilizing the electronics supply chain, mobile-phone production began in the 1990s. Labor and components availability motivated leading contract manufacturers Foxconn (1994) and Flextronics (1994) to invest. Samsung (1992) and Nokia (1995) opened the first global mobile-phone brand factories. Local telecommunications hardware firms Huawei and ZTE started producing mobile phones in the late 1990s. Other indigenous electronics brands followed in the 2000s. More importantly, the region's specific innovational capacities led to the rise of a gray-market innovation—between 2008 and 2012, Greater Shenzhen's Huaqiangbei area became the center of production for *shanzhai* (pirate) mobile phones. These phones used standardized chipsets from MediaTek and standardized internal configurations, differentiating themselves through peripheral hardware innovations. Made by small companies—sometimes a handful of young engineers assembling the phones themselves—*shanzhai* phones incorporated varied hardware innovations: multiple SIM technology to reduce user costs by automatically switching between SIM cards, depending on the caller's network; large keyboards for senior citizens; ringing with both sounds and light for the hearing impaired; broadcast radio and TV receivers; and even counterfeit-money detectors.[18]

The *shanzhai* phenomenon collapsed as quickly as it emerged. Nevertheless, the conditions that enabled small firms to make *shanzhai* phones supported the ongoing and increasingly sophisticated efforts of large electronics companies and former *shanzhai* firms to launch independent smartphone brands. Once smartphones became a stable platform, where competition revolved around incremental innovation and the ability to produce slightly differentiated phones with the same quality as leading brands but at a fraction of the cost, while constantly improving production, Shenzhen companies excelled, taking a growing market share from Western and Korean companies with each passing year. Their stage 4 innovative capabilities were further enhanced due to the fact that Google was not allowed to use the bundling licensing of its Android operating system that it used elsewhere in the world (until this practice was found illegal on antitrust grounds by the EU on July 18, 2018). This allowed Chinese smartphone companies to develop mobile operation systems' (OS) incremental innovational capacities, build their own app stores, and tailor the OS to the specific phones they designed and produced. All these capacities and capabilities were not allowed to be developed and flourish in the West, where Google and Apple used their market position to ensure that this would not happen.[19]

It is important to understand how this stage 4 ecosystem works and its specific limits and strengths. First, all the components and inputs, apart from raw materials and specific high-end components such as integrated circuits sourced from global leaders (Intel, AMD, ARM, Qualcomm, MediaTek, Samsung), are produced and traded locally. However, there is no innovation or production of those high-end, cutting-edge R&D components and systems in the greater Shenzhen area. Thus, the system is dependent on global production networks to supply it with a constant flow of innovation and critical components. This became clear when the Trump administration took issue with ZTE and Huawei, China's most sophisticated and successful telecommunication equipment companies. Within weeks of the Trump administration declaring an embargo that made it illegal for American companies to supply ZTE, the company was on the verge of bankruptcy, and was saved only because the Trump administration relented and relaxed its embargo.[20]

Since Michael Murphree and I started interviewing in 2007, interviewees have consistently emphasized three domains in which local authorities have proved critical in developing and sustaining the greater Shenzhen stage 4 innovation ecosystem: real estate and facilities, R&D and equipment subsidies, and stage-specific human resource development. As a result, the local production network is vast and complex. Leading domestic companies (such as Huawei, ZTE, Oppo, Vivo, BYD, and DJI) and major contract assembly firms (Foxconn, Huabel, and Flextronics) perform final assembly. Dozens of first-tier suppliers, such as Delta Power Supplies, Janus Precision Components, and Aocheng PCB, produce subsystems for brands and contract assemblers. Hundreds of individual component suppliers make the specific parts on which subsystem suppliers draw. Meeting foreign requirements requires constant upgrading of local suppliers' quality to meet global standards. Upgraded suppliers sell their improved components to other customers, since most components are standardized. As a result, local makers have access to the same components and technology as the most advanced global firms. This is true for almost all ICT hardware products. As a result, if you are situated in Silicon Valley, Tel Aviv, or anywhere else in the world, and you just successfully finished your novel-product R&D, and now want to manufacture a top-of-the-line, first-to-the-world ICT product, the best place for you to make it happen is in Shenzhen. There is no equivalent pool of stage 4 innovation skills combined with a production ecosystem in North America or Europe—or, as a matter of fact, anywhere else in Asia.[21]

It is also important to remember what *not* to do in such an environment. A blunt assessment of how to succeed in stage 4 innovation came from a VP of a top local smartphone company:

> China is good in the application of technology, but it does not have a lot of capabilities in fundamental technology because the timeline for such projects is long and the investment requirements are high. We focus on business models that utilize what China's innovation capabilities excel at.

Better advice cannot be given to locales that care about innovation-based growth models that supply vast quantities of good jobs to people with multiple skills backgrounds, instead of a few fabulous jobs that are available only to the graduates of the world's elite universities.

The growth benefits for regions of stage 4 innovation do not occur only in physical production. Have you tried to buy a Dell computer lately, after the company was taken private again? If so, you probably realized pretty quickly that every person you dealt with, from the ordering, to the build-up of your customized machine, to the financial control and the aftercare services, is located in India. We have already talked about the Indian IT consultancies, but Indian firms have mastered stage 4 innovation in many other services. What they have found, to the delight of many gainfully employed Indians, is that the co-location of all components of a service offering, in a very similar way to the production of ICT products in greater Shenzhen, allows them to excel in the innovation, production, and assembly of service products.

Applying the Four Fundamentals

The amount of innovation that is needed to excel in this stage, whether with physical goods or more intangible services, is parallel to none. It is not glitzy, and does not inspire awestruck media coverage, but it produces sustainable economic growth and jobs for millions of people, and arguably more welfare to humanity than most Silicon Valley start-ups will ever produce.

It is important to note how the four fundamentals played out in Shenzhen. We have already seen how the local and the global interacted and how bi-directional flows of knowledge, ideas, and physical outputs became institutionalized. We also saw how the local government has been key in supplying public and semi-public goods, from specialized spaces, to missions analyzing the production networks of specific products, to figuring out what critical capabilities and steps are missing and devising ways to bring them, and the companies that produced them, to the area. The same goes for both human capital and finance.

Especially important for the sustained success of greater Shenzhen has been the co-evolution of those policies with the industry's needs as it grew and become more sophisticated. The case of human capital stands as an ideal example. Within the convoluted system of internal migration in China and the *hukou* registration system, where at least 60 million people are treated as illegal immigrants in their own country, the greater Shenzhen localities are a shining example of humane, and smart, economic growth policies. This might come as a surprise to those who read about the area as the birth-place of the most horrific sweatshops in China. The reality is that the smarter towns and cities understand how to cultivate the "migrant" human capital they need.

From the beginning of the industry, it became clear that in order to expand and excel in stage 4 innovation, the area needed a vast influx of migrants to work in its factories.

The majority of line workers are migrants from China's interior. They lack the independent financial resources, especially upon arrival in the region, to purchase or rent local property. Many workers, however, stay for long periods of time, and thus require room and board. Additionally, migrant workers must also be able to arrange necessary work permits to reside and receive payment in their new home.

Greater Shenzhen's local governments facilitate the availability of pro-duction labor for ICT factories in two ways. First, localities supply factory housing. Second, and much more importantly, Guangdong's provincial government has long encouraged migrant labor. With regard to housing, municipal-, township- and village-level administrations frequently provide housing for workers as part of the industrial-park designs. From the migrant-labor point of view, given that the mandated minimum wage in a city such as Dongguan at the end of 2019 was only about $245 USD per month, in the context of a rapidly rising cost of living, a guarantee of housing is a major attraction. For workers who remain for more than a few years, the localities facilitate the transfer of legal residency (*hukou*) and, in the meantime, adopt a lax attitude toward residency laws.[22]

As the industry developed in sophistication, it needed access to specialized high-skill human capital, so local authorities reacted in tandem. Since the mid-2000s, local authorities have aggressively helped companies recruit and relocate talent from other provinces. *Hukou* regulations have been specifically restructured to facilitate the recruitment of educated labor. While by itself this is not sufficient to attract engineers from places such as Shanghai and Beijing, researchers from strong universities in interior provinces such as Hubei and Sichuan find the *hukou* provisions an important part of the hiring offer. Many of greater Shenzhen's industries' needs are well supported by those universities, which tend to have large research departments in fields that are crucial for stage 4 research—fields that are no longer considered cutting-edge enough for universities that deem themselves top global research universities.[23]

Furthermore, since the growing demand from, and prospect of moving to, greater Shenzhen makes these programs more attractive, the provincial universities are happy to work with Shenzhen companies. This has led to yet another co-evolution in private-public policy, which is also a perfect example of the utilization of shared assets. Over the last several years, local companies and universities from China's interior have been collaborating to supply shared facilities that would not have been profitable for either side alone. For example, a company from Dongguan, Zhicheng Champion, has had long-term research partnerships with Huazhong University of Science and Technology and Wuhan University. With support from the local government, companies and universities co-ran a provincial-level R&D center at the greater Shenzhen's factory campuses. In the case of Zhicheng, the work focused on improved power systems and batteries. PhD students from universities in central China need access to laboratory facilities in order to conduct their thesis research, and the companies benefit from the low-cost talent while building their in-house research capabilities. Similar arrangements can be found at the post-doctoral level. By providing facilities for PhD and post-doctoral researchers, local companies improve their own R&D while keeping it within the company structure, as well as having access to talent for future employment.[24]

Thus, as the case of greater Shenzhen demonstrates, it is not enough to get your fundamentals right. In order to have sustained growth, you need to be able to change your policies and ecosystem in step with the changing needs of the local industry and the ever-more-sophisticated demands from the global production networks.

6

Sewing and Designing—Incrementally—
Innovation-Based Growth

The tinsmiths looked the Woodman over carefully and then answered that they thought they could mend him so he would be as good as ever.

So they set to work in one of the big yellow rooms of the castle and worked for three days and four nights, hammering and twisting and bending and soldering and polishing and pounding at the legs and body and head of the Tin Woodman, until at last he was straightened out into his old form, and his joints worked as well as ever.

To be sure, there were several patches on him, but the tinsmiths did a good job, and as the Woodman was not a vain man he did not mind the patches at all.

—L. Frank Baum, *The Wonderful Wizard of Oz*

Another stage that is too often dismissed by the innovation pundits and consultants is stage 3—second-generation product and component innovation. In this stage, firms improve, expand, and redefine a product or critical component, either by applying incremental and process innovation or by recombining and expanding the product's use and utility. This stage is incorrectly labeled—and despised—by some as mere "fast following" or "incremental" innovation. But it is often the unsung hero of economic growth.[1]

Consider Taiwan.

Since the 1960s, Taiwan has constantly worked to improve its ecosystem and stage-3-specific innovational capabilities across several sectors, from traditional industries such as bicycles to the latest niches in systems on chip design, so that its innovation agents—companies and individuals—can compete globally. As a result, Taiwan has truly joined the ranks of the rich in every imaginable indicator. And its stage 3 success has had wide-ranging consequences elsewhere: from the fact that Taiwan has had the most successful response to COVID-19 in the world, without ever having to go into full or partial lockdown or shut its school system, to, as we have seen in chapter 5, how the stage 3 innovation of Taiwanese company MediaTek allowed stage 4 smartphone producers in Shenzhen to prosper.

While we usually tend to celebrate success, three fine examples of failure show just how far Taiwanese companies were able to reach by focusing on stage 3 innovation. These examples also show stage 3's strengths as well as its limitations. In the first case, the failure was not that of the Taiwanese company involved; instead, it was the spectacular failure of a Silicon Valley darling—Alphabet/Google—and its defunct (for now) Google Glass. We should all be thankful that Google Glass failed, if only for reasons of data ownership and security (we will talk more about those issues in a later chapter). However, what is interesting about Google Glass for us here is the choice of its main technology suppliers. The reason this is interesting is that a key supplier has been Himax—a Taiwanese fabless design house specializing in micro-display technology. Himax was chosen as the supplier of the key chip array for Google Glass on the basis of its strengths in LCOS (liquid crystal on silicon) technology (indeed, as part of the deal, Google became an investor and a significant shareholder of Himax).[2]

Why was Himax chosen? Mark Gomes, the analyst who uncovered Google's decision in March 2013, a few months before it was made public, said it best: "Himax's appeal is not their bleeding-edge technology, it's more the ideal price-to-performance technology."[3]

Over the course of many years, Himax amassed a vast array of patents and inventions—not so that it could develop bleeding-edge technology, but specifically so that it could increase price-to-performance for existing technologies. The original source of Himax's innovational capacities was the Industrial Technology Research Institute (ITRI) and its labs (the foremost being the Electronic Research and Service Organization, or ERSO), which were also where UMC and MediaTek, and indeed almost all innovative Taiwanese companies, originated. To understand the continuous and changing key roles ITRI played in the growth of Taiwan as an innovation powerhouse, we need to go back to the early 1970s, when both the world's and Taiwan's economies went through several waves of severe crises.[4]

In 1971 the Bretton Woods system was dismantled. In 1973 the first oil shock resulted in a steep rise in the price of oil, and many of the advanced industrial economies started to suffer from stagflation. Taiwan's exports, then mainly textile and footwear and low-level electronics, started to face a double squeeze: competition from less-developed countries coupled with protectionists' measures in advanced markets. In addition, with the re-emergence of China on the global political scene and the de-recognition of Taiwan in the United Nations in 1971, the small island started a long period of formal political isolation.[5]

In January 1973, Yun-hsuan Sun, then the minister for economic affairs and later the premier, oversaw the establishment of ITRI near Hsinchu, a strategic location close to Taiwan's two leading engineering universities, National Chiao Tung and National Tsing Hua Universities. ITRI was created through the merger of three existing governmental labs. Using his considerable political power, Sun managed to transfer the responsibility for electronics R&D from the ministry of telecommunication laboratory to the newly formed ITRI. However, it is important to remember that while today we view ITRI as critical, at the time it was seen as a relatively minor policy initiative, and its financing was negligible from the point of view of the region's overall industrial policies.[6]

The idea behind ITRI's creation was to form one lab that would be responsible for the upgrading of the region's industrial technology through technology transfer, development, and diffusion. The objective was that the government would take it upon itself to solve the risky and more challenging part of the R&D process and would then diffuse the results to the industry, which would concentrate on final development and manufacturing. This decision led to a particular division of labor in which the public sector conducted most of the R and the private sector focused mostly on the D when dealing with new technologies. After a few successes, this division of labor became a key characteristic of the Taiwanese innovation system. It had significant influence on the kind of capabilities private firms developed and on the business models and business strategies of Taiwanese innovators. It has been the linchpin of Taiwanese success as a stage 3 innovation-based region.[7]

The semiconductor industry became the template of this development. A year and a half after the establishment of ITRI, in August 1974, Sun met with his friend Wen-yuan Pan, a Chinese-American engineer working at RCA's David Sarnoff laboratories in Princeton, New Jersey. The two agreed on a plan to formulate an innovation policy geared toward the creation of a semiconductor industry in Taiwan. Pan established a group of mostly Chinese American engineers working for leading American semiconductor companies in the United States. The group regularly convened at

Princeton as the Technical Advisory Committee. The committee submitted recommendations for the establishment of a specialist lab in ITRI that would act as the focal launching point for the industry. In September 1974, ERSO was established as a lab within ITRI, with its first goal being the development of technological capabilities to spur the growth of a semiconductor industry.[8]

ERSO started to look for sources of integrated-circuit fabrication technologies. However, it did not manage to find any willing partners until, through Pan's influence, RCA agreed to transfer its already-obsolete technology to ITRI in 1976. RCA had decided to get out of semiconductors and saw this as an opportunity to earn royalties from its old and soon-to-be-unused 7-micron technology, which was already far behind the then-world-limit of 2-microns. A group of forty engineers, many of whom later became the leaders of the semiconductor industry in Taiwan, spent almost a year in RCA's facilities in the United States, and ERSO built its first integrated-circuit fabrication plant with RCA's guidance. During 1977 and 1978, the first trial wafers were produced, and the Taiwanese team started to test its own experimental designs. In 1979 the ERSO team advanced to such a degree that it had better yield (that is, a higher ratio of working versus faulty circuits in each fabricated batch) than RCA's, and it started to sell small amounts of chips to supplement its financial resources.[9]

It was from this process of trail, error, failure to secure better options, and a last-gasp attempt based on what seemed to many at the time an already obsolete technology, that Taiwan found its particular path of stage 3 innovation in semiconductors. This path led Taiwan to rapid, widely distributed, and more equal economic growth, just when the rise of Silicon Valley was generating massive profits that were extremely unequally distributed.

As the ERSO team was perfecting its fabrication skills, the Taiwanese state was establishing the physical and business infrastructure needed for the semiconductor industry. It is here that Kuo-tingLi's leadership over Taiwanese S&T industrial policy became crucial. At that time Li served as minister of finance, after serving as the minister for economic affairs. In 1978 Li organized a special conference on Taiwan's economic and scientific future. The result of this well-attended event was the "Science and Technology Development Program," which was adopted by the cabinet and called for: (i) the creation of a special permanent advisory body for science and technology: the Science and Technology Advisory Group (STAG), to be chaired by Li, that would report directly to Premier Sun; and (ii) the creation of an infrastructure focused on the needs of science-based advanced industries.[10]

The latter project was championed by the president of National Tsing Hua University, S.S. Hsu, who urged the creation of a science-based industrial park next to Taiwan's three prominent engineering institutions in Hsinchu to imitate what he perceived to have happened around Stanford University in California. Thankfully for Taiwan, the implementation of the vision was as far away from what happened in Silicon Valley as possible.[11]

The park, named Hsinchu Science-Based Industrial Park, was put under the jurisdiction of the National Science Council and launched in 1980. Hsinchu Park became an extremely important factor in Taiwan's semiconductor industry's success by enabling the geographical concentration of a complete chain of stage 3 semiconductor-industry firms and suppliers within a half-hour drive of each other. As a result, you now have ODM companies such as Quanta and Acer next to specialized second-generation components and subsystem fabless companies such as Via, Sunplus, and MediaTek, sitting next door to the most sophisticated semiconductor-fabrication companies, from TSMC and UMC to Taiwan Mask Corporation.[12]

However, it was not private business that established the first or many of the subsequent leading firms of the Taiwanese semiconductor industry. In the late 1970s, facing what looked like a large initial investment with high uncertainty, no private entrepreneur, industrial group, or investor was willing to invest capital in commercializing the technologies developed in ERSO. In 1978 the head of ERSO, together with one of the forty engineers who went to RCA, proposed a plan for the establishment of a private-state company. The Ministry of Economic Affairs (MoEA) accepted their proposal and invited some of Taiwan's biggest companies as investors. At first, none of the companies agreed to join. The ministry then flexed its political muscles and organized a coalition of local companies that finally agreed to invest in the project to the tune of the minimal 51 percent of the shares that allowed the company to be private. Thus was the United Microelectronics Corporation (UMC) founded. UMC is not only currently the world's second-biggest pure-play foundry (another stage 3 innovation business model born in Taiwan that changed the global industry, which I discuss in detail later in this chapter), right after another ERSO spinoff, Taiwan Semiconductors Manufacturing Corporation (TSMC), but is also the source of multiple spinoffs, including MediaTek, that have revolutionized many industries.[13]

If you are curious as to how much that success cost the Taiwanese taxpayers, the total sum invested stood between $14 million and $20 million USD, which together with the state investment at ERSO at the time meant that Taiwan invested about $35 million over less than a decade to completely transform its economy. This was quite possibly the most cost-effective innovation policy the world has ever seen.[14]

ITRI's and ERSO's prominence over the development trajectory of the Taiwanese semiconductor industry did not end with the spinoff of UMC. On the contrary, ITRI's story is an almost ideal example of how innovation policy should co-evolve in tandem with the industries and ecosystems that grow around it. At the first stage, the successful launch of UMC encouraged subsequent formal and less-formal spinoffs—that is, teams of engineers leaving to establish their own companies. It is a process that continues to this day, as an analysis of the background of the founders of almost all of Taiwan's main semiconductors companies has revealed. ERSO itself also played a role in steering the Taiwanese industry away from focusing on specific market niches and trying to win global dominance by massive capital investment (a game played by Korea and Japan, with Korea winning both rounds at the somewhat prohibitive cost of multiple hundreds of billions of dollars, first in memory and then in panel displays). Instead, ERSO—without necessarily having a long-term vision, just the wisdom of playing to its locale's strengths instead of having delusions of grandeur—was key over the next two decades in basing the Taiwanese semiconductor industry around capabilities that would allow it to competitively and quickly design and manufacture custom-tailored chips (also known as Application Specific Integrated Circuit—ASIC), and not just around specific products. This was a classic stage 3 innovation model. ERSO rightly contended that by developing these capabilities, Taiwan's semiconductor industry could innovate across the whole spectrum of the ICT industry.[15]

The Keys to Success: OEMs and ODMs

To understand why this is important, let us look at the structure of the Taiwanese industry at the time. That period, the end of the 1970s and the beginning of the 1980s, was also the period in which the current mode of globalization, the global system of fragmented production, was being formed. This allowed Taiwanese companies to experiment with new business models that would later be perfected by Chinese companies. You might remember that Giant, now the world's most prominent bicycle producer, was established in 1972 and first reached success by being an OEM (original equipment manufacturer) for the American bicycle behemoth Schwinn. The business model of being an OEM or ODM (original design manufacturer) is what allows regions around the world to prosper in stage 3 and 4 innovation.

So, what are OEMs and ODMs?

The two are subcategories of contract manufacturing/manufacturers. A company employing an OEM strategy is in a subcontracting manufacturing relationship in which it manufactures equipment for its clients to be sold under the client's brand name and in accordance with the client's detailed specifications. A company employing an ODM strategy is in a subcontracting relationship in which it is also giving detailed and integrated design services to the brand-name company, which supplies it with only high-level design specifications. To hammer the point home, you might think you have an Apple iPhone, but in reality you have a phone produced by Foxconn, the trade name of Hon Hai Precision Industry Co. Ltd. And yes, Hon Hai, the world's largest electronics contract manufacturer, is a proud Taiwanese ODM/OEM.[16]

Another important lesson from Taiwan is the role ITRI played in the creation of the pure-play fabrication OEM model in semiconductors. The pure-play foundry model is one of the best examples of a techno-organizational innovation that enabled new levels of fragmentation in the semiconductor industry's production network. This kind of innovation spurred a rapid process of advances in product-stage specialization and product-stage economies of scope and scale—and, consequently, in stage-specific innovation. The pure-play foundry example illustrates how regions that decide to specialize in different stages of innovation can strategically shape global production networks in order to become key locales within them.

To understand the impact of the pure-play foundry model, let us first understand how the global semiconductor industry operated until the spinoff of TSMC by ITRI. Back then the semiconductor industry consisted mainly of companies that utilized the business model of integrated device manufacturers (IDMs). The IDM model calls for the creation of large vertically integrated firms that perform both design and fabrication in-house (think Intel). The leading semiconductor firms were all IDMs that built their own dedicated fabrication plants. This is an extremely capital-intensive model, since fabrication plants are expensive to build and need frequent "rebuilding," since the production technology is constantly improving as part of the famous "Moore's Law" phenomenon. The industry also consisted of design houses (also known as fabless companies) that were smaller and marginal and needed to secure fabrication capacities from IDMs without accepted standards for information transfer, and with the added risk that comes from sharing IP with potential (read: *probable*) competitors. Moreover, the process was lengthy and cumbersome, putting the design houses at a distinct disadvantage.[17]

The pure-play-foundry model calls for the creation of companies whose sole business is fabrication. Pure-play foundries are specialized OEMs that receive codified designs from design houses and fabricate their chips for them. Thus, they enable stage specialization in both design and fabrication. In 1986 the viability of the pure-play foundry model was still unclear, since critical technologies, such as the technology for full codification of the designs, needed in order for the pure-play foundry can receive the exact directions it needs to fabricate the chip properly, was not yet developed. However, for Taiwan, the value of the pure-play foundry model seems to outweigh the commercial and technological uncertainties that still exist.[18]

After the development of the needed technology and subsequent spinoff of TSMC by ITRI, the pure-play model became the prominent production model in the global semiconductor industry, completely transforming it in several ways. First, the pure-play model enables groups of engineers to quickly bring innovative designs to market with only limited financial resources, fostering even more rapid innovation cycles in the semiconductor industry. Second, the lower costs enable groups of engineers to profitably utilize the business strategy of offering cheaper chips in already developed niche markets using second-generation technologies—the business model that most of the Taiwanese semiconductor companies excel at. Third, the pure-play model transformed the industry by creating virtuous cycles of internal innovation and growing efficiency that make pure play even more profitable than the IDM model. Today, thanks to their head start and continuous innovations on both the fabrication and the design tools, the Taiwanese pure-play foundries, TSMC and UMC, are the global market leaders, and multiple attempts to compete with them on the part of other regions, including Singapore and several localities in China, have ended in failure.[19]

Thus, the strategy of focusing on developing two sets of stage 3 innovation capabilities, ending with a relentless stream of innovations to develop and sustain the quick design and production of tailor-made semiconductors for all industrial sectors, transformed not only the Taiwanese semiconductor industry but Taiwanese manufacturing as a whole. As the island's industry developed and matured, ITRI and the role of public-private policies and partnerships changed, and ITRI was able to assist in the transformation of other Taiwanese industries, such as bicycles, into global stage 3 innovators.

The policy innovation here was the transformation of R&D consortia from a policy tool for advancing cutting-edge innovation into a policy tool for upgrading and sustaining companies' stage 3 innovation capabilities so they could continue to compete in global production networks. By so doing, ITRI has become for Taiwan what the Fraunhofer institutes are for Germany: the key innovation actor around which an ecosystem of stage 3 innovation is developed and sustained. Germany's vast network of Fraunhofer institutes works hand in hand with the country's Mittelstand firms to deliver the economic miracle Germany has been enjoying since World War II. In Taiwan, ITRI has evolved to take on a similar role.[20]

Let us take a brief look at how this co-evolution came to be. As has been vividly argued by John Mathews, the main goals of the Taiwanese R&D consortia have been technological learning, upgrading, and catch-up as part of attempts at industry creation. This is a very different objective from the R&D consortia of most countries, including the United States, Israel, and Japan. In a similar fashion to the Germans, the Taiwanese also realized that the smaller size of their manufacturing-oriented companies, with their lack of sophisticated in-house R&D capabilities, hindered their ability to upgrade and compete in global markets. In more technical terms, the Germans and the Taiwanese understood that in the current state of innovation, small and medium-size manufacturing and production companies cannot be the R&D agents by themselves. Hence, there is a need to create a public-private solution to fix the market and network failures.[21]

The solution in Taiwan was to assemble a series of ITRI-led research consortia, an effort that continues to this day. From the start of this process, the same division of labor in R&D that had been used in semiconductors was applied, with ITRI conducting the R&D and the private companies concentrating on manufacturing and final product development. Even in later research consortia, in which private companies assumed leadership roles, this division of labor has been maintained.

What is at least as important, from the point of view presented in this book, is how these consortia allowed Taiwanese companies to handle potentially devastating attacks by leading MNCs that were aggressively using their intellectual property rights (IPR) (mostly patents, trademarks, and copyrights) to bankrupt or derail their Taiwanese competitors. This is a key lesson that should be learned by anyone who is interested in innovation-based regional development. The tough reality of our current innovation system is that if you do manage to succeed as a region, you should assume that the world's biggest companies and patent trolls will view you as the new juicy prime target to attack. It is not a question of whether they will attack; it is a question of when and how brutal and devastating that attack will be. We will talk more about our global broken IPR system and its implications in a subsequent chapter, but for now let us see how this has played out in Taiwan.

The first few consortia, and some of the most significant, were developed as part of ITRI's multi-client projects in the early 1980s. These projects assisted in the creation of Taiwanese industries that developed and manufactured PCs and, later, laptops. The first such project started after Apple clamped down on the thriving Taiwanese Apple II cloning industry in late 1982. The industry, then highly fragmented and having no prior experience with IP-protection laws, came to MoEA and ITRI for help. ITRI already possessed some experience working with Intel CPUs and advised the companies to concentrate on the new IBM Intel-based PC instead of Apple. The real activity started after February 1983, when Acer approached ITRI/ERSO with a request to develop a PC.[22]

ITRI devised this project as its first multi-client project, code-naming it MCP-1. A decision was made to limit the number of participants to nine. By the end of 1983, Taiwanese companies had started manufacturing IBM PC clones, hoping to ship them to the United States in time for Christmas sales. However, IBM counterattacked, claiming that ITRI's basic input-output system (BIOS) was infringing on its IP. ITRI engineers rewrote the code, but by the time IBM agreed that the new version was legal, it was already May 1984. Some of the project participants followed Acer and used the new BIOS, but others simply sold their PCs in less-IP-strict markets.[23]

Although this project was deemed less than satisfactory, as soon as IBM announced its new PC AT system in August 1984, ITRI announced its intention to launch a new multi-client project. This time the participants were limited to three. The prototype was transferred by ITRI to the companies by July 1985, and soon thereafter the companies started to bring their own products to market. This project was considered a great success and paved the way to a series of related multi-client projects. From this point onward, the projects were formally viewed as research consortia and not as ITRI's multi-client research projects.[24]

The usage of consortia has evolved and changed over the years. One of the most interesting developments has been the extensive training of private firms' personnel, including the transfer of significant numbers of engineers from ITRI to the companies when a consortium concludes. This is yet another similarity between the Fraunhofers' role in Germany and ITRI's in Taiwan. Both ITRI and the Fraunhofers should be seen not only as R&D actors, but also as key human-capital and skills-supply mechanisms for their respective local industries. ITRI consortia have been playing critical roles in the ability of the Taiwanese industry to become a global leader in stage 3 innovation as the industry has continued to change, moving from desktops to laptops to handheld devices and smartphones and every imaginable related subsystem and component. Not all consortia were successful, but their consistency and continuity across sectors ensured that the region's industry continued to prosper, from ICT to bicycles to agrotech. If you like orchids, you should thank Taiwan's stage 3 innovators for the fact that you can enjoy so many of them in your home, wherever your home is.[25]

However, not all is rosy if your locale decides to specialize in stage 3 innovation. There are limits to what your companies can do and what business models they can employ. The story of two once-brilliant stars of the Taiwanese semiconductor industry—VIA Technologies and HTC—and what happened when they got too successful in the eyes of the MNCs that control the ICT global production networks, can serve as an illustrative example.

VIA and HTC are the two brainchildren of one of Taiwan's most successful innovating entrepreneurs, and definitely Taiwan's most successful female ICT entrepreneur, Cher Wang. Cher is also one of the nine children of one of Taiwan's most successful entrepreneurs and richest persons, the late Yungching Wang, the founder of Formosa Plastic. Cher Wang's first company was VIA, at its prime Taiwan's highest-flying and largest chip-design company in terms of sales, a period that ended abruptly in 2001. PC chipsets were then VIA's main product line. As long as Intel's Pentium 3 was the leading PC CPU, VIA gained global market share at Intel's expense, reaching almost 50 percent, in part because of Intel's decision to stick with a more expensive Rambus technology for its own chipset.[26]

In short, VIA followed a classic stage 3 strategy of second-generation component innovation, producing a cheaper and at-least-as-reliable solution to a key component first innovated by a different company. However, Intel is different from Qualcomm and Texas Instruments in mobile telephony or any of the companies in the other niches conquered by MediaTek that focus solely on the lower half of the market. Instead, Intel controlled not just the chipset but also the rest of the computer architecture. That enabled Intel to bide its time and attack at will during a critical time point. With the move to Pentium 4 technology, Intel attacked VIA on multiple fronts: it did not license its P4 technology to VIA, and it took VIA to court over patent-infringement allegations in October 2001. As a result of these moves, all first-tier PC manufacturers, Taiwanese included, refrained from using VIA's chipsets, fearing legal action from Intel. VIA countersued Intel for both patent in-fringement and usage of monopoly status, and the legal battle was fought in five jurisdictions. In April 2003 the two companies reached a settlement that included a patent-swap agreement and a licensing agreement. By that time, however, VIA had lost substantial market share and revenue. Moreover, be-cause it agreed to pay royalties to Intel, it could no longer maintain its former profit margins. In 2001 VIA was the biggest Taiwanese IC design house, with about $1 billion USD in sales; by 2003 sales had dropped to $600 million, and in 2017 (the latest year for which figures are available) revenue was just above $143 million.[27]

The risks of going head-to-head with leading MNCs are even more striking when we consider that this legal battle was fought after VIA had changed its ownership structure to placate Intel. Among other things, VIA had separated from its main shareholder, First International Computers (FIC), which was owned by Cher Wang's older sister, Charlene Wang, because Intel had viewed the combination of motherboard producer, FIC, and chipset producer as a threat.[28]

HTC and Its Fall from Grace

This story leads us to Cher Wang's better-known (to consumers, anyway) company: Hongda International Electronics Co. Ltd., also known as HTC (High Tech Computer Corporation). The story of HTC's rise and decline illustrates what can happen when a company operating in a stage 3 eco-system tries to become a stage 1 innovator. HTC started life in 1997, mainly as yet another Taiwanese laptop ODM. It quickly suffered increasing losses until it strategically changed direction in 1999, becoming one of the world's first ODMs for handheld devices (then called personal digital assistants, or PDAs). In a fortunate series of events in 2000, HTC secured the ODM con-tract from Compaq computers (then still an American computing giant) to develop its PDA—the iPAQ—which was the first to have a color screen and run Windows CE (Microsoft's ill-fated operating system for mobile devices). For HTC, the iPAQ represented a significant change of fortune, with annual orders reaching over two million units. Very quickly HTC became the leading ODM for PDAs operating Microsoft's CE, and Microsoft proceeded to help HTC gain acceptance worldwide.[29]

Following the PDA foray, HTC moved to become a leader as an ODM of (mostly Microsoft-based) mobile and early smartphones, especially for prominent mobile operators such as Vodafone and T-Mobile. This development led HTC to become much more R&D-driven than other Taiwanese companies, with R&D expenditures of over 5 percent. That's significantly above even Silicon Valley stars such as Apple, and twice the average of other Taiwanese ODMs. HTC's success and growing R&D capacity led it to pursue its own brand manufacturing, starting with Microsoft-based touchscreen phones called Touch in 2007. The Touch phones were a great success, but more importantly, they made HTC into a go-to company for all the mobile operators that were seeking ways to fight the iPhone (which at the time was sold exclusively via AT&T). With Windows becoming ever more unsuitable as a platform for touchscreen mobile devices, HTC tightened its relationship with Google and became the first company to ship an Android-based smartphone, together with T-Mobile. This was the G1, also known as the Dream. The move to Android also allowed HTC to cut down on its IP royalty payments (IP licensing costs become a burden to many ICT device makers over time, because the price of license per unit remain the same while final unit prices drop).[30]

HTC quickly seized the momentum, and by the third quarter of 2011 its highly innovative designs had made HTC the biggest seller of smartphones in the United States, with 24 percent of the market share. At that time HTC, which started as yet another Taiwanese laptop ODM, seemed to defy expectations and, unlike other Taiwanese ICT companies, from BenQ and Acer to Asus, successfully moved to stage 1 innovation. Indeed, HTC was seen as such a formidable competitor that in 2010 it was sued by Apple, which accused it of IPR infringement. This success, however, proved fleeting. By early 2012, less than six months after being crowned as the leader of the industry, HTC had already lost its title and quickly became a marginal smartphone maker.[31]

The fall from grace continued, and HTC did not regain market share in the smartphone or tablet markets, even after reverting to an ODM model (in effect it became Google's hardware R&D arm, developing and selling Google's

Nexus and Pixel smartphones and tablets). In 2015 HTC tried to innovate in another cutting-edge, new-to-the-world niche—virtual reality—and together with the Valve Corporation (then the biggest global computer-game vendor), it released the Vive. While the Vive device was a relative success, unit sales languished in the low hundreds of thousands, a far cry from the tens of millions of smartphones HTC sold annually in its prime. In January 2018, in a symbolic move that demonstrated the limit of the Taiwanese stage 3 innovation model, Google acquired half of HTC's research and design personnel, the whole team developing the Pixel, and rights to related IPR for $1.1 billion USD. While HTC has brilliant design and complementary R&D capabilities, perfect for a stage 3 ODM, the fact that it controlled none of the key technologies or components proved to be detrimental when it attempted to recast itself as a cutting-edge innovation leader.[32]

As the analysis of Taiwan demonstrates, in order to become and stay successful, the region had to develop a specific set of solutions around the four fundamentals that allow companies to excel in stage 3 innovation. From early on, local leaders worked to establish and institutionalize local-global knowledge, demand, and input flows. That has been part and parcel of the strategy in Taiwan right from the start, with the establishment of ERSO and the Science and Technology Advisory Group (STAG), all the way to ITRI currently opening branches in foreign locales that are seen as sources of ideas and technologies. ITRI and the Hsinchu Science Park not only provide, supply, and create public and semi-public goods, from specialized human capital to collaborative public spaces, they also constantly co-evolve their policies in tandem with changing global and local industry. We have already seen how the division of labor between ITRI and industry in R&D reinforces the firm-level benefits of the other two factors and allows access to critical resources such as technology and personnel, as well as how the research consortia were reshaped as a dynamic tool for enhancing stage 3 innovation capacities.

Looking at the four fundamentals, the case of venture capital in Taiwan is an important example of two things we should remember. First, it is an ideal example of how to tailor a specific subset of the ecosystem, in this case finance, and optimize it for local stage specialization. Second, Taiwanese VCs, one of the world's most successful VC industries, actually shares very little, apart from the name, with VCs in North America, Europe, and Israel. Accordingly, analyzing what VC really means in Taiwan is an important lesson for local leaders worldwide: Innovation policies, tools, and even industries that share the same name can be as different as one can imagine. Hence, if you copy a tool simply because it worked in particular places at specific times, without carefully analyzing exactly why and how it operated in each of those contexts or how to tailor it to your region's need, you will only end up with failure.

If we want to understand the evolution of the Taiwanese VC industry, we must understand the specific position of Taiwanese ICT firms as stage 3 innovators in global production networks and the specific geopolitical concerns that led Taiwan to an overwhelming political preference for local capital instead of foreign capital as the source of investment financing for, and as a result ownership of, Taiwanese companies. After Kuo-tingLi oversaw the transfer and drastic alteration of Silicon Valley's model of science parks in creating Hsinchu Park, he decided that Taiwan should have VCs, and he understood the need to do the same tailoring to the American VC model. The policy goal was to support local firms, and Li saw a Silicon Valley–like VC market as a solution to "Taiwanese SMEs' insufficient capital."[33]

The policy initiative to create the VC industry started in 1983, with Taiwan's Ministry of Finance issuing the "Regulations for the Administration of Venture Capital Enterprises" and providing a 20 percent tax deduction for investments in local high-technology firms. As discussed in a previous chapter, the usual organizational mode of what we call VCs is a limited-time, limited-liability fund with two kinds of partners, the limited partners that supply the capital but stay passive, and the general partners who manage the funds and make investment decisions. It's the latter that we call the venture capitalists. This is exactly the model transferred from the United States to Israel and to most European countries.[34]

Not so in Taiwan. Wishing to have a VC industry based almost exclusively on local capital (the exact opposite of Israel's VC policy goal), Taiwanese policymakers chose what is known as a "paper company" structure. In such a model the investors (that is, the limited partner in the US model) create a company (not a fund), and it is the investors themselves who not only supply the capital but—unlike limited partners in the US—are also the active managers, controlling investment decisions. Although the hired managers of the paper companies are called VCs, they do not control the investment decisions. In effect, Taiwanese policymakers inverted the American limited partnership to fit their local ecosystem.[35]

Taiwan's regulations succeeded in incentivizing domestic VC activity that, by the mid-1990s, became an "integral force in promoting Taiwan's domestic high-technology (read: ICT) industry." The domestic-centric regulations resulted in a muted foreign, particularly American, investor presence. Further, the domestically oriented Taiwanese VC industry captured its capital gains by listing on the Taiwan Stock Exchange, which had a very different set of regulations with regard to listing requirements. Companies must achieve positive, stable, growing cash flows for several years before being listed. Hence, the Taiwanese VCs' business model does not look for massive financial multipliers reached within five to seven years. Instead, Taiwanese VCs, when investing in Taiwanese companies in Taiwan, prefer to invest in companies with business models of lower technological risk—for example, companies that rely on either second-generation innovation or an OEM/ODM business model. This is a financial business model that fits with stage 3 innovation companies' life cycles. Backed by regulations that made it difficult for Taiwanese companies to list in foreign exchanges before listing on the Taiwanese one, the Taiwanese financial model reinforced the dominance of local VCs, as foreign investors were less attracted by the Taiwanese stock market. The result is a financial industry that supports and profits from the local focus on stage 3 innovation, enhancing its success and specific innovation capacities.[36]

Stage 2 Innovation

Another stage that is too often misunderstood is stage 2: design, prototype development, and production engineering. Part of the reason it is misunderstood is that it is too often mixed with the story of specific companies, or it gets lost within the bigger story of old industrial clusters' "resilience" as they fit themselves into the new global economy. If there is one company that can be blamed more than any other for the former misunderstanding, it is IDEO. This impressive company has become the source of countless business-school cases, articles, books, TV documentaries, TED talks, and guru-like lectures by consultants proclaiming to teach you how to innovate like IDEO, how to engage clients like IDEO, and how to make your employees happy and creative like IDEO.[37]

Indeed, there is much to learn from IDEO. The company is now helping companies and even regions to bring new products and services to the world in countless industries, aptly demonstrating the critical importance of stage 2 innovation. For the purposes of this book, one of the most interesting things about IDEO is almost the opposite of its image of "Silicon Valleyness," and its association with new cool, novel gadgets and technologies. Yes, IDEO is responsible for the ultimate design and production of countless new gadgets, from the first Apple Mouse to more PDAs than one ever thought anyone should buy. However, if you carefully immerse yourself in the histories of IDEO's founders and top leaders, you will find a common and surprising thread: they all started designing within mature industries, designing things that most people would not associate with the word "innovation," or even "technology." Things like a toaster, an "occupied" sign for the lavatory, and even a table saw. As a matter of fact, the ABC show that propelled IDEO to public awareness was focused on the redesigning of the shopping cart.[38]

IDEO immerses itself deeply both in materials and in things that people use thousands of times daily and that they expect to be reliable, easy to use, and yet "cool." This immersion is extremely important for stage 2 innovation. It is exactly here that regions should focus if they are looking for innovation-based growth strategies.

To understand this model, and to see that it is a specific innovation-stage model and not just what many economic geographers broadly and ambiguously term the "resiliency" of old regions, let us go to one of the oldest industries in the world—shoes.[39]

An ancient product in the modern world

In the first chapter, we briefly saw how one area in the Italian northwest, Alto Livenza, transformed its furniture industry in response to globalization to become a successful global node of stage 2 innovation. I also promised you a visit to another area near Alto Livenza—the Riviera del Brenta—where the world's most luxurious women's shoes become a reality. It is a trip that I started thanks to my coauthor and friend Giulio Buciuni.[40]

Riviera del Brenta is one of Italy's oldest traditional industrial districts. It includes adjacent areas in the Venezia and Padova provinces along the Brenta River. As the center of Italian luxury-footwear production, Brenta is globally renowned for upscale women's shoes, chic local brands, and the design, sourcing, and assembly bases for top global brands such as Louis Vuitton, Prada, and Armani. Although the Italian economy experienced a sustained crisis from 2005 to 2015 and many venerable industrial districts contracted, Brenta has thrived. According to Italy's Istituto Nazionale di Statistica (ISTAT), Brenta's number of production units and shoe workers declined by only

1.6 percent (744 to 732) and 4.27 percent (6531 to 6252), respectively, between 2005 and 2014. Brenta's footwear sector endures even as other Italian footwear-production districts such as Vigevano decline.[41]

The reason for Brenta's sustained success? Over the past two decades it has transformed itself into a highly competitive second-stage innovation center, perhaps the most important one in the global luxury women's shoes industry. Three factors have been critical in this transformation: the upgrading strategies of local producers moving to become second-stage innovators, investments by the top MNCs, and the co-development and improvement of local firms and semi-public goods such as Italy's oldest school for footwear producers.

To understand these factors, let us first briefly review the industry. Production of luxury footwear differs from that of mass-market shoes. Luxury brands produce very short runs of distinct, high-quality, high-cost shoes. Designers create multiple collections per year, with the summer and winter collections being the most important showcases for presenting new models. A single large fashion brand introduces up to four hundred new models of women's luxury shoes per year, many of them sourced from Brenta companies and each of them requiring ad hoc product development. Shoe production involves design, modeling, test production, raw materials processing and sourcing (leather, dye, heel and sole glue, heavy thread), cutting, stitching, assembly, distribution, and marketing.[42]

Now it is important to realize that in the real world of business, unlike what viewers of reality fashion-designer TV shows may have come to expect, it is *not* enough to come up with a good design. It is not even enough to produce a prototype. A customer paying hundreds or thousands of euros for a high-end shoe expects it to be luxurious, usable, and aesthetically pleasing at the same time. Customers buy shoes with the intention of using them for walking, with all the physical stress and human-induced chemical reactions (leather interactions with sweat and fungi, for example) that come with repeated use. Further, those shoes need to be designed for production; they are not one-time, hand-made pieces of art. The skills required for designing such shoes and making them into usable footwear that can be produced at certain price points and within extremely demanding timelines are at the heart of second-stage innovation.

Thanks to the global fragmentation of production, only a few firms are still fully integrated shoe producers. Rather, much as with ICT, major brands and design houses often handle upstream (design) and downstream (marketing) services, with specialized contractors performing the remaining activities. Brenta seized on the opportunity presented by this movement to fragmented production. It's not necessarily that manufacturers in Brenta were smarter than others; instead, they combined their knowledge with the opportunity and with local policymakers' willingness to work with them. This combination allowed the manufacturers not only to redefine themselves but also to shape their industry on a global scale.[43]

Brenta's tradition of footwear production dates back to the Venetian Republic. Artisanal production gave way to industrialization in the nineteenth century. With industrial production, Brenta shoes could be marketed across Italy and Europe, and the makers built a reputation for Italy as the location to source or purchase shoes. Industrialization spurred specialization. Lead firms increasingly subcontracted stages of production to smaller, specialized firms. Industrial-production firms served as original equipment manufacturers (OEMs) for foreign brands and retail stores, particularly in Germany, producing on demand.[44]

The OEM business model during Brenta's first opening to global production networks limited the scope for upgrading design, marketing, and distribution. Firms were relegated to the lowest value-added supply and assembly tasks in direct competition with low-cost producers abroad. Some observers questioned the wisdom of local producers' OEM strategy, noting a downgrading of local firms' capabilities—losing the design capabilities they once had as artisanal or small-volume producers. Further, Brenta firms could not match low-cost competitors' prices. Continuing to rely on mass-market orders through global production networks might have undermined the district, as occurred in other Italian industrial areas.[45]

Fortunately for Brenta, during the 1970s a few producers had already begun focusing on designer women's footwear. A handful of local producers initiated a "learning by supplying" process, beginning the transformation from general production to specialization. Aiming to expand sales globally and differentiate their customer portfolios, manufacturers such as Sergio Rossi began traveling to France to meet with fashion brands like Dior. They began offering original design manufacturer (ODM) services to global fashion brands. Brands provided designs that Brenta firms would translate into manufacturable products and produce at scale.[46]

Providing ODM services for luxury brands placed Brenta manufacturers on a different trajectory than those in other locations. By focusing on the highest-end footwear and capitalizing on the existing value of the "Made in Italy" identity, these firms were able to increase their added value. Local firms progressively specialized in translating sophisticated designer footwear into production and focused on absorbing market and innovation knowledge from the global brands. Brenta firms had access to the best global "buzz"—trends in fashion, materials, and techniques at the cutting edge of luxury footwear. This both enabled and pressured Brenta's firms to adhere to the most demanding requirements in order to remain the preferred sourcing destination. This "learning by supplying" process spread throughout the Brenta supply chain as contractors and suppliers all had to meet the exacting standards of high-quality, low-volume, high-value production.[47]

A critical reason that Brenta firms could manage that transformation has been public policy, especially education. Local government, together with Associazione Calzaturifici della Riviera del Brenta (ACRIB—the organization representing local shoemakers) and the Politecnico Calzaturiero run Italy's oldest school for shoemakers. Established in 1923 under the name Scuola di Disegno per Arti e Mestieri, the school attracts students from all over Italy and is a key source of skilled labor. When Giulio Buciuni and I met with the director of the school in July 2014, he described its mission and role in making Brenta into the second-stage innovation hub it is, and sustaining its unique capabilities:

> Our job is a strategic piece of the local puzzle that has been developed here. The school offers a number of services, but what we do best is providing firms in the district with new skills they can utilize to attract global buyers locally. To do that, we had to internationalize our business and adjust our offers accordingly. This is unique in Italy, and I believe this is a necessary step we had to take to keep getting better and hopefully become the world's best school for luxury footwear producers over the next years.

In addition to creating new technicians, the skills-development programs include training for prototype developers. An ACRIB leader we talked with stated this strategy quite clearly when he explained how ACRIB and the school support the upgrading of small suppliers that have yet to participate in global firms' product development. The suppliers are taught how to acquire new-product-development skills:

> Today our programs focus increasingly on the product development side of the production process. We know that production is critical, but product

development is the real competence that makes our local suppliers attractive and suitable for international partnership with global buyers.

The goals of this public-private strategy, focused around a unique educational institution, are to expand the number of firms able to develop new products for global brands and, eventually, generate independent products. By targeting smaller firms, most of which currently specialize in narrow stages of the supply chain, ACRIB aims to support the competitiveness of the entire supply base. To do so, the Politecnico Calzaturiero is actively working to make itself a key second-generation node in the global industry. A first step in this strategy was the creation of a cooperative training and immersion venture with the Parsons School of Design in New York in the mid-2000s. Established to connect local producers with young international designers, the program aims to facilitate knowledge transfer between these key nodes of the footwear-industry chain. Students from Parsons work closely with footwear manufacturers in development and production of their shoe designs. Local producers are exposed to new ideas and market trends, which they use to predict future requirements from global buyers and proactively update their capabilities. Furthermore, local brands gain invaluable experience in being part of the ideation-to-production process. It is not a surprise that when those aspiring designers get jobs, they rely on Brenta firms and their connection with the Politecnico Calzaturiero to act much as IDEO does for many of Silicon Valley's most-admired brands.

This strategy of transformation and of building up the region's second-stage innovation capacities has been working well. Specializing in high-end footwear ideation to production made Brenta suppliers uniquely qualified to supply the types of skills necessary for producing designer footwear. Local companies possess high-quality, not easily replicable capabilities for specific services, including design, fast prototyping, and test production. Accordingly, rather than just sourcing services, starting in the 1990s Louis Vuitton, Prada, Armani, and other global brands established their own facilities in Brenta. Tapping into local design, test production, and sourcing skills, global brands enhance their innovation capabilities and link their brand and market reputations to the "Made in Italy" identity. A director of ACRIB during our visit to Brenta explained this:

Most of the world's fashion brands want to be here because of our reputation. They might produce parts of their collection in Eastern Europe or

China, but when it comes to luxury shoes they need to show that these are made around here. However, without our unique competencies, we will have no reputation; this is happening because of both.

Brenta's specialized production capabilities enable innovation in the luxury-footwear industry, making global-brand firms highly reliant on the locale. Product innovation in the luxury-footwear industry is "process-embedded," taking place through all the steps of the production process, from leather cutting to sewing to assembly. This is a specific feature of luxury footwear: To obtain the necessary quality with sufficient quantity, there must be specialization in distinct, skilled firms. But since innovation requires all stages to innovate in tandem, these firms must be co-located for efficient transfer of tacit knowledge. In contrast, mass-market footwear, where artisanal skill is not required, can be done by firms that simply receive and fill orders to brands' specifications using standardized equipment that can be located and relocated anywhere in the world.[48]

Brenta also developed a specialized financial system that enhances its unique stage 2 innovation system, and in turn profits from its deep embeddedness within the system. This system, devised of numerous small local banks, is called *banche di credito cooperativo* (BCC). The BCC system was developed by local bankers to facilitate new specialized venture formation, often by skilled workers formerly employed in larger organizations. The system addresses the challenge of access to capital by small-scale and highly specialized local entrepreneurs, who are generally ignored by the large banks. This sustains the creation and maintenance of a dense ecosystem of suppliers around which global fashion brands have organized their production networks. The importance of this type of semi-public good is corroborated by local small firms' heavy reliance on credit from BCCs. Nonetheless, the great recession of 2008 and later difficulties of the two major local banks—Veneto Banca and Banca Popolare di Vicenza—have severely affected numerous local firms, putting in question the sustainability of the regional financial system. Currently, a shortage of credit is one of the most critical concerns related to the survival of local small producers and the entire cluster.[49]

Thus, through public-private collaborations, the Riviera del Brenta managed to recreate itself as an important center of second-stage innovation in the global luxury women's shoe industry. This enabled the locale to supply its residents with numerous good jobs for all levels of skills and education.

As we have just seen, this was done by refashioning each part of the four fundamentals: (i) flows of local-global knowledge, demand, and input; (ii) supply and creation of public and semi-public goods; (iii) local ecosystem reinforcing firm-level benefits; and (iv) managing the co-evolution of the previous three fundamentals. An important example in the case of Brenta is the institutionalization of the global-local flows.

The linkage between production skills and global fashion brands' innovation models has had a profound impact on local semi-public goods. While the Politecnico Calzaturiero has been a linchpin of this approach, another tool, perfected to even a greater degree in the adjunct Alto Livenza region, is the utilization of industry expos and shows. To support the integration of producers and designers and encourage foreign luxury brands to continue to deepen their engagement with Brenta, local authorities are taking active steps. Local officials promote Brenta brands and regional shoe design and production capabilities abroad. Supporting this strategy, in 1976 ACRIB established the Consorzio Maestri Calzaturieri del Brenta (Consorzio Maestri), an institution dedicated to the global promotion of the district, mostly through participation in international trade shows, sourcing events, and advertising campaigns.[50]

Alto Livenza leaders took this approach one step further. In 2005 the local chamber of commerce and the Pordenone provincial government established the Salone Internazionale dei Componenti, Semilavorati ed Accessori per l'Industria del Mobile (SICAM; International Exhibition of Components, Semifinished Products, and Accessories for the Furniture Industry).[51]

Within five years of its establishment, SICAM had become one of the most important industrial exhibitions worldwide. By 2012, SICAM hosted 540 exhibitors and 17,000 buyers from as many as 93 different countries, and 30 percent of the participants came from outside Italy. SICAM is a classic example of a coproduced public good. Established thanks to the cooperation between Pordenone Fiere, the chamber of commerce of Pordenone, the municipality of Pordenone, and local furniture entrepreneurs—some of which are members of the SICAM board—the furniture fair was conceived to create bridges between domestic and global designers and between buyers and regional specialized manufacturers. In 2012 SICAM was expanded to reflect the growing importance of the global contract market by creating a focused trade show targeting a specific niche of buyers—that is, contractors—in an attempt to cement close relations between leading global contractors and local firms. The establishment and development of two international trade shows created a stable bridge between Livenza's producers and global pipelines.[52]

As we have seen, stage 2 and stage 3 innovation are a viable option for locales seeking sustained and widely distributed innovation-based economic growth. They are not a panacea—an ecosystem honed to produce and scale-up firms focused on those stages is ill equipped to support and sustain firms that strive to succeed in cutting-edge innovation. The other side of the strengths of complementarities enhancing each other, the gestalt of the system that they form, means that companies needing different sets of public and semi-public goods will be ill-served. Further, as the cases of Taiwan, Brenta, and Alto Livenza show, developing such a system is not a task for a day or even a year, it is a long-haul endeavor of experimentation and development and co-evolution of the four fundamentals that leads to success. Further, the global economic system is not a static one, and hence it is not enough to just engage the local with the global. Public policies need to constantly redefine, improve, and excel in connecting the right parts of the global to the local, changing those connections in time as both the region and the global industry change and evolve.

7

Out with the Old, In with the New!
But in What Ways?

"And now," said Dorothy, "how am I to get back to Kansas?"
"We shall have to think about that," replied the little man. "Give
me two or three days to consider the matter and I'll try to find a way
to carry you over the desert."
— L. Frank Baum, *The Wonderful Wizard of Oz*

Thus, we now approach the last of our four stages of innovation: stage 1,
or novelty—the stage that caught the imagination of so many and to such
a degree that most people think it is the only mode of innovation-based
growth. Further, one specific model of stage 1—the Silicon Valley model
of taking ideation start-ups to stratospheric financial exits in the shortest
possible time—has been elevated almost to the degree of a religious dogma.
We will closely analyze the most impressive case of developing stage 1 innovation since the 1960s: Israel. In doing so, we will see both the strengths
and weaknesses of stage 1 innovation, as well as the particular distributional
consequences this model leads to, and how local policymakers try to alleviate the consequences. For our purposes, the most interesting part of the
Israeli story is not its success, but a careful understanding of how innovation
policy co-evolves with the industry and with global changes to support continuous growth. Israel started from literally nothing and went on to become
a region that led the world in first-stage innovation for over two decades
in a row.

Nonetheless, Silicon Valley is not the only model for first-stage innovation growth, and, as discussed in the first three chapters of this book, it is
not necessarily the most desirable or feasible model for local policymakers
to pursue. To look at other models, we will examine the still partial, still in-
process, transformation of Hamilton, Ontario, from a Rust Belt city whose

best option at one time seemed to be managing its decline in tandem with the fortunes of steel MNCs, to an unassuming, under-the-radar locus of a surprising model of health-tech innovation. This model does not involve massive financial bets on new genetically engineered molecules of uncertain value, but instead relies on a human-problem-centric view of medical technology, backed by experimental modes of moving financial and human capital resources from old industries to new. The model might very well fail or be prevented by misconceived federal and provincial policies from achieving full fruition, but for numerous regions of the world, the lessons it offers seem more promising than attempting to run to the end of the rainbow in search of the fabled gold-filled pots of the Silicon-Hyphens.

Let us start with the story of Israel, a tiny country on the shore of the Mediterranean. Today, Israel is considered an ICT powerhouse, with more companies listed on NASDAQ than any other country, barring the United States, and with investment in R&D amounting to 4 percent of GDP annually for the past two decades, the highest in the world. The Israeli ICT industry is based on an R&D-intensive, novel-product-based, export-oriented business model.[1]

Looking at this impressive record raises a question: How did Israel, a country that as late as 1965 had one of the lowest R&D expenditures as a percentage of GDP in the world, develop such an R&D-intensive ICT industry and become a global leader in R&D expenditure?[2] A critical component has been a public policy that has been developed, experimented with, and implemented over five decades by a tiny agency with very limited resources, the Office of the Chief Scientist (OCS) in what is currently known as the Ministry of the Economy.

The transformation of Israel into what we call today the rapid-innovation-based development path, and what was known back then as science-based industrialization, started with an external shock. A surprise decision of French president Charles de Gaulle to impose a military embargo on Israel just before the 1967 war led policymakers to channel large R&D investments into developing high-technology weapons systems. Similar changes followed in civilian industrial policy.[3]

The most important was the establishment of the OCS in the then Ministry of Commerce. It might be hard for followers of current Israeli innovation policies to imagine, but in the beginning, the OCS was so marginal that the position was filled by a university professor who came to the office only twice a week for half a day each time. Further, most of the budget was devoted to funding several industrial research organizations that had been placed under the ministry's jurisdiction. Only in 1974 did the minister appoint a full-time director, Itzhak Yaakov. While Yaakov had an extensive personal network from his prior positions as head of the armament development and R&D in the military, the OCS budget, even after the increase that had been promised in order to lure him, was barely 15 million Israeli lira (2 percent of the annual budget Yaakov controlled in his military role).[4]

Nonetheless, Yaakov's extensive domestic networks, his educational background as an engineer with an advanced degree in technology management from MIT, and his international connections with the World Bank and other actors made him uniquely able to bring new policy ideas to Israel. His first action was to define the OCS's objective as the maximization of industrial R&D without targeting any specific sectors or technologies. This conceptualization led the OCS to embark on a long series of horizontal technology policies (HTPs), a novel idea at the time. This decision also led him to cut the budget allocated to the various industrial research organizations by 70 percent and channel the funds to the new programs targeting private companies. The first program, which continues to this day, provides conditionally repayable loans covering part of the cost for any approved industrial R&D project originating from private industry that is aimed at developing a new exportable product. The loan is payable only if the R&D project ends with a profitable product.[5]

The OCS's resources were limited. Yaakov commented on this in an interview:

> The small budget had a few reasons, most importantly was that nearly everyone in the Ministry did not understand what is it that they were supposed to be doing. Most of the Ministry personnel thought that industrial R&D is a waste of money—money that can be used to buy meat in Argentina. It was, don't forget, the Ministry of Commerce and Industry.[6]

Given the OCS's lowly status as a peripheral agency, its only hope of infusing an R&D-based development ideology into private industry was to educate more central actors and mobilize them into action. So it took an approach that many early employees described as intensive networking. It engaged in repeated meetings with decision-makers in industry, educating them about the value of R&D and technological innovation. One of the first employees of the OCS described the early years:

We tried to . . . infuse the idea that R&D is something that should be done throughout the industry. To create a sort of paradigmatic change in the way businesses thought about what they are doing. We did not really care who, what, why, when. We just wanted to create an R&D dynamic.[7]

The OCS's new policies received official political support only in the 1980s, after a hyperinflationary crisis in which inflation reached 109,187 percent between 1978 and 1986, decimating the traditional industry. A new R&D law in 1984 stipulated that the OCS would have an "unconstrained" annual budget for its main R&D fund, so all approved projects suggested by private industry to develop high-technology products would be supported. This was possible because the overall demand for R&D funding in Israel was still minuscule. A budgetary limit wasn't reintroduced until the industry had grown.[8]

Many of these new projects proved to be successful in international markets, as evidenced by the rising amount recouped by the OCS as payment for successful projects: from a mere $8 million in 1988 to $139 million in 1999. These payments were immediately injected back into the industry, continuing the growth cycle until the mid-1990s. The influence of the OCS's extended activities on industrial-sector innovative outputs is well documented.[9]

By the late 1980s and continuing at a higher rate in the 1990s, a transformation became apparent: The high-technology industry grew while agricultural, traditional, and mixed industries lost ground. By 1988, 59 percent of Israel's industrial exports were high-technology products, and by 1998 this was over 71 percent. This transformation continued. As early as 2000, according to Israel's Central Bureau of Statistics, the ICT industry accounted for over 70 percent of GDP growth. During the second half of the 1980s and the beginning of the 1990s, many Israeli ICT companies expanded their activities to penetrate foreign markets. In this period OCS grants proved to be critical in the decisions of the founders of key companies, such as Mercury Interactive and Comverse, to come back to Israel to establish their companies.[10]

However, what was at least as important in allowing this trajectory to grow and bloom was the co-evolutionary changes in innovation policy, spearheaded by the OCS. The agency was politically savvy in utilizing windows of opportunity to induce change. That happened in the 1980s with the financial crisis and hyperinflation, and it happened again in the early 1990s with the breakup of the Soviet Union. In 1989, when the USSR started to break apart, Jews who had been unable to emigrate started moving to Israel in large numbers. This wave was perceived to bring the best and the brightest technologically educated workforce from the USSR, and, together with the thousands of engineers who were made redundant by the defense industry, it raised the question of how to tap this body of knowledge. While this convergence was a historical accident, the OCS's two decades of patiently developing and introducing policies using an HTP framework established an alternative model that shaped Israel's S&T policies. A large injection of US financial aid aimed at helping the new immigrants settle in Israel also created an opportunity for the OCS.[11]

In an almost ideal example of how a small, weak public agency with an arsenal of new ideas can utilize its networks to get small amounts of capital to start policies that prove transformative to the whole regional economy, the OCS pushed forward three programs that it had been arguing for for years. The OCS's peripheral status was the main reason why it had multiple innovative policy program ideas, since its status led the OCS to link with diverse groups of heterogeneous and less-mainstream social scientists, economists, industrialists, and civil servants from around the world. Indeed, the ideas for the three programs came from as far away as the United States and Japan. Many of these ideas, in particular the MAGNET research consortia program, came from a group of academics led by Morris Teubal of the Hebrew University, facilitated by the Jerusalem Institute of Israel Studies, which worked closely with the OCS to develop new policy tools based on international comparison of best practices.[12]

In 1991 the Technological Incubators Program commenced operation. It was presented as a solution to two problems: equipping first-time technological entrepreneurs with management skills, and assisting technologically skilled Russian immigrants in integrating into a capitalist society. It established a network of technological incubators managed by local public-private joint ventures across Israel.[13]

The second program, Yozma, started operations in 1992 and kick-started the Israeli VC industry. This time, the OCS decided that the necessary skills and knowledge did not exist in Israel, and that in order to succeed, the VC industry needed strong networks with foreign financial markets rather than the Tel Aviv Stock Exchange. Accordingly, Yozma was created as a government VC fund of $100 million. It invested $8 million in ten private venture funds, which would be 40 percent or less of the total capital; the rest was provided by other private limited partners. To get this financing, the funds' managers had to secure investments from, and partnerships with, at least one local and one established foreign financial institution. The Israeli policy leaders, mainly Yigal Erlich, the chief scientist at the time, understood the position of Israel as a node of stage 1 innovation within the ICT global networks and understood that NASDAQ was already de facto the financial venue of choice of Israeli start-ups. The policy leaders opted not only to copy the US VC model lock, stock, and barrel, but also to ensure that the limited partners would be the same foreign ones that invested in US VC funds. This choice was almost the exact opposite of what Taiwan did.[14]

The last initiative designed by the OCS in 1991 was MAGNET, which started operations in 1992. MAGNET, which, in Hebrew, is the acronym of Generic Non-Competitive R&D, addressed two problems crucial for the development and maintenance of the long-term competitive advantage of high-technology companies. The first problem was that a large number of companies in Israel occupied the same technological space, each one too small by itself to compete with MNCs in cutting-edge infrastructural research activities. The second problem was the underutilization of academic research. To solve this, MAGNET created consortia to develop generic technologies. Consortia are created for a period of up to three years, and all intellectual-property outputs are shared among the members, who also had to agree to license this IP to Israeli companies at a cost that did not reflects the members' monopoly status.[15]

It is critically important to remember that Taiwan made successful use of the same tool—government-backed research consortia—to do the same thing, namely co-evolve with industry. But the two countries aimed to secure the growth of *almost opposite innovative capacities*. The most important lesson in comparing Israel and Taiwan is that in innovation-based economic growth, you can never assume that things that have the same name, such as *research consortia, venture capital*, or even *science parks*, are the same and fulfill the same functions in different contexts and times. Analyze what these tools do in each locale. Do not let their similar names confuse you, no matter what the hired, overpriced consultants whisper in your ear.[16]

The success of these policies moved high-technology industry to the center stage of Israel's economy. Yozma proved to be so successful that it became a model (although with, at best, very limited success) for VC policy worldwide. Today the Israeli VC industry is considered the most advanced and sophisticated in the world outside the United States, with many top US and global funds starting operations in Israel.[17]

Nonetheless, there has been a price to pay for becoming the most successful Silicon-Hyphen region in the world, and it seems to be getting steeper
with every passing year. Since the end of the hyperinflation in the 1980s, on
one side Israel enjoyed years of unparalleled innovation-based growth, concentrated in the high-tech sectors of the economy. On the other side, the
rest of Israel's economy (read: 80 percent of the Israeli population) enjoyed
no positive spillovers. Productivity and real wages in all other sectors of the
economy declined or remained stagnant. The high-tech boom focused almost exclusively on financial exits—rarely on growing companies that would
employ large numbers of non-engineers.[18]

This tendency, which, as discussed in previous chapters, is the natural tendency of a Silicon-Hyphen model in a world of fragmented production, has
gotten significantly worse in Israel. The reason is that Israel has indeed become a part of the global system. The money invested in the Israeli high-tech
industry is foreign and the industry's markets are foreign, which means that
even if an Israeli company grows, it resembles more and more an American
MNC with an R&D subsidiary in Israel. It is an open question whether Israel
created a higher number of good non-engineering jobs (such as management and sales) in Israel or in the United States. Further, when the financial
exits do happen, they occur in New York. And with most of the investors
being foreign, most of the profits are not even channeled through, or taxed
in, Israel.[19]

Last, but certainly not least, the duality of Israel's economy has intensified
as global fragmentation has accelerated and MNCs' behavior has changed.
In the past, the world's leading ICT MNCs, such as IBM, Motorola, National
Semiconductor, and Intel, built extensive manufacturing facilities on top
of their R&D units in Israel. Intel is still the largest ICT employer, by far, in
Israel, and many of the high-paying jobs it offers are not solely in R&D, which
goes some way toward ensuring a relatively wide distribution of the fruits
of the innovation-based economic success. However, since the 2000s, more
and more MNCs have located core research centers in Israel without ever
moving other activities there. At the current count by the Israeli Innovation
Authority, there are more than 320 foreign R&D centers in Israel, almost all
of them employing only R&D engineers—not even sales, marketing, or business development personnel.[20]

The proliferation of the MNCs' R&D centers in Israel not only ampli-
fies the dual-economy situation of good jobs for the very high-skilled and
nothing for the rest; it also now poses a serious danger to the sustainability

of the Israeli model itself. The MNCs will gladly pay significantly more than what Israeli start-ups or even scale-ups can offer. In an ever-tightening labor market for high-quality engineers, this means that the ability of Israeli entrepreneurs to start companies in Israel is significantly diminished, and their ability to scale-up is deeply curtailed. Indeed, when Amazon decided to start an artificial-intelligence R&D site in Israel, it targeted specific people, offering them salaries that were more than triple their then current wages. IIA officials estimated that the immediate result was the destruction of several of Israel's most promising AI companies, and a sharp, longer-term decrease in the capacity of AI startups to be formed and scaled-up.[21]

Israel has truly become a high-tech financial-exits nation, where the extremely high skilled and those who are already wealthy enjoy ever-expanding opportunities, and the vast majority of the population faces an economic future that is bleaker than what their parents faced. Every fifth household in Israel is currently under the poverty line. Israel, the great innovation miracle of the last thirty years, looks more like Mexico and Turkey with regard to economic equality and equity of both opportunity and outcomes, and less like Taiwan, Germany, Denmark, or Finland. In the summer of 2011, the economic tension exploded for the first time in a mass protest movement, known as the "tents protest," which was triggered by the rising costs of housing and living. As a result, a publicly appointed committee was assembled under the leadership of one of Israel's most renowned economists, Manuel Trajtenberg, who incidentally is most famous for his work on innovation, especially on the theory of "general-purpose technologies." The recommendations of the committee were approved by the government with great fanfare. However, inequality has continued to grow, along with the success of the Israeli ICT industry.[22]

These trends have not gone unnoticed by the OCS. As early as 2005 the OCS developed and implemented a program focused on the traditional sectors of the economy. The program tried to tackle these issues from both the demand side (educating firms on how to conduct and utilize R&D) and the supply side (offering incentives and grants for graduate-level STEM students and R&D engineers to work in or research small- and medium-sized enterprises [SMEs] in traditional industries). The program has grown steadily in its first five years and led a significant number of firms from traditional industries to apply for OCS grants for the first time.[23]

Yet it was clear to the OCS that these moves were not adequate. With Israel's focus on a Silicon-Hyphen stage 1 innovation model continuing to intensify and the dual-economy situation worsening, the organization entered into a period of deep reflection, the result of which was a plan to transform the OCS into an independent authority with a wider mandate to tackle social problems. Led by the chief scientist at the time, Avi Hasson, and the OCS's chief strategy officer, Uri Gabai, the plan was presented to the then-minister, Aryeh Deri, who led its approval by the Parliament in 2015.[24]

Restructured as the Israeli Innovation Authority (IIA), the organization continued to focus on technological innovation, but the new mandate allowed the IIA to start divisions to look at social problems, traditional industry (renamed "advanced manufacturing"), and companies' life cycles. The focus on life cycles allowed the IIA to devise policies aimed at increasing start-ups' usage of debt versus equity (that is, bank financing instead of VC), so as to alleviate the pressure for quick financial exits and allow more companies to grow past the stage in which they employ only R&D engineers. In short, the organization is striving to achieve what my students in our joint work with the IIA have termed "complete companies."[25]

This is indeed promising—if there is an organization in the world with a track record of innovation-based transformation, it is the IIA. But there is one critical strategic problem: it is not at all clear to the IIA, or to anyone in Israel, what an alternative model of stage 1 innovation would look like. The central question, therefore, is this: What more equitable model of stage 1 innovation can regions around the world aspire to?

It is here that the story of Hamilton, Ontario, offers an alternative. It is not yet a story of a complete transformation, and it is definitely not a story of foresighted policymakers. Instead, it is a story of how civic, business, and policy leaders built the foundation for the transformation of a Rust Belt steel town into a new model of health-based stage 1 innovation. Lately, Hamilton and its firms have started to attract significant interest from venture capitalists, so it might very well be that its very success as an alternative will undermine its future prosperity. Still, it offers us a different model.[26]

Hamilton is a midsized city of about half a million inhabitants in southern Ontario, just south of Toronto at the southwestern tip of Lake Ontario on the road to Niagara Falls, a short drive from the US border. This location proved to be fortunate to the city's development, as it became the apex of its early development around the two engines of railroad construction and hydroelectric power supply. While the city has always had a large and diverse manufacturing sector, it became the ultimate steel town of Canada between the two world wars, with strong accompanying automotive manufacturing. Hamilton's zenith as economic powerhouse was the period between WWII and the oil shocks of the 1970s. During those years Canada's two prime steel companies, Stelco and Dofasco, were headquartered in the city and conducted large-scale manufacturing and R&D operations. At their prime the companies were the technological leaders of the global industry, which made Hamilton a city filled with engineers and not just production workers. This was further strengthened by the move of McMaster University from Toronto to Hamilton in 1930.[27]

Similar to Cleveland, the city went through a severe crisis with the rapid decline of manufacturing and the demise of both Stelco and Dofasco from the 1970s onward. This led to a sharp decline of employment in the overall manufacturing sector, and in the steel industry in particular, from its prime of 52.2 percent of the total labor force in 1951, to 18.8 percent of total employment in 2001, and 11.68 percent in 2016.[28]

However, throughout this period, the unique set of institutions that led to Hamilton's recovery was set in place, built on three different sources of innovation and the support systems this model of innovation necessitates. The Hamilton model is an interesting mix of what, building on the pioneering work of Eric Von-Hippel on user-based innovation, I term *user-engaged innovation*. Hamilton's new technology companies do not originate from pure "wet lab" basic scientific research. Instead, they grow out of the work of clinicians and researchers in a process by which they figure out significant unmet needs of users and patients, or critical failure of drug and treatment delivery, and build solutions to solve them, many times in interaction with patients.[29]

The reason Hamilton excels in such stage 1 innovations is that the city, more by good fortune then by long-term planning, built the different education and research systems that support and sustain it, as well as alternative financing resources such companies can tap, especially in the very early years of firms' formation. Those institutions allowed resources and knowledge to move from the steel industry into health and material science R&D and engineering services. These resources have been flowing from the management side, as well as through the unique influence of unions and especially union benefits plans. Steel working has always been a dangerous line of work with unique medical needs, which the unions, through their benefits plans, sponsored creative solutions for, sponsoring them to the stage of prototyping and early adoption.[30]

For example, the top management of both Stelco and Dofasco was instrumental in the restructuring of the health system of the city. Not only had steel executives been sitting on the boards of hospitals, and ensuring a flow of needed expansion capital, but in critical junctures they led transformations. The most important such event was the amalgamation of all the main hospitals, but one, into Hamilton Health Sciences (HHS) in 1997. At that time, a group of steel executives, led by Robert Jones, used their knowledge of managing unionized multisite plants to steer the merger of several hospitals to a successful conclusion (this being Canada, all the hospitals involved were public unionized organizations), as well as to secure the $250 million extra capital HHS needed.[31]

Currently, HHS is not only the largest hospital and healthcare entity in the city, it is also one of its main employer and research centers. As part of the management of the HHS creation process, steel executives also rebuilt connections between HHS and the city's other hospital, St. Josephs, which includes an agreed-upon division of labor and joint, cross-appointed vice presidents across the two organizations to improve integration. Thus, since 1997, Hamilton has ended up with a strengthened and deeply integrated care system.[32]

Those flows of capital and management knowledge steering the city's health system to focus on integrated care also played hand-in-hand with the opening, in 1966, of the medical school at McMaster University. The school quickly pioneered and led a different (now globally diffused) model of medical training and research: problem-based learning (PBL). The leaders behind this development were Howard S. Barrows and Robyn Tamblyn, who, under the leadership of the founding dean of the school, John Robert Evans, were given a free hand to develop a new way to teach medicine. The PBL approach to education and research is small groups, patients, and problem-based (cases), instead of the more "what are the trendiest questions in science" and rote-memorization-of-a-body-of-knowledge approach.[33]

Later McMaster as also a pioneer in the development of a parallel research/education philosophy to ensure two things. First, clinicians (that is, practicing doctors) would have the skills to critically read the latest medical research. Second, those skills would then allow them to tailor and change treatments for patients, based on their own observations coupled with a deep critical understanding of the newest medical research behind the new treatments and drugs. Thus, this approach calls for three principles: (1) ensuring that the practicing medical doctors develop and retain the skills to at least critically read the latest medical research; (2) creating a system with which they are kept abreast of the latest research findings; and (3) using those skills and knowledge to tailor treatment based on contextual values and preferences; that is, understanding what are the benefits and downsides for specific treatment options and fitting them within the specific context.[34]

This approach, codified as evidence-based medicine, has by now become the standard approach in North America, but it was pioneered and led by McMaster. One of the fathers of evidence-based medicine, David Sackett, founded the first department of clinical epidemiology and biostatistics in the world at McMaster in 1967 (now called the Department of Health Research Methods, Evidence and Impact), and led a series of innovative randomized clinical trials. The most famous one of them created a new habit for many of us—taking a small-dosage aspirin (baby aspirin) on a daily basis to prevent stroke and heart attacks. One of Sackett's more renowned students, Gordon Guyatt, proceeded to systemize this new approach, coining it "evidence-based medicine" and becoming instrumental in popularizing it around the world. A measure for the importance of this innovation is the fact that when the *BMJ* (formerly known as the *British Medical Journal*) listed in 2007 the most importance contributions to healthcare, evidence-based medicine was judged to be more important than the more well-known and celebrated technologies of the computer and medical imaging.[35]

The success of this philosophy has now reached a peak in which it is influencing (sometimes, alas, the core principals are lost in translation) other fields; for example, evidence-based policy has become a fashionable buzz word. It is important to understand that the philosophy behind evidence-based medicine is sometimes quite different from that of evidence-based something else. Evidence-based medicine calls for two things. First and foremost, is the empowerment (by skill and knowledge) of the user/street-level bureaucrats (the medical practitioner, aka sophisticated users in the innovation parlance), so they can guide development from the front line. From this first principle, it then derives different ways to conduct research and discovery, where evidence from the field (i.e., epidemiology) is used interactively to guide changes in treatments and delivery methods.[36]

This different health teaching and research orientation was further strengthened when McMaster invested in developing a globally renowned research and teaching expertise in population health and clinical epidemiology, as well as point-of-care technologies. These are critical patient-engaging areas, which most elite universities in North America do not see as a source for significant capital from grants and donations, or even as recruitment vehicles for high-prestige researchers. In Hamilton, as part of an overall ecosystem focused on an alternative stage 1 innovation, they had a significant influence on its growth and sustainability. Thus, for example, among McMasters' medical research flagship centers are the Population Health Research Institute (developing specialties in clinical trials), Centre for Probe Development and Commercialization (CPDC), and a joint center with the German Fraunhofers: the Fraunhofer-McMaster Project Centre for Biomedical Engineering and Advanced Manufacturing (BEAM).[37]

Those influences can be seen in the kind of healthcare companies founded in Hamilton. For example, Fusion Pharmaceuticals, which was listed on NASDAQ on June 26, 2020, spun out of the CPDC. Fusion developed a platform for delivering medical isotopes to a precise set of cells. While the first usage is in cancer, where rate and accuracy of delivery (you want all, but only, cancer cells to die and die quickly) is of the utmost importance, the company's main play is in the development of the delivery platform, not the specific treatments. Fusion Pharmaceutical has received a total of $146 million in Series A and B funding from a range of investors. Given that Fusion was able to build on its strengths at CPDC, it was also able to attract more VC investments. For instance, the chair of CPDC, Bob Sutherland, is also a senior investment officer at Fight Against Cancer Innovation Trust, which is one of the key investors in the CPDC.[38]

Another direct spin-off is Adapsyn Bioscience. The company emerged from Dr. Nathan Magarvey's research that established an AI and machine learning method to develop therapeutics and drugs from natural materials. Thus, again, the company's real technology is a platform, not a specific molecule. Adapsyn entered into a partnership and received an undisclosed amount of funding from Pfizer—which will deploy the platform developed by Adapsyn to develop new products. Adapsyn is also entitled to payments worth $162 million on preclinical and regulatory milestones, along with royalties on the sales of therapeutics developed off the platform.[39]

However, the growing involvement of outside investors and venture funds is already leading to some of the problems seen in other aspiring locales, such as Atlanta. For example, Jonathan Bramson, the director of Fraunhofer-McMasters' BEAM also led a spin-out, Triumvira Immunologics, based on his research on immunotherapy solutions for cancer treatments. Specifically, Triumvira developed the technology to extract white blood cells, genetically modify them, and release them back into the body to detect and eradicate cancer cells. However, as a result of its early funding, the company is now headquartered and run out of Austin, Texas, with Hamilton as its R&D center.[40]

Hamilton is also a center of medical device innovation. The early growth of the capacity and willingness to "play" with these technologies was due to the union health benefits (for workers, retirees, and their families) of the steel companies. These acted as a source of both demand and early revenues. This was especially true in the case of trauma, burn, and dental products. Union benefits, generously covering also retirees and their families, coupled with the higher frequency of burn injuries in the steel industry, created a critical mass in both the demand and the ability to pay for such services and products. An example is the growth of the Rotsaert Dental Lab in Hamilton to become a one-hundred-employee strong business, and one of the first in North America to integrate CAD/CAM technologies into its restorative dental business, in the 1980s. This then led the company to expand and establish Emerald Dental Works, which is a contract manufacturer working with dental labs across Canada.[41]

Another example of the user-engaged/based innovation ecosystem in Hamilton is Genesis Pain Relief Light. The company was founded in 2008, when Tom Kerber, an engineer and entrepreneur who runs his own small engineering and technology development company in Hamilton, was taking treatment for soft tissue pain and injury from Dr. Paul Ziemer, a Hamilton-based chiropractor. As part of this treatment, Dr. Ziemer remarked how much more efficient and quicker the treatment and recovery would be if there was a product that would allow patients to treat themselves at home between laser treatments in the clinic. This, in an almost classic user-based innovation case study, inspired Tom to develop handheld light-treatment products, the core technology of which has led to the creation of two companies so far. The first is a handheld product omitting light to help with the recovery of soft tissue injuries, around which Genesis was formed and created. The second is new technology for deep tissues—photodynamic cancer therapy, the core technological breakthrough around which another company, Illumacell, was formed. Both companies have opted not to take VC funding, instead relying on debt and sales to reach positive cash-flow.[42]

The future of this transformation of Hamilton is not clear. While the local ecosystem has become significantly "thicker," with tighter networks and institutionalized processes to increase companies' formation, most local policymakers still view "Silicon-Hyphens" as a goal. This leads many of them to try to form a system for company creation and scale-up that requires venture capital, and hence aims for significant financial exits. Luckily, for now, many Hamilton companies fail to attract out-of-cluster VC, and instead focus on building products and sales as sources of growth revenues. It remains to be seen whether the region will be able to develop alternative capital sources that fit the strengths of its companies, or whether the allure of Silicon Valley and venture capital will doom it to become yet another feeder cluster.

The Importance of Vision

One of the most positive impacts of the globalized fragmentation of production is that local leaders wishing to achieve innovation-based growth in their regions have, in fact, multiple options for doing so—more choices than ever before. These choices affect *how* you succeed and *who* in the region enjoys the benefits. Each choice also entails establishing specific underpinnings to achieve and sustain success.

Accordingly, the most important task for a region is to have a vision. This starts with asking yourself what growth should look like. Should it mean a transformation of the local economy by an onslaught of new companies with nifty new products and services, defining new industries and redefining old ones? Should it mean a resurgence of existing companies as they supply critical components and services in a world economy controlled by global production networks? These questions are intimately tied to two more: Who is going to be employed, and by whom, if your innovation-based growth plans reach fruition? And what levels of equity, inequality, and state intervention do you see as acceptable?

It is only after you answer these questions that you and your region can devise a strategy to get there. In doing so you should consider your current strengths, resources, and position in the global economy, figure out which capacities the region lacks, and determine which of those missing capacities could feasibly be developed.

In too many regions, a failure of innovation-based growth has been the result of a failure to develop a vision of what success should look like, or else a failure to devise a plan for positioning the region for a fair chance of achieving the vision. You should think about innovation-based growth as a journey through stormy, uncharted oceans. You *will* need to recalculate your path, but without an idea of where you hope to go, there is no chance of ever getting there. Even with the best ship in the world, if you go to sea without a destination or a compass, the only thing that is sure is that you will get lost.

Further, developing a vision forces you to face the reality that certain models of innovation-based success might not take the region where you want it to go. You might realize that you do not wish the ultimate outcome on your community. Even if you're determined to turn your locale into a stage 1 innovation center, do you want to find yourself living in a Silicon-Hyphen that suffers from the opportunity inequalities of Silicon Valley and Israel? If not, then look for different financial models, possibly even developing your own.

8

Looking for Better Options

The Science of Innovation Policies and Agencies in a Globally Fragmented World

"Your Silver Shoes will carry you over the desert," replied Glinda. "If you had known their power you could have gone back to your Aunt Em the very first day you came to this country."

"But then I should not have had my wonderful brains!" cried the Scarecrow. "I might have passed my whole life in the farmer's cornfield."

"And I should not have had my lovely heart," said the Tin Woodman. "I might have stood and rusted in the forest till the end of the world."

"And I should have lived a coward forever," declared the Lion, "and no beast in all the forest would have had a good word to say to me."

"This is all true," said Dorothy, "and I am glad I was of use to these good friends. But now that each of them has had what he most desired, and each is happy in having a kingdom to rule besides, I think I should like to go back to Kansas."

—L. Frank Baum, *The Wonderful Wizard of Oz*

Throughout this book we have explored a multitude of cases of regional innovation-based growth. During this analysis, it has become clear that success can be achieved in different innovation stages and different locales, and through a focus on different industries. Yet many of the cases unite in several ways. First and foremost, local leaders in both the private and public spheres have focused their attention on innovation, not on invention, research, or even high-tech. In so doing, each region quickly came to concentrate its efforts on the agents of innovation—companies and individuals—and the ecosystem that allowed it to excel in a specific stage of innovation.

It is at this point that most of the policy confusion arises. There is a critical role in innovation policy for "complementarities"; these include institutions of research and higher education as well as knowledge of the latest technologies and technological trends, such as advanced manufacturing, artificial intelligence, or nanotechnology. Nonetheless, one of the most common ways for regions to fail is to focus on the trendiest complementarity, be it venture capital, university parks, green tech, or artificial intelligence. Regions too often assume that if they fix this one complementarity, then they will magically overcome their failure to achieve the primary aims of creating and growing the agents of innovation. Innovative companies and entrepreneurs will appear like mushrooms after the rain and will proceed to happily grow and scale up.

In all of our successful cases, local leaders, instead of bowing to fashion (and intellectual laziness), figured out why and where their agents of innovation were struggling (or in some cases why these agents did not exist) and then devised specific public policies with regard to particular domains in order to solve problems in particular points in the locales' growth cycles. This meant understanding the current competitive advantages their regions could utilize, what future advantages were feasible to invest in, and what capacities the envisioned local future agents of innovation should have. Only after developing a clear vision of those issues did the leaders go on to develop complementarities.

For example, only *after* Israel had twenty years of IPOs on NASDAQ did the OCS implement a focused venture-capital creation policy. Only *after* multiple Taiwanese firms were already operating in specific industries and it became clear that alone they did not have the R&D capacities to compete globally did ITRI develop its research consortia programs. And only *after* Brenta's leaders figured out their companies' business and growth models in the globalizing women's luxury shoe industry did they revise the educational programs of their dedicated professional school and tie them to the global buzz via the Parsons School of Design in New York.

A fascinating finding from our cases is that three of the most common obsessions of innovation consultants worldwide—venture capital, science parks, and globally competitive research universities—very rarely played roles in the regions' successes. Further, when any of those elements did play a part, its role was peripheral, limited to a particular time point, used in a very specific way, and extensively tailored to fit local conditions.

This is a lesson learned long ago in the private sector, yet somehow forgotten in public policy: the importance of the division of labor. A perfect example is the confusion around institutions of higher education and research. Their specific role in the division of labor appears prominently in their title: research and education. These are the domains where they excel. Locales that understand this can enjoy the immense benefits and competitive advantages that institutions of higher education and advanced research provide to their regional economies. However, places that assume that if they just fix their universities, ordering them to become more entrepreneurial, then the Good Witch Glinda will wave her wand and innovation-based growth will be had for all, will wind up disappointed.

Yale University in New Haven, Connecticut, is a case in point. Starting in the 1990s Yale has indeed been the impetus and originator behind the city's growing biotech industry. However, as detailed research by Professor Shiri Breznitz has showed, this is not only because the university changed its internal policies on IP and entrepreneurship—it is mainly because Yale, which had always been a top research university, in effect transformed itself into the region's de facto innovation-based economic development agency, bringing together investors and industries, allocating space, and coordinating its own efforts with those of the city and the state. In that role it created a set of highly successful innovation policies that focused not so much on its own capabilities as on New Haven's innovation agents, the ecosystem they needed, and the dynamic processes in which the ecosystem changed over time. Focusing on just one set of institutions, instead of on your innovation agents and the ecosystem they need, will almost always end in tears.[1]

The same goes for almost any other policy program whose premise is that if we just fix that one thing, whether it be finance, spaces, or intellectual property rights, in just one specific time point, then all will be solved. This misunderstanding, coupled with the fetishism of novelty and the misunderstanding of innovation, is the main cause behind the Boulevard of Broken Dreams that Josh Lerner describes in his book on entrepreneurial and VC policies.[2]

This leads us to a crucial point about devising policies for innovation-based growth. As we have seen (but it bears repeating), innovation policy should attempt to achieve three things: (1) equip the agents of innovation with the capacities they need in order to excel; (2) develop, support, and sustain the ecosystem those agents need; and (3) stimulate said agents to action. Yet human society is a dynamic, and most importantly a learning, system. Ergo, to be effective, policy must co-evolve in tandem with society. That means that as times and local and global industry change, growth models must change too. One set of policies is appropriate when you attempt to spur new companies where there are none, but a different one is appropriate when those companies grow to become the new global competitors. To ensure long-term innovation-based growth in your locale, you need to ensure that your region has the capacity to constantly co-evolve its innovation policies.

But no one knows in advance which changes will work and which won't. At the time you devise polices, you can have very little understanding of what the desired future products, services, customers, business models, and sometime even the industry will look like. Accordingly, to succeed over time, locales need to have the capacity to constantly, quickly, and efficiently experiment with their innovation policies. Successful regions manage to institutionalize a continuous cycle of innovation policy experimentalism. As the old proverb goes: a central banker can work from sun to sun, but an innovation policymaker's work is never done.

How should regions institutionalize continuous experimentation with innovation policy?

Many of the most successful places have done it by creating an independent organization whose mission is to develop and implement innovation policies. A common name for these organizations is *innovation agency*. It is a somewhat misleading name, since their legal structures are widely diverse, from policy units to private-public enterprises to endowment-based public-mission foundations. But they do have a core mission in common: They focus, long term, on innovation-policy experimentation so that policy can co-evolve with the regional industry.

Understanding the Innovation Agency

Surprisingly, when in 2010 my friends in the World Bank and the OECD, Yevgeny Kuznetsov and Dirk Pilat, asked me and my colleague Darius Ornston to look at how such organizations operate and evolve, we discovered that very little systematic research had been done on this critical issue. The rest of this chapter describes our journey of discovery alone and with friends from Nesta UK, the Inter-American Development Bank, multiple innovation agencies on five continents, our colleague and former post-doc Steven Samford, and our friend Rainer Kattel, one of the very few scholars to publish academic work on the subject.[3]

Policymakers modeling new innovation agencies on the example of successful organizations could be forgiven for becoming quickly and completely confused. Effective innovation agencies include large, powerful, pilot organizations as well as small, lightly funded ones. Some public agencies have clear technological objectives and manage much of the research themselves, while others have delegated these decisions to private-sector actors. Some organizations have thrived by insulating themselves from political and industrial networks, while others have successfully promoted innovation by embedding themselves within these same structures. In short, there is considerable variation in the design of successful innovation agencies, and no clear lessons for reform-oriented local leaders.[4]

Nonetheless, those findings appear to be confusing and contradictory only if you make the classic mistake of equating innovation with stage 1 innovation—novelty. Once you understand that there are different kinds of innovation and different stages of innovation-based growth a locale can excel at, it becomes quite clear that the real question is: What kind of innovation agency excels at what kinds and stages of innovation?

Since every stage of innovation is associated with a different set of capabilities, designing an effective innovation agency depends on the regional innovation-stage specialization and the particular modes in which the locale aims to sustain its advantage in that particular stage. Even so, there is no clear one-to-one fit between specific innovation agency design and innovation-stage specialization. In our joint work we identified four distinct types of innovation agencies. As we will see later, each one of them fits better with specific stages of innovation, but there are at least two models to choose from in each stage. The questions local leaders need to ask themselves are: What are the resources at hand that can be devoted to this agency? And what are the sociopolitical norms with regard to the proper role of public policy in private business, and of private business in public policy?[5]

The four models of innovation agencies are: *productivity facilitators, directed upgraders, state-led disruptors*, and *transformation enablers*.

Productivity facilitators are modestly financed innovation agencies that introduce small-scale, incremental product and process innovations across a wide range of established industries. This mode of innovation-policy development works best in cases in which there is already an existing industry, mostly focusing on stage 4 and/or stage 3 innovation, and where the local community's vision for innovation-based growth is of sustaining and upgrading already established activities by infusing them with the latest technology. The state's role is seen as one of assisting private industry, focusing on fixing the most obvious market and network failures in R&D, and fostering information flows. The aims and the mission are modest, and there is no aspiration for significant economic or industrial transformation.[6]

Two examples of this model are the Danish GTS Institutes and the Canadian Industrial Research Assistance Program (IRAP). The GTS Institutes (in Danish, *Godkendt Teknologisk Service*, which can be translated as Approved Technology Service providers) vary in size and specialization, but all work closely with private-sector partners to identify and solve technological challenges. The government views them as an important policy instrument and funds roughly 10 percent of their activities. Nonetheless, they operate at the periphery of public sector, with almost all of their budget coming from private industry. Instead of viewing the GTS Institutes as public agencies, it is better to view them as operating on a quasi-commercial basis, selling services to individual firms, which define their own needs and appropriate technologies. The institutes are heavily tied into Danish industry, particularly to established firms.[7]

The GTS Institutes' close proximity to the private sector, very modest independent budgets, and need to sell services in order to continue operations, discourage them from conducting high-risk, long-term research or getting involved in the creation of start-ups in new industrial sectors. In fact, while several of the larger institutes engage in significant research, the GTS Institutes as a whole are a relatively minor player in the Danish innovation system. Collectively, the GTS Institutes represent roughly 7 percent of Danish public R&D expenditure and less than 2 percent of total R&D spending. They act more as research translators and combinators, drawing on local university research and foreign technologies to meet local corporate needs.[8]

The GTS Institutes' inability to conduct ambitious, long-term, large-scale R&D is an asset in that it encourages them to apply existing technologies in pragmatic and effective ways. Learning from these exchanges, the GTS Institutes have emerged as an important vehicle for technological diffusion throughout the Danish economy, either distributing knowledge to Danish firms or organizing local production networks, most notably in the "network initiative" of the early 1990s. As such, they have been credited with upgrading the Danish innovation system, enabling firms to continue to occupy their positions within established low- and medium-technology industries even when facing cost-based competition from lower-labor-cost areas.[9]

Their perceived success has enhanced their profile and they are considered key actors within the Danish innovation system.[10]

However, there is an opportunity cost to this structure. The institutes' limited public budget and research capabilities prevent them from conducting the kinds of sustained, focused, and large-scale industrial policies that characterize other industrial R&D-conducting innovation agencies, such as Taiwan's ITRI and Germany's Fraunhofer Institutes. Further, their reliance on private-sector partners and established firms discourages the development of radically new technologies or business models. By responding to industrial needs as expressed by individual firms, the GTS Institutes have focused on solving short-term problems with practical solutions.

A similar role is played in Canada by the Industrial Research Assistance Program. IRAP is a modestly financed agency that relies on strong networks with the private sector rather than generous government funding to develop new technologies. Structurally, IRAP is a subdivision of the National Research Council (NRC), and as such exists at the periphery of the broader public sector. IRAP is also an extremely flat organization (unlike most state bureaucracies). Industrial Technology Advisors (ITAs), the frontline agents within IRAP, are given geographical regions to manage. In that role they are granted vast authority and are responsible for building networks with firms, research organizations, and educational institutions in their industries of expertise and their geographic areas. ITA recruitment favors candidates with industry experience, so they bring knowledge of technology development as well as networks of contacts in their target industries.[11]

IRAP's official mission is to assist SMEs with technological innovation and diffusion. Like the GTS Institutes, IRAP relies on its ITAs' deep networks within multiple industries to effectively address barriers to innovation. Moreover, rather than solving particular issues by developing technological solutions themselves, the ITAs use their networks to locate other organizations that can assist with necessary R&D. Thus, IRAP acts as a bridging/networking agency across its ITAs' local ecosystems. In so doing, the ITAs construct a framework for technological diffusion and continuous, incremental innovation. The contact between ITAs and firms is intimate and constant, with ITAs using their knowledge about firms' products and processes to identify other organizations or firms that may have solutions to particular technological problems. A small proportion of these R&D relationships (roughly 20 percent) are funded by IRAP; this occurs in cases where firms are judged to be especially promising but lack the financial resources necessary to take advantage of the partnerships proposed by the ITAs. The agency's mode of operation has enabled IRAP to secure a high return on its investments in the private sector. One of the great benefits is the ITAs' contextual knowledge, which allows them to accurately distinguish client firms that need funding from those that would perform R&D without it. Another is IRAP's ability to build networks of organizations to help fulfill clients' needs.[12]

At the same time, IRAP's approach has a clear trade-off: far-reaching radical technology development is not even considered. Because the ITAs are engaged with firms that have specific barriers to innovation and their funding is dedicated to projects with tightly defined goals, the agency does not promulgate broader or more-radical innovations. While ITAs do have contact with one another, they are deeply engaged with particular client firms and the particular geographic regions in which they work. This pragmatic focus comes out in the language of the agents when asked about broader technology-development projects: "We are very application-focused. . . . We don't support blue-sky research." Thus, the agency's effectiveness at fostering innovation and growth stems from the aggregation of piecemeal productivity improvements experienced by a large number of small firms, usually operating in established industries. This incremental effect is evidenced in the particular benefits that firms cite from working with IRAP: whereas 90 percent of businesses improved their technical knowledge or capabilities related to their businesses, and 70 percent reported improved productivity, only 30 percent reported the development of novel technologies or other intellectual property. This does not diminish IRAP's importance as an instrument for promoting innovation and growth among SMEs in traditional Canadian industries. However, it does illustrate trade-offs that the productivity facilitator innovation agency model embodies: locales can promote incremental innovation very efficiently by embedding modestly endowed innovation agencies within the private sector, but the same features that allow the agency to excel at this mission effectively preclude it from promoting broader, more radical innovation.[13]

Directed upgraders also specialize in incremental innovation, but in comparison with productivity facilitators, their time frame is longer, their focus is on a narrower set of industries and activities, and the resources they mobilize are greater—sometimes immense. As a result, directed upgraders facilitate large-scale change and foster a much deeper involvement of the public in directing the trajectories of private industry. Directed upgraders also fit better in cases where the aspiration for innovation-based growth is for a significant industrial upgrade but not a full socioeconomic transformation.[14]

Utilizing this model necessitates a vision and social norms that see the public-sector role as leading and steering the technological trajectory of private business. This means that the aim is never truly novel innovation, since a technology or industry needs to be deemed already important enough or promising enough (that is, operational and growing in other locales) for it to be "strategic" and state-led. A classic directed upgrader is Singapore's Agency for Science, Technology and Research (A*STAR). In 2001 the tiny island state of Singapore established A*STAR with great fanfare and positioned it at the heart of public policy and the civil service. A*STAR is one of the richest innovation agencies on earth, and its mission is no less than spearheading industrial R&D in Singapore. This profile is almost the opposite of that of the humble, under-the-radar, peripherally positioned IRAP and the GTSs. [15]

As a result of its position, importance, and ability to spend abundantly, A*STAR is deeply connected to private industry, most notably to the multinational corporations that dominate Singapore's economy. Unlike productivity facilitators, A*STAR also maintains a tight network with other public-sector actors and actively collaborates with leading institutions such as the Ministry for Education, the Ministry of Health, and the Enterprise Development Board to steer Singapore's entire R&D system. Furthermore, it coordinates and directs the activities of dozens of research institutes that it or its predecessor, the National Science and Technology Board, established. This is not a humble, flat organization that relies on private-industry matching funds to conduct specific, small-scale R&D projects.[16]

Indeed, A*STAR actively attempts to guide the technological development of the regional economy. In contrast to the productivity facilitators described earlier, A*STAR has been launching big-ticket, large-scale, long-term initiatives targeted at specific industries such as biotechnology. These focused efforts have benefited from A*STAR's formidable resources. For example, A*STAR established a series of new research institutes without ever needing private-market buy-in or financial support. By 2005, A*STAR-funded institutes "accounted for 38% of total biomedical R&D spending, more than then the entire private sector." A*STAR's efforts were not limited to research institutes or biotechnology but extended to a wide range of other areas, from technology parks to human capital.[17]

Directed upgraders are limited by their close ties to big industry and the rest of the public sector. These connections restrict their ability to experiment and take risks with radical innovation, both technological and policy-wise. A*STAR's high-profile position within the government discouraged it from taking risks with public funds. Instead, the agency has gravitated toward conservative policy instruments, many of which were established by its predecessor. Second, the agency has faced intense pressure to cater to the needs of existing, politically influential firms, most notably multinational corporations. The biomedical initiative just mentioned, for example, was a priority of the Enterprise Development Board (EDB), which sought to upgrade foreign direct investment in this space. By colonizing A*STAR's leadership and applying political pressure, the EDB reoriented A*STAR toward its own strategic vision.[18]

This is the true meaning of choice: Your choice of policy tools, in this case innovation agencies, has real consequences, both positive and negative. In the case of A*STAR, the agency's resources and strategic focus allowed it to upgrade Singapore's research infrastructure on a scale that dwarfs anything that productivity facilitators could even dream of. New research institutes, technology parks, and PhD programs enabled A*STAR to reach beyond SMEs to attract investment by large multinationals such as Nestlé, Proctor & Gamble, and General Electric. Nonetheless, while it succeeded in upgrading foreign direct investment within a handful of targeted sectors such as biotechnology and financial services, A*STAR has not had the radically transformative effects that policymakers envisioned when creating it. The agency was unsuccessful in its efforts to cultivate indigenous industry, and its failure to develop fundamentally new industries has confined its impact to specific sectors.[19]

Successful utilization of the directed-upgrading model is not limited to East Asia. In Latin America, the Chilean Economic Development Agency (CORFO) operates in a radically different context, within a democratically elected, economically neoliberal, and largely resource-extractive economy. Despite these stark differences, CORFO has been very effective as a directed upgrader in what has been one of the best economic growth stories of Latin America in the last forty years. CORFO, in a similar way to A*STAR, has tight connections with private-sector actors. Following consultations with industry, CORFO has taken leadership in seven "high potential" sectors. These sectors have been defined conservatively, focusing on existing national strengths: mining, aquaculture, agriculture-food, special-interest tourism, construction, creative economy, and advanced manufacturing. Again, in a similar fashion to A*STAR, in defining those sectors, and the specific programs for each, CORFO has been working in concert with, and as a coordinator of, numerous other government organizations.[20]

CORFO has been playing a leading role in the technological development of these seven sectors. For example, the agency famously spearheaded the transformation of Chile's traditional fishing industry into salmon aquaculture. There was already a clear potential for export of seafood, but the agency identified and solved significant technological and operational leaps in the transition from traditional fishing to aquafarming. In an effort that resembles A*STAR and far outstrips the scope and resources of productivity facilitators, CORFO worked with other agencies to fund public research, establish the Salmon Technology Institute, determine the most auspicious locations for aquafarms, and define and implement the standards necessary for local producers to export to North America and Western Europe. As a result of those efforts, by the early 2000s Chile had become one of the largest salmon-exporting countries in the world. CORFO's program further co-evolved with the industry when the aquaculture industry faced a crisis due to widespread fish disease. CORFO funded and led a collaborative effort to develop vaccines. Similar policies and approaches can be found in mining (where Chilean firms now lead the world in several technological niches) and the five other sectors (although with more mixed results).[21]

Nonetheless, the same constraints that limit the directed-upgrader model in Singapore can be seen in Chile. CORFO's centrality in the public sector and its tight networks across it limit the extent to which it can behave experimentally. CORFO's directory council (i.e., board) includes not only the minister of economy, CORFO's parent ministry, but also the ministers of foreign relations, finance, social development, and agriculture. One consequence of CORFO's accountability to other ministries, and by extension to incumbent stakeholders, is a pressure to target established industries. For example, in 2016 only five of sixty-two new instruments developed and implemented by CORFO were aimed at new sectors. Coordination with government agencies, which have their own agendas, and constant contact with existing private-sector organizations have meant that CORFO is mostly focused on promoting incremental change and innovation in existing sectors, which it has done very well.[22]

State-led disruptors represent another model in which the public sector not only conducts the industrial R&D but aims to lead the industry as well. However, the mission statement is radically different from those of directed upgraders or productivity facilitators. The aim of local leaders here is to foster

significant socioeconomic change by stimulating the creation of new industries and activities, where new can be new to the world or new to the local
economy. As such, these organizations are what can be called economic-
activities hedging organizations. The agency's mission is to utilize innovation
in order to diversify and expand the portfolio of economic activities in the locale. As such, state-led disruptors do not cater to the current mainstays of the
economy. Accordingly, while controlling more resources than productivity
facilitators, they are lean and poor in comparison with directed upgraders,
and are situated on the periphery in their relations to both the public and private sectors. This position allows them also to be much more experimental
and to take more-radical and long-term views and actions.[23]

We have already encountered one of the most renowned successes of state-
led disruptors: the Industrial Technology Research Institute (ITRI), which
was created specifically in order to spur the development of new industries,
activities, and technologies in Taiwan.

Perhaps the most celebrated example of state-led disruptors is the US
Defense Advanced Research Projects Agency (DARPA). Interestingly, even
after becoming internationally famous, DARPA sits at the periphery of the
public sector, much like ITRI. Further, both DARPA and ITRI are actively
involved in continuous network creation with an ever-changing set of private
firms. The agencies sit at the central node of those networks, charting out
technology trajectories up to the level of specific early-stage products. The
main difference between the two is that whereas ITRI is actively engaged in
R&D itself, DARPA contracts out R&D to external researchers, private firms,
and universities. DARPA's role is specifically to hedge, to be the small (in relative terms—in absolute terms its budget dwarfs the total R&D budgets of
several nation-states) initiative that ensures that the United States will never
be surprised by new technologies.[24]

For that reason, DARPA was also structured very differently than any
other US federal agency. Its mission is to define cutting-edge defense-related
technological projects and problems and then build up and bring together
new networks of researchers from academia and industry to explore a variety
of new technologies. Erica Fuchs's discussion of the role of DARPA project
managers clearly specifies their leadership role in setting the direction of the
research and its overall management.[25]

The process of determining the direction of technological development
reflects the needs of the military. The agency brainstorms possible research
directions with scientists and engineers that would meet those needs and

then works with military officers to help them understand emerging technologies. Fuchs emphasizes that the first part of this process is critical and less discretionary than the latter parts. Senior military officers, present in DARPA facilities, act as liaisons and help managers understand the nature of the military's needs. Managers also visit military installations and observe operations throughout the country in order to better grasp particular military operations. Working closely with and taking guidance from the defense branches is a primary step that "managers cannot escape." The direction of innovation is thus determined by the Department of Defense rather than by the private sector.[26]

At the same time, DARPA differs from A*STAR and CORFO in that its relationship with the US military shields it from short-term political pressures, giving it flexibility and making it into a "collaborative space" so that it can allow experimentation with radically new technologies. Historically, the agency has developed "proactive" rather than "reactive" technologies. Those technologies are by definition not foreseen as necessary by industry, although many times they quickly become essential after they have been developed. In short, unlike either directed upgraders or productivity facilitators, DARPA's networks explore more radical solutions in areas that are deemed important by the state, instead of addressing the immediate concerns of established companies.[27]

Nevertheless, DARPA's gloried successes as a radical innovator should not obscure its weaknesses. While DARPA has been contributing to technologies from the Internet to the iPhone, robotics, and new-material semiconductors, its autonomy from the private sector can lead it astray, and not all projects are successful. Indeed, at any given point in time, DARPA works on several major projects, and while the (rather rare) successes are widely celebrated, the vast majority of the projects do not have any revolutionary impact, even after an investment of several years and hundreds of million dollars in each. This rate of failure is a necessary condition for DARPA to fulfill its mission of being the ultimate hedge on the cutting-edge of defense-related technologies. However, from the point of view of economic growth, if one's aim is mainly growth, one has to wonder if the DARPA model does not inherently breed many more expensive dead ends than successes.

At least as importantly, the agency relies on the formidable capacity of the US private sector to commercialize its transformative technologies. With its relatively weak ties to industry, the organization is poorly equipped to facilitate the diffusion and adoption of new technologies, particularly as they apply to traditional industry. Regions seeking to replicate DARPA's model should recognize its limitations, and they need to be sure that the absorptive capacity of their industry is high enough to be able to take the outcomes of a DARPA-like organization and make them into innovations that can be the bases for new industries. It remains to be seen whether even the United States can replicate the DARPA model in other sectors. For example, a DARPA-like agency in the energy sector, the Advanced Research Projects Agency-Energy (APRA-E), started operation in 2009, and after more than a decade the jury is still out on whether it has had, or ever will have, a DARPA-like transformative impact.[28]

A different limitation of state-led disruptors becomes apparent in the case of ITRI. Because the agency operates in an ecosystem where industry has a significantly lower absorptive capacity than in the United States, ITRI devised, implemented, and tailored a set of tools to ensure diffusion. These include the research consortia and official spinoffs that were discussed earlier. However, this different path of co-evolution led to a different problem: the division of labor that developed between government and private industry, with ITRI conducting much of the research and industry focusing on development. This limits the innovative capacities and the business models pursued by Taiwanese industry. Although the sophistication of the industry has grown tremendously, interviews with some of the most advanced Taiwanese semiconductor companies still sparked comments such as: "Sometimes, I wish I was still in ITRI. It is the only place in Taiwan where real R&D is taking place."[29]

The comparison between ITRI and DARPA also serves to remind us that different models can be tailored to enhance different innovation capacities that fit different stages of production. Thus, we have one state-led disruptor, ITRI, that has successfully focused on enhancing its regional industry capacity to engage in new industries, but with the aim of becoming a critical node of stage 3 innovation. On the other side we have DARPA, a state-led disruptor solely focused on advancing the ability to do cutting-edge innovation in industries and technologies that do not yet exist—the optimum stage 1 innovation.

This leads us to *transformation enablers*. Transformation enablers are the ideal Schumpeterian developmental agencies (SDAs)—that is, organizations that are the main agents of Schumpeterian change in their economies. They are stimulators of qualitative innovation-based change. As such, this is the only model of innovation agency that clearly fits only one stage—stage 1, novelty. Transformation enablers seed large numbers of small-scale private-market experiments, rather than taking a narrowly focused big-ticket approach. When the seeding approach is allowed to work and hone itself in a two-loop learning process of co-evolutionary adjustments over the course of several decades, we have the very rare creation of successful Silicon-Hyphens. Since we have already analyzed at length the story of the OCS in Israel, let us look at Finland.[30]

Most studies of Finland's miraculous transformation from a resource-based economy heavily reliant on barter trade with the USSR into a global ICT powerhouse attribute the change to large, well-funded agencies such as Tekes and big-ticket national bodies such as the Science and Technology Policy Council. The historical truth is that those organizations were critical only in the scaling-up of new policies. The organization that developed, implemented, experimented with, and refined those policies was Sitra, a small public enterprise with extremely modest resources, created as a minor and marginal hedge in an effort to diversify the structure of the Finnish economy by innovation (operationally defined in those years as new technologies, companies, and industries). For a long period of time Sitra was a truly experimental innovation-policy innovator. This was partly out of necessity, since as soon as Sitra's new policies proved themselves, they were poached by more powerful actors. This forced Sitra to constantly launch new initiatives. However, as its recognition and prestige grew, Sitra was scrutinized and became highly politicized, and as a result lost most of its ability to experiment and innovate.[31]

This, as Darius Ornston and I have shown, is the main threat and limitation of following the transformation-enablers model. In order to continue to be experimental and policy-innovative, the organizations must remain marginal, avoiding public scrutiny and politicization. However, if their policies achieve success, their status grows, and so does the public, media, and political interest in what they do—effectively censoring their ability to innovate. Currently, with innovation becoming such a politically prominent subject, it is questionable whether any region can create and maintain the conditions that allow transformation enablers to succeed. Hence, even if your locale strategically decides to focus on stage 1 innovation, it is not clear whether you can utilize this model under current political conditions.[32]

Historically, Finland possessed one of the lowest-technology economies in the OECD. Even "high-technology" companies such as Nokia derived half of their international revenue from noncompetitive, bilateral trade with the USSR. Macroeconomic policy was devised to reinforce this trajectory. The Bank of Finland, in close collaboration with the major banking groups, incentivized investment in capital-intensive industries by fixing interest rates below market-clearing levels, strategically allocating foreign exchange, and repeatedly devaluing the currency. Industrial policy was focused on the same goals. The Ministry of Trade and Industry (KTM) used grant aid and created state-owned enterprises to successfully target mature, capital-intensive manufacturing industries such as copper, steel, and chemicals.[33]

In this context, Sitra—formally, the Finnish Innovation Fund—was created as a minuscule hedge in policy innovation. The idea for Sitra was proposed by Klaus Waris, then the governor of the Bank of Finland, who was worried that the economy was overconcentrated on resource extraction and its USSR trade. He managed to get Sitra approved by parliament in 1968, on the pretext of celebrating the Finnish parliament's fiftieth anniversary. Sitra was established with a broad mandate to promote the competitiveness of the Finnish economy, reflecting both a growing consensus about the inflationary consequences of the devaluation cycle and continued disagreement about how to escape it. Sitra's budget was modest in the extreme—the organization operated off the interest from its 145-million-euro endowment.[34]

Sitra's small budget and unconventional mandate effectively insulated it from political interference. It was forced to become a policy innovator, since the larger, more powerful actors such as KTM and the Bank of Finland monopolized traditional instruments such as state-owned enterprises and credit rationing. Inspired by his extensive international contacts, Waris, who became Sitra's first president, sought instead to promote entrepreneurship by using grants and soft loans to cofinance risky long-term research by private corporations. Sitra's low political profile also enabled the organization to target nontraditional, private actors. For example, during the first ten years, over a quarter of Sitra's funds were allocated to electronics.[35]

Lacking capital, the organization sought to raise awareness of an alternative, R&D-intensive, developmental model by writing reports and inviting elites to participate in courses on economic policy. These efforts bore fruit in the early 1980s, not because of an emerging high-technology coalition (which was still in its infancy), but because of deteriorating economic performance and geopolitical vulnerability. The OPEC-induced oil crises of the 1970s increased bilateral trade with the Soviet Union to worrisome levels, while high-profile failures delegitimized traditional industrial policies. In this context, Sitra's research program provided a proven model to promote restructuring. Nonetheless, reflecting Sitra's marginalization within the Finnish public sector, a new actor was created to take over this domain, the Finnish Funding Agency for Technology and Innovation (Tekes). Tekes's initial budget was four times higher than Sitra's and increased rapidly from 40 million euro in 1984 to over 400 million by 2000. By then, Finland led the European Union in public R&D spending as a share of GDP and ranked second only to Sweden in gross expenditure on R&D as a share of GDP.[36]

With the decision to establish a much larger agency dedicated to research, Sitra was forced to develop a new set of policies to advance its core mission. To identify new instruments, Sitra policymakers looked beyond the established companies that they worked with in the 1970s, which were now the focus of Tekes, and beyond Finland to the United States. Inspired by a visit to Silicon Valley in the mid-1980s, Sitra managers used their endowment to purchase equity in high-technology firms and support private VC funds. Because Sitra was not deemed important enough to merit intervention, its moves into early-stage risk-capital markets provoked little resistance.[37]

Given its budget limitations, Sitra again relied on education, generating awareness, and building networks. For example, Sitra established the Finnish Venture Capital Association in 1990 and worked with private-sector venture capitalists to lobby politicians, KTM, pension funds, insurance companies, and other major investors. By the early 1990s, when a severe recession and banking crisis delegitimized established policy routines and industries, Sitra had again pioneered and refined a promising alternative model that could be copied and scaled by national politicians. Kera, a regional development fund, was the first to copy Sitra by launching the first dedicated public VC fund, Start Fund of Kera (SFK), in 1991. In 1995, parliament established an even larger fund, Finnish Industry Investment (FII), under the supervision of KTM.[38]

These two funds, coupled with a successful campaign to entice institutional investors, rapidly increased VC investment in Finland. For example, investment in early-stage risk capital climbed from 0.003 percent of GDP (2.8 million euro) in 1989 to 0.103 percent of GDP (135.4 million euro) by 2000, leapfrogging every EU member-state for which data is available, to rank first within the European Union. The creation of FII and an increasingly vibrant private sector led Sitra to exit from the VC industry. From 1996, Sitra shifted its role from direct provider of capital to network builder, providing planning assistance to firms, launching a networking service to link firms with business angels, and matching young enterprises with experienced managers. Sitra's new role in the VC industry reflected a broader shift away from the provision of hard resources toward the coordination of various actors in the innovation process, particularly end users and citizens.[39]

By 1999 Sitra had adopted the concept of "social innovation" and subsequently launched initiatives in areas as diverse as healthcare, municipal reform, and energy efficiency. This more holistic approach to innovation has since been adopted by other actors in the Finnish innovation system in response to recent economic shocks. By 2008, Finland's national innovation strategy had addressed the concept of social innovation, prompting agencies such as Tekes to launch programs on public-sector reform and workplace cooperation.[40]

It is unclear whether Sitra still has the capacity to generate disruptive new ideas. While Sitra still publicly claims to be a radical thinker, new policy innovations are scarce. This should not be that surprising if one looks at the politics surrounding Sitra. The organization now has a much more prominent position in the Finnish innovation system. While its endowment remains modest, Sitra's increasing profile has attracted political attention. A former executive noted, "Sitra had built up a very good reputation, not only nationally, but also internationally. . . . It became prestigious for politicians to sit on its supervisory board and show to their constituents that they impact its policies." Growing parliamentary interference was most visible in the appointment of former prime minister Esko Aho to lead Sitra in 2004, but political appointments are now common at lower levels as well.[41]

Political interference affected Sitra's strategy. Sitra's board has pressured the organization to focus on high-profile social problems such as healthcare and municipal reform. One senior employee acknowledged, "We were led to understand that we cannot say no to a national problem. So, for example, we have to do something for healthcare, even if it is an old problem that should have been resolved, like municipal IT systems, twenty years ago." This focus—more on social and political issues and less on innovation policy—has become Sitra's mainstay. In 2019 Sitra proudly said its main themes include inducing and sustaining societal change and redefining the social dialogue and the Finnish welfare system. Sitra's commitment to solving urgent social problems is admirable, and the organization performs a valuable consensus-building function. However, one cannot but wonder how political interference has managed to effectively move an agency that was formally titled the Finnish Innovation Fund to focus on things so far removed from innovation.[42]

It is too early to declare that the transformation-enablers model is politically doomed to fail as soon as it reaches success—after all, we have seen that similar political dynamics led the Israeli OCS to an almost opposite trajectory, with the agency changing its role to become the Israeli Innovation Authority so that it could regain the ability to experiment in innovation policy. Nonetheless, it is clear that prominence on the public-policy stage can cripple an innovation agency's ability to keep experimenting—and sometimes, inevitably, failing—with policy ideas over long periods of time.

As we have seen throughout this chapter, innovation agencies come in all shapes and forms. Some are not even public agencies. Nevertheless, they all unite in being the actors responsible for the continuous creation, implementation, and management of innovation policies focused on the two agents of innovation: individuals and companies.

One important lesson is the need for a good fit among the mission, the vision for innovation, and the structure and organization of the innovation agency. In Israel, the structure and organization of OCS, one of the world's best transformation enablers, was an excellent fit for both the mission and the vision, which favored stage 1 innovation. However, in Canada the structure and organization of IRAP, one of the world's best productivity facilitators, *is no longer* a great fit for the mission and vision, at least to judge from the public debate. People in Canada constantly lament the country's failure in stage 1 innovation; consequently, IRAP is given an ever-growing set of new policy programs to manage, with stage 1 innovation the aim. Yet IRAP will never succeed in that role. No set of new programs and responsibilities will ever make IRAP effective in fostering Silicon-Hyphens. However, they might very well make it less effective in what it does well.[43]

Another lesson in creating innovation agencies is the importance of setting realistic expectations. Take a careful look at three things: the current and future capacities of the local innovation agents, the resources that can be given to the innovation agency, and the local norms about public intervention in the market.

On the matter of local agents' capacities: Creating GTS or a Fraunhofer copycat in an industrial desert or within a thriving start-up scene would be less then helpful. The model of such organizations is to deeply engage with an already established industry. If there are no companies or industry to work with, creating the world's best productivity facilitator would not do much good.

On resources: If you happen to have several billion dollars to allocate to your innovation agencies, your choice of models is drastically different than if you can allocate at best $10 million a year. The same goes for talent: If the public sector has the best applied researchers and the resources to employ them, your choices are strikingly different than if you are in a locale where no self-respecting R&D engineer would be willing to work in the public sector.

On local norms: In devising an innovation agency that achieves the best fit with your mission and capacity, you must be keenly aware of the political constraints you might have to work within. But beware: assessing the consensus on market intervention is not as easy as you might think. For example, the United States is the home of neoliberalism and the so-called Washington Consensus, calling for minimal public intervention—there is a long history of aversion to the idea of the state leading the way in innovation. Yet in the United States we find DARPA, which underscores that norms may shift when it comes to arenas such as defense. In healthcare, too, there appears to be tolerance for greater market intervention. Indeed, some researchers argue that the United States has, in effect, the most complex and effective apparatus of innovation agencies the world has ever seen; it's just that it is hidden.[44]

These lessons are hardly quantum computing, or even rocket science. Nonetheless, in the old Greek mythology, Pandora has left humanity with hope, not wisdom. This is the only reasonable explanation as to why trillions of dollars are wasted annually in attempts to create Fraunhofer and DARPA look-alikes in environments without industries that can act as absorptive partners, or in attempts to spur innovation by "creating" VC industries in locales without any start-ups.

PART III
THE THREE DYSFUNCTIONALS

"Oh, 'tanstaafl.' Means 'There ain't no such thing as a free lunch.'
And isn't," I added, pointing to a FREE LUNCH sign across room,
"or these drinks would cost half as much. Was reminding her that
anything free costs twice as much in long run or turns out worth-
less." "An interesting philosophy." "Not philosophy, fact. One way or
other, what you get, you pay for."

A rational anarchist believes that concepts such as "state" and "society" and "government" have no existence save as physically exem-
plified in the acts of self-responsible individuals. He believes that it is
impossible to shift blame, share blame, distribute blame . . . as blame,
guilt, responsibility are matters taking place inside human beings
singly and nowhere else. But being rational, he knows that not all
individuals hold his evaluations, so he tries to live perfectly in an
imperfect world . . . aware that his effort will be less than perfect yet
undismayed by self-knowledge of self-failure.
                    —Robert A. Heinlein, The Moon is a Harsh Mistress

A Short Introduction to Part III

This part of the book is slightly different from the first two parts, and if you,
the reader, so wishes, can also be read as an essential addendum. So far we
have analyzed what innovation is, how we can constructively understand
the current global system of production to devise different local innovation-based growth models, and how to plan for such growth. This part of the
book looks at three critical domains of innovation-based growth that, from
the point of view of communities seeking sustained prosperity, are not only

deeply dysfunctional, but also that regions and communities have very little influence on: intellectual property rights (IPR), finance, and data.

It is important to understand what I mean by dysfunctional here. Unlike the common current use, dysfunctional does not mean that something does not function at all, but that it does not function properly. The way IPR, finance, and data currently function is dysfunctional from both the general human welfare enhancement sense and from the particularity of communities that try to secure their own innovation-based prosperity. There are many people, some of them are even my friends, who became fabulously rich thanks to the way these three systems work. To them, what regional leaders and common citizens see as dysfunctions to be fixed are rather features to be exploited with the right rent-seeking business models.

Further, the current state of affairs is not going to change any time soon. Unlike my colleagues, who still think that there is a chance to change those systems and make them function, I see no hope for such change. Instead, what all rational local leaders (à la Robert A. Heinlein or not) should strive for is for them and their communities to fully understand those systems to the point they become the savviest users of their own dysfunctions as they work to mitigate their negative influence and maximize the chances that their own innovation actors succeed.

Accordingly, what the next three chapters, in a succinct and clear-eyed way, try to explain is how these domains now work and why they have become dysfunctional, and to offer a few, out of the multiple available, venues for strategic action by locales striving for innovation-based growth.

9

Our Anti-Intellectual Property Rights System

> Clearly, economic freedom, in and of itself, is an extremely impor-
> tant part of total freedom.
>
> Milton Friedman, *Capitalism and Freedom*

One of my true pleasures as a professor is teaching the foundations of political economy to doctoral students. It is one of the only courses where instead of looking at forms and techniques, we delve deeply into economic
theories and their implications for the real world. Every year when we discuss Marxist economic theories, my right-leaning students get incited and
vehemently oppose everything until we reach the "ten commandments" in
the *Communist Manifesto*. Reading them, they realize that by now most of
the commandments are part of the common-sense tools and policies of advanced economies. A similar thing happens when we look at modern lib-
eral economists: my left-leaning students storm the barricades until we read
Milton Friedman's "ten commandments," and then realize that, again, almost
all of them are now common-sense policy tools used around the world. It is
at that moment that all students realize the importance of carefully reading
and analyzing the worldviews behind the equations and seeing how the logic
they present leads us to analyze different problems, which in turn leads to
specific sets of policies. As a class we move from reacting to names into analyzing substance for the rest of the semester.[1]

It is a great teaching moment.

However, for me it is also a moment of great sadness. I keep asking myself
how much better our world would have been if Milton Friedman, instead of
focusing too much of his attention on the legitimacy of national parks, had
focused instead on the biggest government-run machine of monopolies and

rent creation the world has ever seen—our current system of IPR, mainly patents, trademarks, and copyrights.

To understand how a system established with the best of intentions— aiming to maximize innovation and its diffusion—ended up as the most dysfunctional system of economic-freedom destruction humanity has seen since the beginning of the Industrial Revolution, let us go back to the basics and understand the inherent economic dilemma of innovation.

Intellectual property rights are socially constructed tools (sets of regulations, laws, and the institutions governing them) originally developed to solve an inherent market failure—namely, that under conditions of perfect free-market competition there will be an underinvestment in innovation. The reason is that innovators face too much uncertainty and risk about both whether they will have success and whether if they succeed they will enjoy any economic gains from their innovations. In technical terms, the issues with innovation (defined as the application of ideas to any stage of the production of goods and services in a way that leads to an increase in supply in the market of new or improved goods and services for the same or lower factor costs) fall into three categories.[2]

First, when trying to innovate, you face high risk and uncertainty. You cannot know in advance whether your R&D efforts will be successful or whether, even if they are successful, customers will buy the resulting products or services.[3]

Second, innovation is information. Once it is in the market it is easily copied by people with sufficient technical skills. Hence, without some way to enforce property rights, you will not be paid for your innovation.[4]

Third, once you innovate, your competitors will start with your innovation as a baseline from which they will advance. A classic example is the wheel. Once the wheel was invented, it was immediately incorporated into other innovations (and as a result, all of us have to suffer people telling us not to reinvent the wheel). Hence, by innovating you also improve your competitors' offerings without being compensated fully for it.[5]

Faced with these obstacles, private actors would allocate fewer resources to innovation than would be socially optimal—a classic public-goods supply problem. Thus, policy intervention is necessary. Society needs explicit and enforceable tools to reduce innovators' risk and to protect their ability to gain from their ideas.[6]

Innovation is necessary for economic growth and for generating useful, sometimes life-critical advances in welfare, such as improved medicine and hygiene. It is also crucial to remember that innovation has its positive impact only when it is widely diffused and becomes the basis for later (and constant) improvements. It is exactly the large and wide impacts of innovation, what economists like to mystify with terms, such as externalities or spillovers, that make innovation so important for economic growth. It was not the first internal combustion engine that changed the human condition; it was the constant improvements to it and their diffusion across industries and places. Thus, solutions such as trade secrets and anti-compete laws, even in cases where they are feasible (for example, keeping secret the precise formula for a cola drink), have negative effects on growth and welfare. True, in certain cases trade secrets and anti-compete laws may lead to increased innovation, but at the high price of undermining innovation's positive spillover effects, a classic case of the cure being worse than the disease.[7]

In its ideal form, IPR is a tool designed to solve the two dilemmas of supply and diffusion. Take patents: in their original form (before things such as software, business methods, and fundamental scientific discoveries become patentable), patents were a deal in which society grants the creator of an original and significant invention a monopoly that is limited in both time and usage, in exchange for disclosing enough detail about the invention that anyone with common technical skills could understand how to manufacture and improve on it. Done properly (a very hard, if not impossible, thing to do), a patent system solves both sides of the dilemma—it allows the innovator to collect a tidy profit but also increases the diffusion and sharing of knowledge, enhancing both welfare and rates of innovation.[8]

A patent that solved both sides of the dilemma very well is US Patent 139,121, which was granted on May 20, 1873, to one Jacob W. Davis of Reno, Nevada, and assigned to him and to Levi Strauss and Company of San Francisco. In this patent, titled "Improvement in Fastening Pocket Opening," Davis detailed his invention for reinforcing the weak points in denim pants. This turned out to be a truly useful invention, leading to the creation of one of the world's most popular pants—jeans. Further, the patent makes it very clear how one should manufacture, and improve upon, denim jeans. As a result, while Levi Strauss has since made billions of dollars (annually) on this invention, the diffusion of the innovation has been rapid and wide, thanks to a patent system that allowed others to constantly improve on the original. This process is still in motion almost 150 years later, with noteworthy positive results for human welfare. One small example: profits from jeans manufacturing allowed the Italian fashion tycoon Renzo Rosso, nicknamed the Jeans Genius, to sponsor, in 2013, the latest renovation of the famous Rialto Bridge in Venice.[9]

It is extremely important to remember the dual target of patents: allowing appropriation but only for increased diffusion, and, it is hoped, ever more rapid follow-up innovation. Sadly, this duality seems to have disappeared from most current debates on patents and IPR. Instead, the discussion follows a very narrow read of Ronald Coase's work. Coase, most famously in his paper "The Problem of Social Cost," showed that strict and clear property rights solve the issue of externalities (i.e., spillovers) and allow for market solutions based on internalized prices. Thus, the thinking goes, a strong IPR regime (a legal system in which patent, trademark, and copyright owners have very robust claims that are strongly enforceable by the court system) would fix the problems of innovation inappropriability and allow markets for technology to flourish. By creating such lucrative markets, strong IPE regimes would also incentivize innovators to innovate even more.[10]

There is only one tiny problem with this thinking. The main, and maybe the only, reason for public support of innovation is the externalities—that is, the significant positive spillovers effects of innovation. Hence the reason for the original duality of the patents social contract. Once you "solve" the problem of externalities and "internalize" all the transactions, you ensure that innovation will have a significantly less positive public-welfare impact. This has become even worse with the linguistic trick used by proponents of using IPR and patents to create effective rent-seeking monopolies. Instead of calling *monopoly* by its name and admitting that they think monopoly power is a good idea, they have divided IPR legal systems into "strong" and "weak" regimes. Who in their right mind would like to be "weak" as opposed to "strong"? As a result, everyone runs to strengthen IPR monopoly power, and only those of us who think that economic freedom is important are appalled.

There has been extensive research into the impact of these moves on the economics of innovation. The results are clear and tragic. Patents tend to slow down innovation. That is, the more patents there are (especially patent "families" that allow you to completely block competition in specific technologies by creating "patent thickets"), the less innovative a technology becomes. This especially hurts new companies that try to work on follow-up innovation (which, we should remember, is the main way in which innovation positively affects welfare and increases economic growth). Further, due to the recent wisdom of the US Supreme Court, which somewhat limited the ever-expanding power of patents and what is patentable, we can run experiments on whether strong IPR systems are indeed more innovation-facilitating than weak ones. The answer, if you are wondering, is no.[11]

This machine of economic-freedom destruction is not only growing, it is growing faster and faster with every passing year, and to that we should add ever more draconian copyright laws. Below are graphs summarizing the rapid growth of IPR, patents, technology standards essential patents, and trademarks. As you can clearly see in Figure 9.1, patenting activity in all major patenting offices rose rapidly starting in the 1980s and then exploded in the 2000s. By 2017 the number of US patents granted per year had risen to over 325,000, with the Chinese patent office blazing ahead to above 400,000. It seems as if governments around the world now grant patents as if they were chocolate chip cookies and not what they really are—legal monopolies. Further, this massive growth in intellectual legal-rent extortion has been happening in the exact same period during which leading scholars argue that innovation has slowed down.

Even more rapid rates of monopoly creation can be seen if we look at one of the most lucrative subsets of patents, technology standards-essential patents (SEPs) as shown in Figure 9.2. which tracks the trends in the stock of active USPTO (United States Patent and Trademark Office) patents that that have been declared as SEPs.

Even worse is the rate in which trademarks now confine our economic freedom, as shown in Figures 9.3.1 and 9.3.2.

If these graphs are not enough to help you realize that our global IPR system's dysfunctionality is now a serious risk for our future welfare, let me share with you a game I developed to help my students understand how much of the English language they are no longer allowed to use. I call it the trademark word puzzle. There are a few versions of this; the simplest way to play is to take a paragraph from a book you admire and then run it through the USPTO trademark database, scoring 1 for each™ you hit. A "hit" means all the words (from one to X) of a™ are found in the paragraph; order does not matter, and length of ™ does not matter (shorter and longer trademarks count as one). Below is an example using the paragraph from L. Frank Baum's *The Wonderful Wizard of Oz* that opens this book's introduction:

"Tell me something about yourself and the country you came from," said the Scarecrow, when she had finished her dinner. So she told him all about Kansas, and how gray everything was there, and how the cyclone had carried her to this queer Land of Oz.

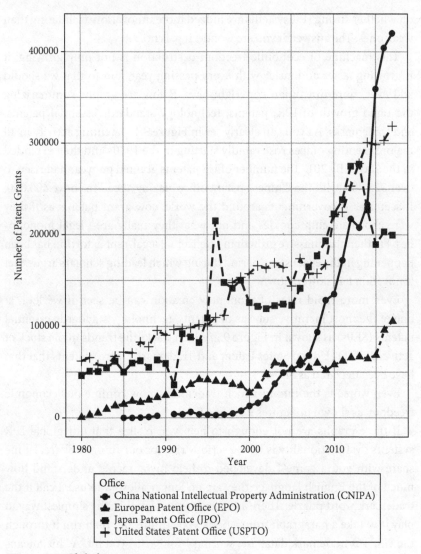

Figure 9.1 Global patenting activity since 1980.
Source: WIPO Statistics Database, https://www3.wipo.int/ipstats/.

The Scarecrow listened carefully, and said, "I cannot understand why you should wish to leave this beautiful country and go back to the dry, gray place you call Kansas."

"That is because you have no brains" answered the girl. "No matter how dreary and gray our homes are, we people of flesh and blood would rather

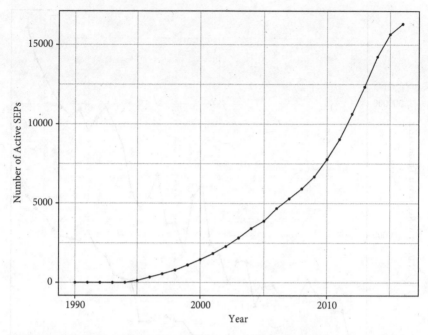

Figure 9.2 Here goes more economic freedom: Growth of SEPs since 1990.
Note: Data taken from Justus Baron and Tim Pohlmann, "Mapping Standards to
Patents Using Declarations of Standard-Essential Patents," *Journal of Economics
& Management Strategy* 27, no. 3 (2018).

live there than in any other country, be it ever so beautiful. There is no place
like home."

The Scarecrow sighed.

"Of course I cannot understand it," he said. "If your heads were stuffed
with straw, like mine, you would probably all live in the beautiful places,
and then Kansas would have no people at all. It is fortunate for Kansas that
you have brains."

With the help of my research assistant, Reuben Aboye, using the USPTO data
set of October 16, 2019, we found 514 different trademarks using 49 words
in this short paragraph alone. By the time you read this paragraph, there are
probably even more. The English language™ was never so legally limited in
the ways it can be used.

As if all of this were not enough, there is one more fact that is even more
detrimental to innovation in our current dysfunctional IPR system. Patents

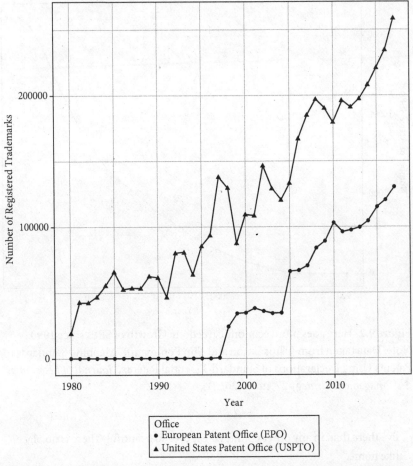

Figure 9.3.1 You are not allowed to use those words anymore: Growth of TM Part I.
Source: WIPO Statistics Database, https://www3.wipo.int/ipstats/.

are granted to the inventor, not to whoever figures out how to use the invention to come up with new and improved products and services—that is, the innovator. This gives rise to a new rent-seeking, extortion-based business model: patent trolls, also known as "patent assertion entities."[12]

Here is the sad truth: if you want to make money out of technology, you are probably better off not innovating. Instead, what you should do is acquire a nice pile of patents (preferably in information and communication technology) and send letters threatening to sue everyone who is stupid enough

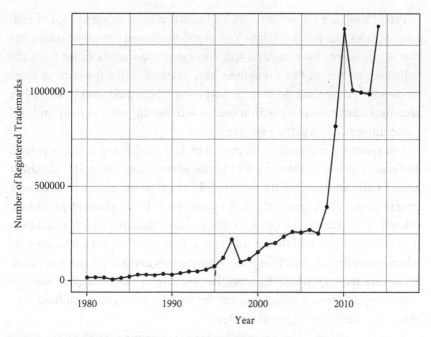

Figure 9.3.2 NO! Not allowed in Chinese either: Growth of TM Part 2.
Source: WIPO Statistics Database, https://www3.wipo.int/ipstats/.

to try to innovate in areas that remotely resemble anything that is covered
by any of your patents. Hire lawyers and then just sit back, kick off your
shoes, and watch the "royalty payments" accumulate in your bank account.
You can even do it without anyone knowing it is you. Patent trolls are mas-
terful at setting up shell companies to litigate patents. The negative economic
impact of this behavior has become so big that that the US Federal Trade
Commission was allowed to use its power of subpoena to conduct a study of
patent assertion entities. The very lengthy report is sad reading, even in its
very politically correct and careful final form, for anyone who cares about
growth and innovation. A more entertaining source of information for those
of you who want to get depressed (and very similar in its conclusions) are the
"When Patents Attack" collection of *This American Life* episodes on National
Public Radio and John Oliver's *Last Week Tonight* episode dedicated to the
subject. For those of you with an entrepreneurial streak who might be wondering whether similar business models now exist to "assert" copyrights and
trademarks, the answer is yes. The market for rent-seeking behavior seems
limitless.[13]

Patent trolls are not evil or even malicious. What they are is a set of economic actors that follow to their logical end the flawed economic incentives that we ourselves have constructed. Too many economists suffer from the delusion that the way to strengthen "free markets" is for the state to grant monopolies. They should not be surprised when their very own policy recommendations end up with more lawyers making more money and real competitive markets getting weaker.

IPR systems are socially constructed tools for balancing multiple private and public goods. Problems start to arise when companies and individuals acting rationally employ the best minds to devise strategies to maximize profits in ways that divert the IPR system from its original intent and diminish innovation and welfare. Political economists like myself should expect that to happen and should not react with holier-than-thou fake surprise when entrepreneurs legally exploit opportunities to make billions of dollars. If you care about economic freedom, be very careful when you grant monopolies, especially monopolies that can be bought, sold, and combined with others to make them bigger and fatter.

Because intellectual property rights are not dynamic enough on their own to change in tandem with technologies and the business strategies developed to use IPR to maximize profits, those of us who care about innovation-based growth for our communities advocate constant and dynamic policy intervention. First and foremost, there is a need to address the freedom-to-operate problem—the usage of IPR by incumbents and patent trolls to prevent competition and/or extract rents.

This is mostly discussed as a general problem—that is, excessive patenting slows all innovation in a particular technological domain. However, for the purposes of this book we should also acknowledge that it is jurisdiction-specific. It is all too common for communities that try to spur the creation of new technology-based companies to find that these firms are blocked from the market by aggressive IPR litigation by incumbents and/or patent trolls.[14]

A second reason for policymakers to care about IPR is the tight relation between intellectual property rights and three things that are at the heart of economic policy: jobs, profits, and taxes. There is a strong co-location effect between IPR ownership (which can be in a different locale from where the underlying invention was created) and growth in jobs, profits, and companies' tax "strategies." Further, this connection has recently became stronger by means of the OECD's (the club of mostly rich countries) agreement on Base Erosion and Profit Shifting (BEPS). Even without any specific "tax-avoidance" strategies, locales with a lot of IPR ownership will gain significant and rapidly growing economic benefits within the current global production and trade system. A perfect example is the change in the trade balance between Canada and the United States under NAFTA (which will be even more pronounced under the new trade deal), where the United States now enjoys an annual $6 billion positive inflow solely from IP trade and another $80 billion on non-energy-related goods (tightly connected to the increased importance of intangibles—read IPR—in the production of both goods and services), after having a negative imbalance with Canada until 2006.[15]

However, policymakers should also keep in mind that by playing with the residency of IPR ownership, multinational corporations (MNCs) have managed to take advantage of public (that is, taxpayers') money without having to give back benefits such as increased jobs or taxes. Consider Ireland's relationship with Apple, which is representative of its ties with numerous MNCs. Since 1958, Irish economic development policy has been built on one pillar: special treatment of MNCs in exchange for job creation. One of the most important special treatments that MNCs enjoy in Ireland is very low tax rates—in the past, the tax on corporate income was 10 percent; now it is 12.5 percent, still far below the US rate of 21 percent, and taxes on R&D and IPR are even lower. Moreover, producing in Ireland allows MNCs to bill all their sales in Europe, the Middle East, and Africa to their Irish subsidiaries, effectively minimizing their global tax bills. For many years this worked like a charm. Numerous MNCs (mostly American companies) built significant manufacturing and sales operations in Ireland, the MNCs significantly reduced their tax bills, and Ireland got hundreds of thousands of jobs. Both sides were happy.[16]

But the supposed connection between job creation and tax benefits was severed when the reality of IPR taxation came to light. With IPR revenues becoming an ever-larger share of its total revenues, Apple utilized a sophisticated ownership structure to minimize taxation. Utilizing the best accountants and tax lawyers possible, Apple constructed a dazzling and complex structure of companies, all to ensure that it will pay no taxes. To do so it first set up Apple Operations International (AOI) as a firm wholly owned by Apple. AOI was officially classified as a manufacturer and in theory was supposed to buy materials from companies and sell manufactured goods. The key to this part of the structure is that while AOI was incorporated in Ireland, it didn't have Irish tax residency, since it was treated as a fully owned-and-managed subsidiary of a fully owned subsidiary of a US corporation. AOI in turn owned Apple Operations Europe (again incorporated in Ireland, but without tax residency), which in turn owned Apple Sales International (ASI), yet another company incorporated in Ireland, and, yes, you guessed it, also without tax residency.[17]

Apple had a cost-sharing agreement with its subsidiaries that allowed for the sharing of risks and research and development between Apple Inc. and ASI. This agreement entailed dividing the economic rights to intellectual property. The revenues of goods sold using Apple's intellectual property in Africa, Asia, Europe, and the Middle East would be routed through ASI, while revenues from items sold in the Americas would be routed directly to Apple Inc. In theory, ASI would contract out manufacturing to its Chinese affiliates, buy the assembled goods, then resell them in Africa, Asia, Europe, and the Middle East at higher prices. However, ASI never took physical possession of the goods, but instead traded that possession to distribution centers in Ireland for European markets and to distribution centers in Singapore for African, Asian, and Middle East markets. The main loophole that has allowed Apple's subsidiaries to pay little to no taxes is that they don't have tax residency in Ireland, as they continue to be managed through a US-based subsidiary.[18]

The US Senate Permanent Subcommittee on Investigations, headed by Senators Carl Levin and John McCain, found in 2013 that ASI paid an average effective tax rate of 0.06 percent between 2009 and 2011. Since all three companies (AOI, AOE, and ASI) have very few employees in Ireland, the result was that Apple managed to not pay US taxes on the work of its thousands of R&D engineers in California, but employed virtually no one and paid virtually no taxes in Ireland. Since almost all the technologies that Apple utilizes are based on publicly funded (that is, US taxpayers' money) research to the tune of hundreds of billions of dollars, the company's behavior called into question the basic assumptions behind, and the financial sustainability of, US innovation policy.[19]

The revelation of this behavior led the Irish government to tighten its rules in 2015. But with such profits to be made by first claiming all revenues are due to IPR and then shifting the ownership of IPR to lower the tax bill, the action of the Irish government proved futile. Apple's response to the changing of roles was to make ASI and AOI residents of Jersey, a tiny self-governing island off the coast of Normandy, while designating Apple Operations Europe as a tax resident of Ireland. This structure allowed Apple to use the aptly named Double Irish with a Dutch Sandwich, by inserting Dutch subsidiaries in between two Irish subsidiaries. This "sandwich" allowed it to continue to not pay any taxes on revenues it attributed to its IPR while still not increasing employment in either Ireland or the Netherlands. The practice was found to be illegal by the EU, which demanded that Apple pay $6 billion USD plus interest in taxes to Ireland. If you own stock in Apple you should not worry—those funds have yet to be paid, nor will they be paid in the foreseeable future.[20]

A favorite way for companies and jurisdictions to play this game is to use a tool called a "patent box," in which a jurisdiction (national or subnational) defines how (as in what set and what level of activities) corporations can declare their IPR ownership to reside in the jurisdiction and then qualify for a reduced (sometimes zero) tax rate. Jurisdictions hope these attractive patent-box regimes will lure corporations to move their activities (especially R&D) to the locales. The results have been in the range between negligible and catastrophic in terms of local economic development; however, the MNCs are always very happy with the tax benefits.[21]

One of the worst such policy initiatives was Canadian—the infamous British Columbia patent-box policy. After an expansion of its patent-box regime in 2008, the Province of British Columbia is estimated to have doled out $140 million, through the misleadingly titled International Business Activity program, with the beneficiaries' identities legally kept secret from the public.[22]

The result?

There was some investment into real estate in the greater Vancouver area, but no increases in jobs, innovation, or R&D activities. However, it took ten years until a newly elected government abandoned the patent-box policy in 2018, together with the rest of the International Business Activity program.

This situation, in which an international tax regime no longer fits the new reality of innovation and global trade, led to the enactment of the OECD's previously mentioned Base Erosion and Profit Shifting agreement. BEPS was intended to solve these issues as well as modernize tax regimes to fit with the reality of modern global production. The principle behind BEPS is that taxes should be levied in the locales where the activities take place. Hence, corporations should register their IPR ownership, and pay taxes on that IPR, in the locales where they conducted the R&D leading to it. This is known as the "Modified Nexus" approach. This approach ties the preferential tax regime to the amount of R&D expenditures made in the jurisdiction, so that the benefits of IPR flow to the local economy. Under the BEPS framework, many countries modified their patent-box regimes or developed new regimes to align with the proposed framework. This also meant strictly defining parameters such as companies' qualifying income, where the R&D expenditures would take place, and where the R&D would be performed.[23]

By incentivizing corporations to allocate IPR ownership and the accompanying taxes on R&D and IPR to the appropriate locales, BEPS clearly benefits regions that already have significant R&D activities, such as Israel, Silicon Valley, and Boston. But it is questionable whether a patent box can be effectively used to persuade a corporation to locate R&D and innovation to an area where it doesn't already have such activities or doesn't already intend to start such activities for other reasons, such as access to talent.

It seems more plausible that as part of a comprehensive innovation-policy regime, a patent box can be used as an enhancing tool. Further, under BEPS, any jurisdiction (national or subnational) that wants to offer IPR tax benefits is required to implement a patent box. In short, all savvy locales should implement a BEPS-compliant patent box, but they should view it as a minimal requirement, not an effective innovation-policy tool.

So what IPR policies should jurisdictions focus on as part of an effective innovation-policy program?

This leads us back to questions about the freedom to operate and the broken link between the locales where innovation occurs and locales that accrue the economic-growth benefits from it. For a jurisdiction to enjoy the benefits of its "own" innovation (whether conducted by local companies or MNCs), those innovations need to lead to increased numbers of (and preferably better-paying) jobs, as well as greater profits and tax revenues. In a world where companies and entrepreneurs can easily acquire IPR anywhere and move them elsewhere in the blink of an eye for the purposes of conducting job-creating and profit-making activities, it is not enough for innovation policy to focus just on increasing local R&D or early-stage innovation (also known as start-up formation). Here issues of freedom to operate are crucial, especially if a locale has any scale-up aspirations for its local companies, start-ups, and entrepreneurs.

It is exactly in this area that most regions fail miserably. The province where I reside, Ontario (and as a matter of fact the whole of Canada), has been doing a horrible job. As an example, let us look at Ontario's current claim to innovation pride: artificial intelligence. Both Canada and Ontario made the right decision to invest public funds in the fundamental research that led to the techniques known as deep learning. Twenty years later, deep learning has become the basis for rapid advances in AI globally. Further, recognizing their R&D and inventiveness advantage, the governments of Canada, Ontario, and Quebec sponsored both the Vector Institute in Toronto and the new AI "super cluster" in Montreal, with the aim of translating the regions' inventive power into innovation and growth. Sadly, their complete disregard of IPR policy, both in the past and in the present, means that these two initiatives come too late and will end up benefiting foreign companies and economies more than Canadians. The reason is that the publicly subsidized R&D into AI has already been embedded into IP that is owned by foreign organizations. To put it in perspective, as of July 2017, when these two initiatives were first designed, the number of machine-learning patent applications in the previous ten years by Microsoft stood at 1,030, and by IBM at 580. Intellectual Ventures, the world's most feared patent assertion entity (patent troll) had 50. The total for all Canadian firms, research institutions, and individuals put together was 48.[24]

The results of such a naïve non-innovation policy are substantial and long-term. Those patents represent not only missed streams of revenues, jobs, and taxes, they also represent legal monopolies that prevent both current and future Canadian entrepreneurs and companies from operating and building viable and innovative businesses in a domain opened to the world thanks to Canada's far-sighted and generous science policy.[25]

In short, IPR policy is a crucial part of any regional innovation policy and is necessary for such efforts to reach their ultimate goals of sustained local economic growth and welfare. However, it is questionable whether IPR policy can either lead to increased foreign direct investment or replace instruments such as grants and other direct transfers in fostering the growth of a local innovation-based industry. This is especially the case in a context of a locale with low levels of R&D and IPR ownership, in a post-BEPS world. On the other hand, without having a clear IPR policy, a locale might do all the right things, only for its growth to be stymied as innovative companies find they lack the freedom to operate due to the IPR strategies of incumbents and patent trolls.

How should a community try to safeguard its freedom to operate?

The world's IPR system is deeply and irrecoverably dysfunctional, and any possible solution leaves a lot to be desired; hence, we should aspire to what is achievable under the circumstances, not to ideal solutions.

A practical strategy should be three-pronged: (1) If you can't beat them, *join them*; (2) *be smarter* (and more educated); and (3) have *zero tolerance* toward bullying.

Join Them

As a locale, you should aim to generate and own as much IPR as possible. Because you will never succeed on quantity alone (you cannot compete with Silicon Valley), your aim should be to accumulate high-quality patents and IPR whose availability (and both the offensive and defensive options they grant) is as wide as possible, preferably to all local companies and entrepreneurs. Pay extra attention to strategic and publicly funded R&D efforts, and think about solutions such as IPR/patent pooling, in which a complete "pool" of patents is available either for free or at nominal prices to current and future local companies and entrepreneurs.[26]

Make sure your card deck includes a few "jokers"—weapons that can stop others from using IPR to stifle your companies' freedom to operate. One such weapon is a strategy of maximizing firm-level IP competitiveness. Local companies need to be encouraged to participate in the international deliberations that lead to agreements on such things as IP licensing and sharing. Particular attention should be given to embedding local firms' IPR in international technology standards. For example, travel, membership, and employee-training support should be offered to firms to encourage their participation in ITU, IEEE, and the Electronics Industry Association standardization meetings. Such support should include participation in both national- and international-level bodies. Regions can maximize their benefits from IP, and enhance their firms' global reach, by encouraging participation in these forums, which include multiple organizations—government, nongovernmental, and private.

Technology standards are the platforms on which current markets evolve and future innovation is developed. They determine the winners and losers of technological battles. Further, firms (and their regions) that manage to insert their patents as standard essential patents secure to themselves and their communities a reliable source of income and jobs, as well as increased opportunities to shape the global trajectories of technologies and industries. Only the firms that participate can advance their interests in these deliberations. Firms absent from negotiations on key platform technologies will be unlikely to have their technologies included, and their access to others' technologies may be restricted.[27]

For example, by increasing their participation in IEEE and ITU forums, Chinese firms have had their technologies and protocols internationally recognized. The results of this sustained effort are stunning. In mobile telephony, Chinese companies such as Huawei and ZTE moved in one decade from being underdogs to dominating the world in fifth-generation technology, causing much alarm in the (strategically clueless) West due to their close connection with the Chinese state. Moreover, the wider the representation of firms from a specific locale, the better the chances that their technologies will be the ones around which new products will be developed.[28]

There are benefits to this kind of participation even if companies don't make significant technology contributions of their own. Working with the world's best minds on setting the development paths of industry-defining technologies gives companies future market knowledge and technological understanding that's impossible to acquire by other means. And it's not just large corporations that benefit from participation. In my research with Michael Murphree, we observed how in the case of the IGRS standard, part of the Internet of Things for home networking, small firms that joined working groups derived significant benefits from such factors as increased orders from large players and access to publicly funded R&D.[29]

Be Smarter

The second prong of a local IPR strategy should be to make your local actors smarter than anyone else. Ensure that your community members are highly IPR-educated, to the degree that they become the savviest IPR strategists. The strategic position from which local leaders are now facing our world of dysfunctional IPR systems is this: we are outnumbered and poorly armed, and hence we must be better players in the IPR game than the competition. What is needed is a comprehensive effort, from online programs open to all residents; to seminars and mentorship programs for entrepreneurs, mangers, and innovators; to university courses and diplomas; and even changes in the K-12 curriculum. Again, and not that surprisingly, a clear global leader here is China, which developed an encompassing IPR curriculum starting at the high school level, with specialization in various aspects of IPR strategy and policy, from patenting to standardization. The impact of this comprehensive effort is already being widely felt by American and European companies that find themselves beaten again and again in what they view as their game—IPR manipulation and monopolization.[30]

Zero Tolerance

The third strategic prong should be to recognize patent trolls and incumbents for what they are—bullies. As any parent and teacher knows, the best way to treat bullies is by showing them zero tolerance. Bullies and patent trolls share many things. First, they always look for the easiest wins and shy away from any target that is sure to offer significant resistance. Second, they prefer to work in the dark. Going to court is expensive, and many times the trolls are not sure their claims would hold up in court anyway, so they much prefer to extort settlements. Moreover, out-of-court settlements are secret, and the secrecy allows the attackers to extract the maximum from each target, since no victim know what the other victims paid, but the trolls know, and they also have detailed knowledge of how much each target can pay, and can extend those rents for as long as possible. Another reason why patent trolls prefer to work in the dark is that they are fully aware that the morality of their business model is questionable. That is why all patent trolls work through a complex web of shell companies, and the real owners prefer to never reveal themselves in court.[31]

To increase the chances that their targets will opt for out-of-court settlements, trolls and incumbents time their attacks for moments when getting embroiled in a court case would inflict the most damage and distraction on their targets (for example, in the midst of a crucial scale-up phase). To this end, efficient attackers accumulate detailed information on start-ups that show promise.

Entrepreneurs and regional leaders should assume that all their companies will be IPR-attacked. The question is never if, only when. To fight back, first make it clear that if any of your companies is attacked, there will be a very costly and very public legal and media fight. Second, make it even clearer that the fight will not end there, that you will go to extensive lengths to make the attacker pay, by going after its patent portfolio and creating alliances with its other victims. The aim is not to fix the dysfunctionality of IPR systems, but to make sure that the bullies start to avoid you and look for easier targets.

A locale should adopt policies to support all local companies and entrepreneurs attacked by trolls and incumbents, with both funds and expert legal advice. The aim is to ensure that the battle extracts the highest possible cost to the attacker, while costing as little as possible in time and money to your local entrepreneurs. You might even want it to be known that you have an ongoing relationship with some of the world's best and most tenacious IPR lawyers. And make it personal. If trolls are trying to hide behind shell companies, expose them. Make it clear to the jury that on one side there is a community of hardworking families doing the right thing, and on the other there is a shadowy group of immoral lawyers and their investors. Name and shame them. Sunlight and intense media attention are two of the world's best bully disinfectors.

However, this is not enough. You also need to make sure that you have strong counter claims (such as patents) that are of the highest quality, which is the aim of the first prong in our strategy. In addition, you need to weaken the other side's claims. Indeed, you want it to be known that you will ensure that any other patents they might hold will also be weakened as part of your strategy of zero tolerance for bullying.

One way, out of many, to do this, which will also enhance your IPR education efforts, is to focus on *prior art*. Prior art is a legal term that refers to evidence of publicly known work that precedes an invention and renders it unoriginal. In theory, patents should be granted solely for original inventions; hence, part of the process of patent validation is checking for prior art. That is, did anyone, anywhere, at any time, already make this invention? A patent can be declared invalid if it can be shown that prior art existed and was not weighted properly by the patent examiners.

A big part of the problem with the current patent system is that slightly over two decades ago USPTO (still the world's de facto patent office) started issuing significant numbers of low-quality patents, without properly checking for prior art, and it granted those patents vast general application. This has stifled innovation to such a degree that both the USPTO and the US Supreme Court have started to intervene in the hope of fixing the quality problem. The USPTO has opened more opportunities for third parties—individuals and organizations not directly involved in the original filing of a patent—to offer information about prior art.[32]

How can prior art be a strategic tool for communities that want to defend the freedom to operate?

For the last half-century at least, many of the fundamental stepping stones to new technologies were publicly funded. We the taxpayers have been funding the research that led to the prior art that companies and individuals then gladly patented as theirs. Thus, pushing for prior-art examination can create four positive effects for a community: (1) it diminishes, and sometimes eliminates, the legal arsenal that trolls and incumbents can use against local companies; (2) it ensures that the results of research paid for by our taxes can be used without fear by our own companies and entrepreneurs, now and in the future; (3) it creates an effective deterrent against aggressive behavior toward local innovators by IPR owners, who would prefer not to run the risk of having their own patents invalidated; and (4) the region can use a prior-art initiative to educate its residents to become the world's savviest users and producers of IPR.

A fruitful way of getting a prior-art initiative started is crowdsourcing. Ideally, such an initiative will recruit and train student-volunteers from all disciplines in the rough-and-tumble world of IPR, and specifically in the skills of doing thorough prior-art checks. These (ideally) highly motivated and trained students will be mobilized to crowdsource the world's most complete prior-art research (1) whenever a local company is attacked on patent infringement, focusing on both the patents in question and the overall portfolio of the attacking entity; (2) whenever patents are filed in the USPTO in areas that are strategic to the locale; and (3) as part of the international patent-filing activities of local companies in order to ensure that their patents are known to be of the highest quality possible. Thus, the prior-art initiative will create a significant deterrent against the predatory behavior of patent holders toward the locale's entrepreneurs and companies; ensure that local research, technology, and innovation are fully and openly embedded in patents in areas that pertain to the region's strategic objectives; and educate generations of students in the highly applied skills of obtaining and retaining IPR.

IPR, very much like finance, is a social construct. As such, it balances multiple public and private goods, and hence can never be counted on to be the basis of a real competitive and efficient market. Further, the current solution of giving extensive monopoly rights as part of our IPR system should make each and every one of us afraid for our economic freedom. This is especially true in the current situation, with the global IPR system becoming increasingly more dysfunctional with every passing year. Under such conditions, local leaders should aim to defend the interests of their communities, without having any illusions that the system can be fixed.

10

The Road to Hell Is Paved
with Good Intentions

The Age of Financialization

*If the state of affairs assumed by the theory of perfect competition
ever existed, it would not only deprive of their scope all the activities
which the verb "to compete" describes but would make them virtually
impossible.*

Friedrich Hayek, *The Meaning of Competition*

Today Friedrich Hayek is famous for his political views, in particular those
in his widely read book *The Road to Serfdom*. There is a good reason for this.
I fully agree with many of my colleagues and masters of the field in their critique of Hayek's work in economics, succinctly stated by none other than
Milton Friedman: "(I am) an enormous admirer of Hayek, but not for his
economics." This is why the only Hayek works I give my students to read are
his essays about the role of information, knowledge, and learning over time,
and how these should lead us to a better inquiry into competitive markets
and their function in society. It's highly ironic—and too bad—that so many
economists, especially in financial economics, no longer read these essays,
given that Hayek won the Nobel Memorial Prize for his "pioneering work in
the theory of money and economic fluctuations."[1]

If I were a benevolent, smart dictator (the kind of ruler Hayek argued always leads to tyranny), I would make it a rule that all PhD students must
read his 1946 lecture "The Meaning of Competition" before they are allowed
to submit papers for publication. Every several years the good and great of
the field gather to discuss the ailments of the discipline. After much hand-
wringing, a consensus is usually reached: it is declared that the discipline has

detached itself from reality and disengaged from the world. Therefore, there is a need for economists to re-engage and become relevant.[2]

Here lies the mistake. The greatest problem in economics is *not* disengagement from reality. The problem is the exact opposite: economists fall so much in love with the neatness and internal logic of their theories that they try to force reality to resemble their economic models. The original sin of economics consists of economists changing laws and regulations to ensure that real markets act like the imagined markets of their models. This is the exact problem Hayek warns us against in "The Meaning of Competition."[3]

It is, consequently, obvious that Hayek was not a great economist, since the market, which he viewed as the greatest vehicle for information exchange and social learning that has ever been created, has not only failed to teach us anything about this recurring error in economics, but has actually amplified this failing over and over again for the past eighty years.

This problem is most common in finance, for two interrelated reasons. First, as any self-respecting economist will confess, financial markets should not be treated as "natural" markets. Second, partly due to the same inherent characteristics that make financial markets a special case, financial economics is the easiest domain in which to develop clean, "pure" models of "perfect" competition and "efficient" markets. From here it is only a small logical step to argue that if we only made financial markets slightly less like reality and a little more like our models, then human welfare would improve. Not that surprisingly, like any endeavor that starts with hubris and false assumptions, it always ends in tears. Sadly, those tears are never shed by financial economists or investment bankers.

I vividly remember the very first time my belief in modern financial economic theory started to shake. It was just after I finished my field exams and submitted my PhD proposal for approval. I was invited by my supervisors to join them for a research trip and conference in Taipei. It was an amazing conference. Leading scientists from multiple fields came onstage to explain their visions of markets and society. Especially memorable, to me, was a talk by people from a lab working on RFID tags on how the then-new technology would interact with logistics and global markets. The term "Internet of Things" had not yet been coined, and Google was just another private company touting yet another search engine. On the bus back to the hotel, humbled and badly jet-lagged, I found a seat next to a rising star in finance who was then teaching at an Ivy League business school. He was holding court, explaining how we were all wrong in our analysis of the ills of American car manufacturers. The year was 2000, and he was telling us how we all missed the reality of the industry. He said we were wrong to believe that the Japanese car companies were still more successful than their American counterparts, and our error was that we were analyzing production, innovation, and technology. He contended that the American car industry had already recovered and was in glowing good health, while we were looking, literally, beneath the hood. Highly impressed with his arguments, I asked him how he knew that the American car industry had recovered. "Well," he answered, looking at me as if I were a slow learner who was studying with the wrong people, "look at their stock price. It has fully recovered and is performing extremely well."

This was the first time I realized that the efficient-market hypothesis (EMH) had left the lab and become a religion with its own disciples. EMH, whose revival is partly attributed to Hayek's work on information and markets, and whose modern variant was developed and made famous by Eugene Fama, states that the price of an asset fully reflects all available information. This led, in somewhat logically stretched jumps, to two conclusions. First, in our very own world, not in a perfectly modeled world, stock exchanges actually approach that level of knowledge, and hence stock prices are always "fair" in the technical economic sense—that is, they represent all knowledge about firms. Second, and consequently, if a company's stock is performing well, then the firm is obviously doing brilliantly in whatever it is supposed to be doing—for example, developing and selling cars. Not that surprisingly, EMH is now seen as one of the main culprits leading to the financial crisis of 2008 and the Great Recession that followed.[4]

The price of stocks is one of the main reasons that any economist worth her or his salt will admit that financial markets are not really markets. The issue is this: It is not at all clear what the benchmark for a stock price should be, and there are always ways to manipulate it. As a result, we get cycles of boom and bust driven mostly by narrative and only slightly by facts. In each cycle you will find economists and pundits claiming that this time is different. For example, the financial crisis of 2008 was caused by a complete miscalculation of the price and risk of financial assets based on "re-engineered" high-risk mortgages. The derivatives of those re-engineered toxic financial assets (aka subprime loans) were praised, during the hype, by too many financial economists and pundits (who should have known better) as brilliant innovations that allowed for lending to poorer households.[5]

Today, if you are looking for a likely candidate for the next crisis, I highly recommend focusing your attention on stock prices. The reason is the practice of stock buybacks by companies.

For years the idea of companies' purchasing their own stock on the open market with the specific aim of impacting the price was deemed illegal as a form of insider trading. However, stock buybacks have been allowed by the SEC since 1982. Proponents claim that buybacks are very useful, especially since they help to convey information. That is, they are allegedly used when insiders (management) feel that the market, even after supposedly accounting for and evaluating all information available, sets a price that the insiders "know" is too low. To fix this alleged market failure, the company spends money to buy back some of the stock. Somehow this financial maneuvering is said to convey management's firm belief in the company.[6]

This narrative is based on four logically bizarre ideas: first, that the world's most sophisticated financial markets continuously make mistakes in judgment when evaluating stocks (if this is true, then stock markets are suffering from a systemic failure in their one main function: the setting of stock prices); second, that the mistakes are worth fixing only when the markets err on the side of undervaluation; third, that the best people to judge whether this undervaluation happens are those with the most to gain from a higher stock price (that is, management and shareholders); and fourth, that markets should react positively to a company buying its own stock instead of using the money to invest in new lines of business that could generate more profits.

Somehow the people with the most to gain from this blatant price manipulation have managed to create a narrative that makes these four bizarre assumptions acceptable, and that portrays stock buybacks as a legitimate tool to systematically manipulate prices. Thus, investors and analysts do not view a buyback as a desperate ploy by managers who have been cornered by activist investors and are running out of ideas on how to artificially inflate the price of their companies' stocks, but as a badge of good business practice.

Buybacks already reached over a trillion dollars annually in 2018. To put this in perspective, President Obama's stimulus package, enacted in February 2009 to kick-start the economy after the worst financial crisis in ninety years, was budgeted at $787 billion. Hence, we have now reached a stage at which companies are buying their own stock to the tune of 130 percent of that stimulus package. The main effect of that trillion dollars is to enhance the bank accounts of the same people who decide whether or not (and how much) to spend on buybacks. Not surprisingly, they tend to want more of the same every year, no matter the situation of the companies' underlying businesses. Given all this, my real fear about the distortion caused by buybacks is that stock prices (which in turn affect an array of prices in both the financial and the real economy) convey very little information about firms' performance. Therefore, when the music stops (as it always does), the crisis will be especially severe. We will suffer the consequences of several decades of underinvestment by our main companies, in the midst of a situation in which we discover we have very little trust in what stock prices mean. Under such conditions the most rational thing to do is to assume the worst and sell everything. If that happens, the result will be a horrific crisis.[7]

Interestingly, the fact that everyone is aware of the falsity of this narrative became clear when one of the first demands by the federal government from the management of publicly-traded companies that got financial help during the COVID-19 pandemic was a ban on stock buybacks. Tragically (and puzzlingly) this was construed as a "temporary" thing, with the expectation that once the crisis passes executives and investors can go back to partying with their companies' money as if there is no tomorrow.

By the time you read this, the bubble might have already burst, and stock buybacks might have been made illegal (as they should be). Nevertheless, do not worry, the financial markets will cook up yet another mechanism that distorts prices while posing as a tool to enhance information, and the bubble will soon begin re-inflating. This is the inherent dynamic of financial markets and the reason they should not be treated as real markets.

However, the failure of financial economics would not have been so severe, and fixing finance would not be as hopeless as it is, without a parallel movement in redefining the purpose of companies and, consequently, how they are managed and how their performance is judged by investors, analysts, and, even more importantly, the courts. The common name for this movement is *financialization*. The concept has been used and overused lately, but it is in essence quite simple. The idea is that all elements of the economy, companies and workers included, should be viewed, managed, and valued as financial assets. Thus, Walmart and IBM are not a retail company and a computing services company, respectively, but rather financial assets that maximize their returns by pursuing opportunities to deploy their capital in retail and computing. We should judge them purely and simply by analyzing how good are they at creating financial gains from each dollar employed, no more and no less. Further, the main goal of this wealth creation should be to maximize shareholder value (which might not be aligned with maximizing profits, in case you were under the illusion that profit maximization was what companies should do). How should we judge shareholder value? By management's ability to increase the price at which its shares are bought and sold on the stock exchange.[8]

You might find this view a bit weird, but it is now not only how financial markets judge companies' performance, but also a legal obligation. Courts in the United States, all the way to the Supreme Court, have espoused this view when deciding cases brought by shareholders against management, even allowing the usage of EMH as partial evidence.[9]

The effects of financialization is that companies, managers, investors, and financial markets engage in behaviors that, from the point of view of locales wishing to stimulate and sustain local innovation-based growth, lead to complete dysfunction.

It is very important to understand what I mean by "dysfunction."

If you view finance as a stand-alone activity in which fortunes are made (and lost), without regard to the rest of the economy, then finance is currently functioning extremely well. Indeed, if you are smart and mathematically gifted, do not waste your time on developing new technologies. Focus on finance instead. Your chances of becoming fabulously rich for much less personal risk and sacrifice are vastly better in finance than anywhere else in the economy. This fact, by the way, has not been lost on the young and brightest, and they have been flocking to finance in droves.

But if you believe that, as a society, we should hope (and regulate) for maximizing local innovation-based growth, then finance is completely dysfunctional, because it doesn't do what is urgently needed: efficiently allocating capital toward productive activities. To maximize local growth, finance should re-assume its classical role as a matching activity, channeling capital to where it is needed and can best be utilized. I will gladly be proven wrong, but I for one am worried about the implications of the current dysfunction, especially since I think the chances of changing the finance system are approaching zero.

I am first going to provide an example to show how dysfunctional finance is, and why we should have no illusions that it can be changed. Then I am going to suggest a pragmatic approach to what can be done by locales to maximize their growth prospects under such conditions.

Ending in Bedlam

In 2013, MIT concluded a large, multidisciplinary, multiyear, multi-location study aimed at figuring out how to revive production in the United States.

The results were published in two books: *Making in America* (2013) and *Production in the Innovation Economy* (2014). The authors found that both productivity trends and trade flows were not enough to explain the sharp (and sudden) decline in manufacturing jobs in the United States versus other OECD countries since the beginning of the twenty-first century. What did explain it was the move toward maximizing stock price on a quarterly basis, and with it a focus on "core competencies." The idea that companies should narrowly prioritize core competencies sounds very logical, but it has effectively destroyed many of the activities that supported manufacturing and innovation in the United States, as companies became leaner and smaller. In technical terms, the move toward core competencies has destroyed the industrial commons, leading to what we saw in chapter 5—Apple having difficulties procuring things as simple as screws in Texas. The MIT team strongly decried "short-termism" among investors, but stopped short of criticizing finance as a whole. Instead it sang the praises of state pension funds and other sources of "patient capital."[10]

As part of its study, the MIT team identified regions and companies that offered models and hope to the rest of America. One paragon of regional development it highlighted was the Timken Company of Canton, Ohio, a firm that was first publicly listed on the Cleveland Stock Exchange when Cleveland was America's innovation hub almost a century ago. In 2013, when the company was employing about 20,000 people in three countries, it was still led by a member of the founding Timken family. It focused, among other things, on high-end steel and power transmission. Its advances in material science allowed it to develop large (two meters in diameter), heavy, durable bearings for applications such as windmill towers. Further, Timken was deeply involved in the local community, participating in the creation of semi-public goods such as skills and shared assets that are vital for local sustainability and competitiveness.[11]

Then, stunningly, Timken came under attack. In May 2013, just after the first book was published, shareholders demanded a vote on breaking the company into two. Investors claiming to stand for "shareholder value" used the "core competencies" logic to contend that by doing both materials and industrial components, Timken was limiting its stock value. They said shareholders would do better if the company were broken into two firms that did "pure play." As has happened elsewhere in the United States, the activists won the vote against management, and the company was broken up.[12]

The real kicker is that the shareholders who attacked Timken were led by none other than the California State Teachers Retirement System (CalSTRS) pension fund, which is the second-largest public pension fund in the United States and for decades has been cited as an example of patient capital and "good" finance.[13]

There was nothing anomalous about CalSTRS's involvement—public pension funds' investment officers are bound to uphold their duties, which are very clearly set forth in laws and regulations established by the citizens of the United States through their elected representatives. Accordingly, it is very important to realize here that none of CalSTRS's managers or board members have been evil or derelict in their duties. Exactly the opposite. Everything they did was rational and proper. They simply maximized the utility function that they were incentivized to uphold. The question is whether this corporate behavior is what we, as a society, should want. One has to think that by now the idea of financialization has reached the stage in which it has become, in John Maynard Keynes's words, "an extraordinary example of how, starting with a mistake, a remorseless logician can end in Bedlam" (which, interestingly enough, was his critique of Hayek's book *Prices and Production*).[14]

The Timken story illustrates that those of us who put all the blame on "short-termism" have been in denial about finance as a whole, like a smoker who believes his breathing problem is the result of him having just run up the street, and not his two-decade-old chain-smoking habit. The myth of short-termism allows the denial of reality. Finance as a whole, including the regulations underpinning it, has become a hindrance to local growth.[15]

Instead, we have preferred to believe in a narrative that is an almost Star Wars–like view of growth and financial markets in America. On one side are the evil hedge funds and activist investors whose "short-termism" aims to maximize stock price on a quarterly basis. On the other, standing as the last hope of the republic, right next to Luke Skywalker, are long-term investors and their patient capital, working to make America great again.

The shock of the CalSTRS attack on Timken led to a special public forum of the *Boston Review* where Suzanne Berger, the lead author of *Making in America* and my friend and mentor, acknowledged that finance itself now stands as an obstacle in the way of growth. Too bad for the people of Canton, Ohio, or any other locality that pins its hopes on the Timken model.[16]

Given the immense and concentrated fortunes made in finance, and the aggressive political lobbying that supports them, there is no real chance that finance as we know it will change. The reality is that if local firms become successful, there is no practical way to guard against the forces of finance. At some point, successful companies will achieve financial exits in the form of acquisitions by bigger companies or transformation into public firms, which will expose them to the usual shareholder-value pressures.

As regional leaders devise ways to enhance local growth, they must take into account this reality and work around it. Since I see no real hope of fixing finance, I recommend a strategy of *growth and delay*.

Growth and Delay: Taking Action in a Financialized World

What do I mean by growth and delay? And why might one think this is a good idea?

The reason we are interested in innovation in this book is that innovation is the key to *local* economic growth. This happy outcome occurs when new and existing companies are not only funded but grow and supply large numbers of good jobs in a sustainable way over long periods of time in the locale. The key, therefore, is to ensure that such companies are not only created, but also grow while staying put.

Thus, our aim is to achieve an interrelated outcome of innovation: local growth of companies in a way that produces a large number of good jobs. Preferable, but not necessarily achievable in all innovation stages, is not just a large number of good jobs, but also jobs for people with diverse skill sets. Given that finance is dysfunctional, the way to maximize the chances that we can reach these aims is to enable as much growth as possible, for as long as possible, before local companies have to face the consequences of financial exits and financialization. Indeed, such a strategy might be even more important to stage 1 Silicon-Hyphen regions than to other stages. If you know that the ultimate outcome of most of your start-ups is to be bought out, your main policy aim should be to ensure that they grow enough—that is, reach a critical mass of operations—in your region so that buyers would prefer to let them grow, or even make them into strategic divisions of their global operations, instead of relocating away the activities and key people. Further, the more a start-up develops and moves into full business operations (such as actual sales and after-market services), the greater the chances that it will provide employment opportunities to people who are not only R&D engineers.

Accordingly, it should not come as a surprise that the Israeli Innovation Authority has embraced this strategy of growth and delay in recent years. Specifically, the IIA growth division has been working extensively on increasing debt funding for scale-ups. Debt financing allows young companies to mitigate some of the pressures for financial exits, as well as incentivizing them to focus on revenue growths (so they can repay the debt). Accordingly, it can act as a key tool in a growth and delay strategy. The main effort of the new programs is to develop knowledgeable supply and demand for growth-debt for high-technology firms. Currently, almost all the capital available to high-tech companies is equity, with the accompanying pressure for quick financial exits instead of long-term growth. The IIA aims to, first, supply guarantees to entice banks into extending debt to high-tech companies. Second, it offers extensive training so that those bankers will have the skills to decide which projects to loan to and under what conditions. Third, the IIA aims to train the financial managers of high-technology start-ups to effectively use and manage bank debt. Currently, debt financing, and the knowledge of how to use it, or even secure it, is lacking among the CFOs of Israeli high-tech companies, which are focused almost solely on equity finance.[17]

But this is the case not only for stage 1 innovation locales. Taiwan, maybe the world's most successful stage 3 innovation region, is very much aware that to secure continuous prosperity it needs its SMEs to innovate, grow, and stay in Taiwan. To do so, its public and private leaders have made the region a best-in-class example of SME debt-financing policy and environment. Not only is there a vigorous and diverse use of loan guarantees, but in order to lower risk and reduce information asymmetries, a centralized information-sharing system was created and maintained. The result is that loans to SMEs now amount to more than 60 percent of all bank loans to private businesses, a 20 percent rise in less than fifteen years.[18]

In both cases, local leaders focused on mixed-debt-based financing as a vehicle to allow companies to realize profits even before—and, it is hoped, to avoid—financial exits. There are a few critical components to such a strategy. First, since the aim is companies' growth in the region, local leaders should focus on companies that either already are or have a good chance of becoming deeply tied to their community and will derive a great deal of value from being in the locale. This should, again, remind us about the unfulfilled potential of the tech teens discussed in chapter 1. By definition, tech teens are deeply tied in to the community. Further, their owners and managers have no plans to relocate and are committed to growing all business activities of their companies locally. Another example of companies that are tied to the community is those whose business models derive a lot of value from local resources, such as the supply of unique skills, the presence of specific assets, or the locale's particular brand. What local leaders should avoid targeting is companies with business models that clearly call for quick financial exits by sale.

Mixed-debt-based financing may sound logical and simple. However, this approach has proved to be quite difficult to implement, especially with regard to new companies and SMEs, for multiple reasons. The two main problems are the challenge that companies face in using debt to fund innovation-based activities, and the challenge that funders and companies face in making risk-versus-profit calculations.[19]

Using debt for innovation

A company that borrows to fund innovation needs to repay the debt on a regular basis from current cash flow—an obvious stumbling block for start-ups without any cash flow. But even for more mature SMEs, debt financing can create more problems than it solves. Imagine that a visionary manufacturing SME needs to pursue its revolutionary ideas about additive manufacturing by purchasing the newest 3D printers. It submits its plans to various publicly financed innovation programs and gets a low-interest loan. The company needs to start repaying the loan immediately, but cash becomes an issue. It takes time for the new machines to arrive, it takes more time for the company to learn how to run them efficiently, and it takes even longer for customers to appreciate the new products and services (this is known as the time-interval problem). Meanwhile, the cash flow from the old line of products is diminishing as workers are moved to the new machines and product offerings are shut down. The company's financial position soon becomes so precarious that even a slight ripple in the market could drag it under.

And then there's the debt service, a problem that grows as loans accumulate. Even if a company has a substantial cash flow, the cash can be eaten up in servicing the debt, leaving the firm with limited resources for growth. Further, if a company has a lot of debt on its books, it is viewed as toxic by private investors. The sad result is that even the most promising companies stagnate instead of achieving the hoped-for rapid growth and happiness for their founders, employees, investors, and communities. This is the SME equivalent of becoming a house-poor family. So much house, so little life.[20]

Problems like these make debt financing one of the most common sources of failure in many government-backed innovation-funding programs around the world.

There are ways for communities to help companies deal with these challenges. On the cash-flow side, publicly financed programs can offer grace periods of twenty-four months or so before payments have to start. This is similar to the logic behind student loans: the aim is to achieve both a public and a private good, and the borrower's ability to repay is much higher after the initial period. To further ease cash flow and alleviate some of the debt-service burden, funders of start-ups and SMEs can provide money in the form of conditional "grants," rather than traditional loans. Suppose, for example, that a company needs money to fund product development; the lender's terms could stipulate that only when (if) revenues from that product begin to accrue does the firm need to start repaying the money, preferably as a percentage of the new revenue—much like a royalty. An added benefit of designating such funds as a grant is that a grant is not recorded on the books as a liability, even if it is conditional.

The Israeli innovation agencies have been using conditional grants as their main tool in transforming the country into a stage 1 innovation powerhouse since the 1970s. Even today, companies that successfully approach the IIA for funds get it as conditional grants toward specific projects to develop exportable new technology-based products. If a project—for example, development of a computer-memory technology—is successful, the grant, usually limited to less than 50 percent of the R&D cost of the project, will be paid as royalties on sales of the product. If the project fails, the company does not need to repay the IIA.[21]

Another variation is an agreement stating that a certain portion of the borrowed money will be converted to equity, which the owners can purchase within a given period for a specified sum, such as three times the company's current valuation. This allows the companies more flexibility and less fear of not being able to pay on time, and it gives borrowers extra security and an option to enjoy higher returns.

However, before any of these loan alternatives can be implemented, local policymakers need to ensure that funders, companies, and the community have a sophisticated awareness about the issues and the potential of using debt to spur innovation-based growth. Indeed, the main point in dealing with these issues is not that the problems are hard to solve, but that there is no awareness of the problems to begin with. Regional leaders should make sure, as they devise their innovation policies, that these problems do not cripple the vulnerable companies in their locales. Thus, seminars, online courses and materials, and even mentorship programs should be viewed as an essential part of the policy. As a matter of fact, this education effort should also be aimed at the general population in order to garner not only understanding, but also the necessary political support.

Risk-versus-profit calculations

Financial risk is part of the reality of the market. There are essentially two sources of risk. First, there is the risk stemming from lack of knowledge and information. Most places in the world are not the Riviera del Brenta, meaning that they are not supported by a system of lenders, such as the *banche di credito cooperativo* (BCCs), that can draw on deep knowledge of the local industry and technology to calculate the risk of lending to specific enterprises and to devise profitable portfolios of loans. Most places in the world also lack companies whose managers know how to utilize debt effectively and deal with banks as the main suppliers of finance.

This latter lack of knowledge is, sadly, too often unacknowledged and dealt with. I still remember a story I heard from the cofounder of New Dimension Software, one of Israel's earliest globally successful software companies. Early in its life, in 1987, the company found itself in acute financial difficulties. It had booked several million dollars in future orders but was running out of working capital. The founders, all brilliant technologists without any business education, frantically started to look for outside equity investors. Fortunately, Kobi Alexander, Comverse's cofounder and CEO, agreed to meet with them. After recovering from his shock at their lack of financial literacy, he advised them to use the simple financial tool of bridge loans. Without this chance encounter, New Dimension probably would have folded just as it was on the verge of reaching its big breakthrough.[22]

Reducing this kind of risk requires overcoming the lack of knowledge on both sides. There is a need to create the skills of technology-savvy debt issuers, and there is a need to educate SME managers about debt instruments. This is exactly why a key component of the Israeli policy includes the education of bankers, as well as extensive courses for high-technology companies'

CFOs. The bankers need to understand how to evaluate risk and opportunity, as well as how to design a financial product that will appeal to (and help) high-technology companies in their early growth stages. CFOs need to know how to approach, talk to, and deal with bankers, and how to effectively utilize and repay debt. Further, the CFOs need to understand the different options, the pros and cons of debt versus equity, and when one instrument would be more beneficial than another.

Done properly, this education component of a venture-financing policy intervention promises to have bigger and longer-term positive impacts than just creating yet another dedicated capital pool. First, it allows a locale's companies to devise multiple growth patterns that are focused on ensuring long-term expansion and survival, rather than solely on the metrics that would increase valuation in the next investment round. Further, it might change the companies' time horizons, allowing them to grow their local activities to the maximum. Third, it can inject new growth dynamics into a large set of companies that, under equity-only financing, are stuck in low-growth inertia due to their inability to secure capital for new ideas. Last, but certainly not least, it can stimulate innovation in innovation financing, something that the world is badly missing.

An additional advantage of such a comprehensive solution is that if you train a group of capable and ambitious young bankers and equip them with the right skills, they will want to make sure that this new line of business grows, and will lobby for it within their banks. In technical terms, you have now aligned their career prospects with the growth of debt financing to innovation-based SMEs.

The second source of risk is the inherent uncertainty around financing innovation-based businesses—particularly those with socially important goals and those in markets that seem shaky. The intent should be to reduce the risk enough to maximize private investment in these companies. There are two ways public officials can do this. The first is to offer public-investment capital, which acts as a leveraging instrument. This can come in the form of direct public investments or loans to companies, or as extra capital given to an investment vehicle for distribution as the vehicle's managers see fit. An example of an investment vehicle is the Small Business Investment Company (SBIC), a program of the US Small Business Administration. Approved SBICs get two extra dollars to invest on top of each one dollar they commit. Thus, for every dollar given by private investors, the state adds two more (paid back to the state). Accordingly, SBICs can leverage three times their privately committed capital toward their companies.[23]

The second way for public policymakers to reduce risk is by offering insurance against losses—in case of default, the lenders are paid back in part or whole from the public purse. An instrument widely used by development banks all around the world is the loan guarantee: banks pay a very small annual fee (for example, 1 percent of the value of the loan), and in case of default they are guaranteed to be paid back a percentage of the loan, usually 50 to 80 percent. Loan guarantees significantly lower the risk while keeping the upside. With this approach, a small amount of public money can leverage loans that are several orders of magnitude larger. For example, if a community asks a 1 percent fee from lenders and gives an 80 percent guarantee, the cost of stimulating $1 billion in loans for a period of three years would come to only around $30 million annually, even assuming a very high annual loss rate. Loan guarantees are popular because there is no transfer of money from the public purse to a private entity unless there is a default. And once the loans are repaid, the public money can be rolled over and utilized again and again.[24]

Regions should compensate for the systemic failure of finance by enhancing what they can do, as a practical matter, to increase the chances that their innovation-based companies grow—and continue to grow locally. The goal is to create opportunities for local companies to secure sufficient financial resources to achieve rapid growth, without forcing them to resort to business models whose main aim is to secure the quickest and largest financial exit in order to satisfy their investors.

Determining which financing approach to take requires a careful analysis of local companies' needs and funders' resources and objectives. For example, loan guarantees provide substantial leverage in comparison with direct grants—the $30 million that could stimulate $1 billion in loans via guarantees would generate only $60 million if it were provided in the form of a direct grant at the rate of one-to-one private-public. Nonetheless, in some cases, such as very-early-stage companies or the development of radically novel technologies, the risk and uncertainty are too high for private investors—indeed, you should expect failure to the tune of 90 percent. In those cases and stages of companies' growth, direct grants are necessary. Regions should use both instruments for different companies at different points of their growth cycles.

Whatever the funding instrument, the goal should always be to ensure that companies' financial exits happen only after they are big enough, sophisticated enough, and embedded enough—and that they derive enough value from the region—that they will continue to grow locally after going public or being acquired. For example, when Intel bought the Israeli image-processing company Mobileye in March 2017 for $15.3 billion, it moved its global automotive division to Israel, in effect ensuring that Israel would continue to enjoy growth in terms of jobs and knowledge. Thus, the hope for local leaders is to develop a financial infrastructure that will maximize the chances that companies will grow locally to the point where if they are bought by an MNC, the most logical decision for the parent firm would be to encourage the continued local scale-up of the acquired company's activities.[25]

The strategies I have presented in this chapter should be viewed as just a few out of many possibilities. I hope that local leaders will stick their necks out and experiment with new ways of financing innovation-based growth in their locales' chosen industries and stages of innovation. If they—and we— are lucky, some of the experiments will pay off and be scaled up.

Regions that are able to develop new and effective modes of venture financing will gain a tremendous advantage. It is important to remember that, throughout history, regions that spearheaded successful new models for venture financing—from England to Lyon to Turin to Frankfurt to New England to Cleveland, and all the way to California—enjoyed long periods of rapid economic growth. If we and the experimental local leaders become *truly* lucky, the financing models that grow out of the successful experiments will radically change the national and international landscape and will come to replace the old, tired, and no-longer-effective current VC model.

11

Data

Why Mining Us Is the New Boom, and for Whom

Information wants to be free.

Stewart Brand, Hackers Conference, 1984

On the Internet, nobody knows you're a dog.

Peter Steiner, *New Yorker*, July 5, 1993

Personal data is the "gold" of a new category of companies.

Helen Nissenbaum, *Privacy as a Contextual Integrity*, 2004

If you are not paying for it, you're not the customer; you're the product being sold.

posted by blue_beetle at 1:41 p.m. on August 26, 2010
(attributed to Andrew Lewis)

Is data the new oil?

Perry Rotella, *Forbes*, April 2, 2012

In the end, all roads lead back to Cobalt. The good people of that tiny Canadian mining town discovered long ago that the communities supplying raw ore to the world's economy are almost never the ones that enjoy the long-term prosperity that flows from it. The real growth happens in communities—Toronto, in Cobalt's case—that come up with innovative ideas about how to capitalize on commodities.

This is a lesson that must be fully—and quickly—absorbed by communities, because a new commodity is bubbling up out of the ground all around us, in great abundance. It is there for the exploiting, and MNCs are racing to grab it, to the detriment of unenlightened local policymakers.

The commodity is data, and it is one of the most dysfunctional policy domains. The reality is that we do not even have a decent understanding of how data should be used, who should use it, what technologies it might spawn, who should regulate it, who it should be regulated for, or how it should be regulated.[1]

The dysfunctionality of this domain is one of the reasons I have included a discussion of it in this book, along with the equally dysfunctional domains of financialization and intellectual property rights (the previous two chapters). In fact, as you will see, there are significant parallels between the data domain and IPR. In both fields, locales attempt to recruit MNCs to stimulate innovation-based growth. In the IPR domain, as we saw, the (misguided) focus tends to be on various types of tax incentives. In data, cities and regions offer up local denizens' personal information as test beds or data mines. In both cases, no attention is given to how benefits to the locale would accrue, and locales end up finding that they give up a lot—and get no innovation-based growth, or money or jobs, out of the deal.[2]

Just as in the IPR domain, locales need a well-informed and well-thought-out strategy on data. I will show how to go about thinking about a data strategy, but first let's take a clear look at the data problem that locales face.

Tens of Googols of Data Points

When we talk about personal data, what are we talking about? To get a handle on it, think about a particularly voluminous biographical tome, such as Walter Isaacson's biography of Steve Jobs, which runs to 656 pages, weighs 2.2 pounds, and painstakingly details the life of the person who cofounded Apple. This very lengthy book might seem to be an extensive, maybe even obsessively detailed, account of one human being's life.[3]

But for data scientists, companies, and software systems (specifically those based on so-called artificial intelligence), the Jobs biography would seem a disappointingly sparse, not-detailed, and not-long-enough story. When today's collectors and users of data talk about the details of a person's life, they talk about a millisecond-by-millisecond account of everything the person does. For Jobs, this would include his vital signs, his facial expressions, data about his sweating, tracks of his eye movements, and more. Then, to make the data into something useful, they would merge it with similarly detailed information on millions of other life stories into what we euphemistically call "big data."

Give a data analyst several streaming minutes of your life as you walk down a busy street, and she and her trusted "expert" system will know much better than you do many things about you, including what your real sexual orientation is, and, at least as profitably, what must be done to maximize the chances that you will buy a specific product, be it a cup of coffee or a candidate in an election. More often than not, an even better option for their paying customers would be to know how to maximize the chances that you will *not* bother to do something—for example, vote in the next election—and to know what deals they should *not* offer you, since you are either not worthwhile, too risky (for example, unhealthy or of the wrong ethnicity), or just so gullible that you would buy the same things at much higher prices. And bear in mind: technology is advancing so quickly that, before long, new methods of gathering and analyzing personal data will make today's technology look crude and unsophisticated by comparison.[4]

The leading global corporations are right to want to get their hands on this lode of personal data. On a global scale, they are already doing it, collecting data from sources as diverse as fitness apps and music-streaming services. But there is a world of data that is locally rooted, ranging from location information generated by Internet-connected cars to messages from renters to their Airbnb hosts.[5]

Locally generated data is potentially an important business resource for communities seeking ways to boost innovation-based growth, and a number of regions are already trying to capitalize on it by partnering with tech companies in data-sharing ventures. In Toronto, an attempt (now thankfully defunct) was made to permit Sidewalk Labs, a company owned by Alphabet, Google's parent, to develop a twelve-acre high-tech site where homes, offices, and stores would be integrated with traffic-control and waste-disposal systems, all of which would generate data that the company would amass. Arizona has offered itself as a testbed for autonomous vehicles. Apart from assuring that the state is written into the history books as the place where the first pedestrian was killed by an autonomous vehicle, it is not clear what Arizonians are getting out of the MNCs using the extensive road infrastructure, paid for by their taxes, to busily gather data from their experimental drives and services.[6]

You might have heard some of my fellow economists telling you that the frenzy of data sharing that we call modern life is good for consumers and good for locales. For example, after your online-purchase data is shared with advertisers, you will be offered only the deals you really want, and after your driving data is shared with a tech company, your city will be able to unclog some of its traffic jams. But data sharing is not good for consumers or cities. Nothing could be further than the truth, in fact. Firms that gather data do it because it helps them with one important task: selling the most products at the highest possible prices. Thus, the end results of data-gathering efforts are higher profits for the companies and worse deals for the buyers and the communities that help generate the data.[7]

Unless the data is specifically designated otherwise (for example, in health), information that is gathered by a corporation belongs to the gatherer, which can utilize it for free, with no limits whatsoever on time, place, or type of usage, while enjoying full exclusivity and monopoly. The company can deny anyone else access to the data and/or sell it to whoever it chooses at whatever terms it deems most beneficial. Further, the gatherer is not required to let people know what data it has collected; whether it is accurate; where and how it is stored, used, and sold; or to whom it is sold.[8]

In other words, each corporation does its best to collect at least as much data as all other corporations, and then to prevent the others from having access to that data. From your watch to your mobile device, computer, TV, home alarm, heating and cooling systems, cars, and fitness equipment, the same data is collected again and again by competing corporations. As a consequence, the lives of most humans, whether they live in democracies or authoritarian regimes, are under such intense surveillance by multiple organizations that it makes the data-collection efforts described by George Orwell in his book 1984 look like a semiprofessional attempt by benevolent amateurs. In addition, neither citizens nor their communities see any of the economic-growth benefits that are the fruits of the intensive efforts to gather, process, and utilize their own data. This current situation is by far the worst imaginable for citizens, locales, and future growth.[9]

If this description of corporate excess and lack of transparency and accountability sounds eerily similar to the conditions that turned the relatively minor issue of higher-than-expected subprime mortgage defaults in the United States into the great global recession of 2008, it is because it is indeed frighteningly similar. Worse, with data there is much more collection, trade, and storage than in the mortgage world, while even less is known about who owns and uses what, the quality and accuracy of both the data and the algorithms built on top of it, where the data is stored, and how safe it is.

How can locales learn to refuse the drugs and dreams that are pushed by MNCs and instead secure maximum freedom of innovation for current and future local agents of growth? As with the two other critical domains I have discussed—financialization and IPR—local leaders need to be aware of and understand the dysfunction of data. And they need to ensure access to the data that is locally generated. To do that, they need to understand a few basic things about this newly abundant commodity.

Data: A Different Kind of Commodity

Data supposedly became the new "gold" or "oil" of our "age of big data" almost two decades ago. Indeed, data has become the source of all new riches.[10]

In several senses, the physical-commodity analogy holds up: For example, data, like gold and oil, requires extraction and processing before it can become a valuable and usable asset. But data is very different from other commodities because of three factors that are critical for economic growth. These are: the ease and marginal cost of reproduction and use, the potential for increased value over time coupled with the advantage of scale, and the central importance of usage and business-model experimentation.

Ease of reproduction and use

Once you have collected and stored data, the marginal cost of creating a copy approaches zero, as does the cost of transporting it to the other end of the world and back. Moreover, data, unlike gold or oil, is a nonrival good. If I use a chunk of data to build a financial algorithm, you are physically capable of using the same chunk (though I may try to block your access) to build as many different algorithms as you wish, and all these algorithms will work at the same time, leaving the data undiminished and just as useful tomorrow or many years into the future, in any location. It doesn't wear out. This is the opposite of what happens when you use oil to drive your car.[11]

Potential for increased value over time

Unlike oil, whose usefulness per unit remains the same, data can become more useful as time passes, especially if more of it is acquired to complement the original collection, a phenomenon known as "increasing returns to scale." The more data you have, the more valuable each piece of it becomes.

Neural networks, which are behind what we now call "artificial-intelligence applications," have the ability to learn, from influxes of additional data, to produce better and better algorithms. The more data they have, the better the algorithm will be. Thus, those who have more data have an advantage over others, and data gatherers have a strong and clear incentive to try to hoard as much data as possible and to monopolize the use of it. It is already questionable whether anyone can compete with incumbents such as Alphabet, Facebook, Microsoft, Acxiom, Amazon, and the Chinese state.[12]

Importance of usage and business-model experimentation

This point is particularly critical for economic growth. While we can assume that we know most of the commercial uses for oil and gold and the business models around them, we can only guess how data will be used in the future. Since data is the raw material for innovation, we cannot know what kinds of data will have value or why—nor can we imagine what the business models might look like.[13]

Accordingly, by far, the best way to maximize both welfare and growth is to allow technology to diffuse rapidly and to encourage enormous amounts of experimentation and radical and incremental innovation. Hence, it is vitally important for local leaders to ensure that both current and yet-to-exist local entrepreneurs and firms that will try to develop yet-to-be-thought-about products will have access to data so they can experiment and innovate. Communities that don't ensure innovators' access to data will undermine the basis of future innovation.[14]

There is one other element that decisively sets data apart from all physical commodities. *Data* is a very clean word for what can only be called *coded life*. The loyalty-card information that you enter when you buy a pair of shoes, the address book that you upload to Facebook, your location data, your heart rate as recorded by your Internet-connected watch—these are your life, encoded.

Mistakenly, public debate assumes that the main issue with data is your ability to decide what is known about you and by whom—essentially, that it's all about privacy. In reality the issues are much deeper. The consequences of corporations owning your coded life, selling it as a commodity, and being able to use it as they see fit are at the core of the fabric of society. This is much more significant than privacy intrusion. Choices about data are choices about democracy and the kind of society we would like to live in.[15]

Devising a Data Strategy

You can see why it would be a criminal dereliction of duty for a community *not* to develop a data strategy, and why it would be preposterous to develop a strategy that did not take into account data's inherent qualities and its effects on life and society. The differences between data and tangible commodities— ease of reproduction and use, advantage of scale coupled with the potential for increased value over time, and the importance of usage and business-model experimentation—can serve as the basic principles underlying data strategy from the point of view of local economic growth.

Locales need to know that they should not permit locally generated data to be simply given away. Policy should be aimed at ensuring that well-functioning data markets with efficient price-setting mechanisms exist to enable the optimal allocation of resources, incentivizing growth and innovation. This means establishing property rights, which amount to rules around data gathering and usage: who is allowed to collect what data and for what purpose, and how said rights can be transferred in whole or in part.[16]

Currently in most countries, such rules either do not exist or are at best aspirational. The result is that the corporations doing the data gathering have de-facto full, exclusive, and unlimited (in time and usage) rights to the data they gather. It is here that the confusion between data issues and privacy is the most damaging to society and economic growth.

The rules established by communities should also include mechanisms for enabling accurate pricing that is based on the level of data collection and the rights of use. Allowing accurate market pricing based on real use and value would also have the wonderful effect of optimizing the allocation of resources to the collection, acquisition, and processing of data. Currently, those valuations are based on hype and dreams, and as such lead to inflated bubbles and a massive waste of resources. Fixing this would have a positive impact on economic growth. This has become an even more pressing issue due to the rise of so-called platforms, ranging from the general (Facebook and Amazon) to the niche-specific (Airbnb, Uber, and Lyft).[17]

Corporations would have to ask, and pay, to collect and then use personal data, and they would have to accurately price their services, since individuals would have a choice to pay in cash or with data. Under such rules, I might, for example, give a company permission to take some of my personal data in exchange for allowing me to use its taxi-ordering app. I could allow the company to license my data to others, but I would retain the property rights, which means I could use the same data to pay for other things. Another benefit is that my data would have to be collected only once.[18]

For such a system to work, there must be accurate records of all requests for any data, by whom, and for what reason; all individuals would need to have the ability to find out exactly what data has been collected about them, verify it, and challenge it; and there must be an accurate map of all the transactions and licensing agreements that individuals have approved, as well as of all requests for the data. In addition, there would be a need for data-storage facilities that would enable the quality and accuracy of the data to be checked and assured.[19]

This is where government plays an important role. A government entity must ensure that the data goes into a (publicly or privately managed) repository; that the gatherers make an effort to adhere to the principal that data is "collected once"; that all licensing and approvals are in order; and that individuals and others can check the data for accuracy and correct it if necessary. In the example of a ride-sharing app, a government-enabled system would record what data is collected (not the data itself), what the fitness-app company is allowed to do with it, and all further transactions on that data. The government would also ensure, at the very least, minimal security standards and establish criminal and civil penalties for theft and misuse. Regions that pioneer in these comprehensive infrastructural regulatory frameworks have a competitive advantage in attracting large capital investment projects. Indeed, the surprising success of biotech manufacturing (not only R&D) in the very high cost area of Cambridge, Massachusetts, since the late 1990s owes much to the fact that Cambridge was the first city to establish clear and strict regulations, zoning ordinance included, about biotech manufacturing that not only ensured long-term certainty, needed for such big capital investments, but also that biotech companies which followed those regulations will be protected from litigation—a critical issue with new-to-the-world manufacturing processes with possible unknown environmental impacts.[20]

Governments must be thoughtful about intervention, or they will leave citizens with inadequate protections and a false sense of security. A perfect example is the European Cookie Law, which requires all websites that use cookies for collecting data to remind visitors that if they enter the sites their data will be collected using cookies (strangely, there is no requirement to declare the use of much-more-intrusive techniques, with the predictable result that those techniques are incentivized relative to cookies). The flawed assumption here is the idea that if people are reminded about privacy issues, they will think twice about entering websites. In today's economy and society, not entering websites is just not a viable option. Also, the issues are not whether or not you are aware that your life is now coded to become the commodity called data, but rather who has a right to collect what data, and who has the right to define what the data can be used for and how it can be used.[21]

For communities, there is a continuum of approaches to regulation, ranging from market-based to fully licensed. At the market-based end, all comers would be allowed to gather data as long as they and the individuals providing the data agreed upon on a price, and as long as the individuals are allowed to retain their property rights—that is, the data gatherers are not allowed to sell it to third parties or use it for any other activity but the one for which they paid. At the other end of the continuum would be systems similar to those regulating and certifying doctors, accountants, lawyers, and other professional-services providers. Under such a system, data gatherers will have to purchase licenses, and only those that adhere to the regulations that come with such licenses are allowed to collect individuals' data. Locales must decide where they wish to stand on this continuum.[22]

Whatever the specifics of the approach, the most elegant solution would be to grant individuals full property rights to their personal data and establish fully transparent rights to all the data gathered as part of public activities, such as transportation services.

Thus, for example, app services such as Waze, and transportation-for-pay services such as Uber and Lyft, should make their data readily accessible to the cities in which they operate as well as to their residents, in exchange for the right to use this data. With regards to personal data, this could be collected in a universal reservoir (which would be either centralized or fragmented, depending on security and efficiency concerns), and individuals could then both check its accuracy and sell the right to use it to specific vendors or government agencies. For that to work, full transparency also would be needed on who asks for access to this data.

While many, especially lobbyists for industry, might argue that these conditions are too complex and that implementing them would be technologically unfeasible or so cumbersome that they would be unworkable, reality has already proved them wrong. These conditions currently underlie Estonia's e-Government policy, which is considered the most advanced and competitive in the world. Indeed, Estonia's data strategy is now a competitive advantage that the country skillfully uses to lure international business and talent to make Estonia their base of operations. Further, other countries are now adapting Estonia's solution, creating an international system in which Estonia's chosen principles, technologies, standards, and solutions are embedded into the infrastructure.[23]

The technological issues, and many of the regulatory issues, have therefore already been ironed out at least once, and making this policy effective with regard to both public and private services is feasible. Further, as Estonia has proven, regions and countries that become policy leaders gain a significant competitive advantage.[24]

In addition, if history tells us anything, it is that greater prosperity is enjoyed by the places where most of the experimentation with new "factors of production" take place, not those where the commodities are mined or tested. Accordingly, local leaders should do their utmost to develop strategies that grant their locales competitive advantage, knowing full well how dysfunctional data gathering and markets currently are.

It is important to understand that we have very little knowledge of how the data economy should ideally work. At best we have very questionable economic models—little more than logic games—that attempt to estimate the distribution of very badly defined welfare, according to who will have de facto and de jure property rights (the gatherer or the individual).[25]

That is why significant experimentation should be conducted on various business models, from full open-source to two-level licensing, where a license to use is granted to the gatherer in exchange for sharing the data with current and future local citizens and companies, either for free or for nominal fees. It's also why any data strategy must be aimed at securing the greatest possible access to data for a community's future innovators. In order to ensure that its present and future entrepreneurs can succeed and scale up, a locale must have a data strategy that incorporates the shadow of the future as a core principle.

The point about which communities prosper the most from resources is important to remember. If you need a reminder, come and visit me in Cobalt one of these summers. Just remember that the train does not stop there anymore, so you better get a car.

Conclusion

In Defense of Experiments, Mistakes, and the Right to Choose

And since we find that two successive reigns of valiant princes, as of Philip of Macedon and his son Alexander, suffice to conquer the world, this ought to be still easier for a commonwealth, which has it in its power to choose, not two excellent rulers only, but an endless number in succession. And in every well-ordered commonwealth provision will be made for a succession of this sort.

Niccolo Machiavelli, *Discourses on Livy*

If there is one lesson that I hope you, the readers of this book, will take away from it, it is to believe in human ingenuity and the ability of communities to chart their own future even under the worst global headwinds. This is the real splendor of innovation. Whenever we are told that there is no choice, that the forces of the market, technology, and globalization continuously limit our ability to act, communities prove those pundits wrong by devising innovative ways to chart their own growth paths, demonstrating again and again that human choices, creativity, and actions matter, and that social structure is malleable to the, always underestimated, human agency.

Furthermore, both the importance of innovation and the incentives to innovate exponentially grow the closer the economy is to reaching a stable equilibrium state, and the more experts and pundits alike think that they finally got that one-perfect-model of how to organize it. The periods in which old models of behavior and organization achieve, at best, declining growth rates, and as a result spend more and more effort on creative financial engineering and securing monopoly status, are the best times in which to innovate. They are also the perfect times in which to differentiate and disrupt, and for communities to believe in themselves and their ability to devise their own unique way forward. Those that devise a vision of what society they want to be, think about how innovation would allow them to reach that goal, and then go on to experiment and contextualize their growth models to their position in the global system, will achieve prosperity. Those that opt to go for "proven" cookie-cutter models slightly rewarmed by consultants, like my very own country of Canada, can be sure that their productivity figures and socioeconomic prosperity will slowly, but surely, decline.

Throughout this book we developed a framework with which communities can understand, and plan for, innovation-based growth under our current system of globally fragmented production. To do so we first needed to understand (i) what innovation is (and what it is not), and why should we care about it; (ii) how innovation translates to prosperity; and (iii) how the current global system of fragmented production influences these processes. This allowed us to see that there are a multitude of innovation-based growth models, each with its pros and cons, especially with regard to the socioeconomic distributions and what fruits of its own success the locale should expect to retain from each model.

A key to understanding innovation-based growth is to understand that innovation is not invention, nor is it only high-tech and the creation of new technology and gadgets. Innovation is the whole progression of taking new ideas and devising new or improved products and services. It comes in all stages of the production of goods and services, from the first vision, design, development, production, sale, and usage to the after-sale. Contrary to common belief, and the proponents of the Silicon Valley and venture capital models, the true impact of innovation is not in the inventions of new technologies or even in their introduction to the market. The true impact of innovation is the continuous stream of implementation of large and small innovations, making those inventions more useful in more sectors of the economy, more reliable, and significantly cheaper, while constantly innovating in their sale, marketing, and after-sale services.

Once we realize this, we become aware of the large number of available options with which to reach prosperity, as well as the futility (and perhaps the stupidity, if we care about inequality) of only trying to become a Silicon-Hyphen. The smart community lets others try to become Silicon Valley North, Silicon Vale, Silicon Hill, Silicon Isle, or Silicon Shade, and instead focuses on developing its own model of innovation-based growth. This is especially true with the current model of VC-to-financial-exits reaching the end of its steam as a growth model, and with the impact of globally fragmented production of considerably limiting the local positive spillovers of stage 1 innovation.

As the divergent fortunes of communities under COVID-19 attest to, it is time we start to appreciate the widely distributed growth and the greater resiliency that focusing on stages 4 to 2 innovation grants. Thus, as you think about your own region, think carefully about whether its current capacities and capabilities, and at least as importantly its potential capacities and capabilities, would allow it to excel as stage 4 (production and assembly), stage 3 (second-generation product and component innovation), or stage 2 (design, prototype development, and production engineering), instead of becoming another locale that failed to become Silicon Valley, or one that cursed the day it succeeded.

As you think about these options and develop a way forward, you should also keep in mind that the only economic actors that innovate in the economy are individuals and firms; therefore, the focus of innovation policy should be on changing the behavior of, and the environment for, those actors. Thus, before investing billions in complimentary assets and actors, from accelerators to VCs, science parks, and research institutions, be very clear how that investment would end up in a changed (preferably positive) behavior of your of innovators. Otherwise, you can call your policy whatever name you fancy, but innovation policy it would not be. It is crucial to remember that innovation policy's goals are to (i) equip the agents of innovation with the capacities they need in order to excel; (ii) develop, support, and sustain the economic ecosystem that innovators need in order to thrive; and (iii) find the most effective ways to stimulate those agents to innovate and grow their businesses, while staying locally embedded.

As you plan, implement, revise, change, and perfect your policies, it would be useful to constantly focus on the four fundamentals. The first being the local *flows of local–global knowledge, demand, and inputs.* Since we live in a world of fragmented production, continuous success requires that a region establish and institutionalize modes of ensuring constant bidirectional flows of these three critical components. That means institutionalizing the modes in which the local interacts with the global and the global interacts with the local. These activities represent key strategic decisions for firms, and different modes of engaging with those flows are compatible with building and sustaining the specific capacities that are needed in each different stages of innovation.

The second fundamental is *the supply and creation of public and semi-public goods*. Innovation, by its very essence, is a collective endeavor that requires an array of public and semi-public goods, from the supply of specialized skills, be they craftspeople or R&D engineers; to shared assets, such as testing facilities, trade shows, or specialized prototyping-to-production facilities; to what I call collaborative public spaces, the socioeconomic places where an industry moves from sharing knowledge to becoming a community. Those first two lead us to the third fundamental, building a *local ecosystem that reinforces the firm-level benefits* of the previous two fundamentals and allows access to critical resources, such as finance or legal services, that fit the business models and the local stage of innovation specialization. In time, the elements of the ecosystem support one another as the locale develops in a specific innovation-based-growth trajectory. Reflecting on the different approaches Taiwan and Israel took, very successfully, to using similarly named policy tools, from research consortia to venture capital policies, to enhance their very different local ecosystems, is a useful reminder here.

The last, but not least, fundamental is the *co-evolution of the previous three fundamentals* and the role of public policy as the locale grows and excels. One of the classic mistakes of policymaking is the assumption that what works in one time and one place will always work across time and space. This is a perfect example of inflexibility, a textbook failure to change policy instruments in tandem with the environment. In innovation policy, even more than in any other policy domain, the forces of evolutionary change mean that those who do not change become extinct.

Nonetheless there are critical policy domains over which local leaders, maybe even global ones, have no control. Worse, from the point of view of communities aiming for innovation-based sustained prosperity, they are badly dysfunctional. Three of those domains—finance, intellectual property rights and data—are crucial for innovation, and yet the ability of local actors to influence them is minuscule. Instead, regional leaders should be widely versed in these issues, and develop strategies to mitigate, or even take advantage, of their systemic dysfunctions to maximize the success and growth chances of their local innovation actors.

The act of innovation is what led us to profoundly change our world and natural environment, it is what makes us humans. As such, innovation is hope—hope in the human ability to bring change, and hope that, more often than not, human-brought change will lead us all toward a better world.

Notes

Introduction

1. For a wonderful book on the history of Cobalt, see Douglas O. Baldwin, *Cobalt: Canada's Forgotten Silver Boom Town* (Charlottetown, PE: Indigo Press, 2016).
2. Mark Zachary Taylor, *The Politics of Innovation: Why Some Countries Are Better Than Others at Science and Technology* (Oxford: Oxford University Press, 2016),140–141, 142, 146, 153, 155, 156–157.

Chapter 1

1. Wiebe E. Bijker, *Of Bicycles, Bakelites, and Bulbs: Toward a Theory of Sociotechnical Change* (Cambridge, MA: MIT Press, 1995), 92–93.
2. Akira Takeishi and Yaichi Aoshima, "Case Study Shimano: Market Creation through Component Integration," in *Management of Technology and Innovation in Japan* (Berlin: Springer, 2006), 36–38, 41–43.
3. Jason Dedrick, Kenneth L. Kraemer, and Greg Linden, "Who Profits from Innovation in Global Value Chains?: A Study of the iPod and Notebook PCs," *Industrial and Corporate Change* 19, no. 1 (2010): 53.
4. Wei-Li Wu and Yi-Chih Lee, "From OEM Supplier to a Global Leading Company," *Journal of Business Case Studies* 10, no. 3 (2014): 226; S. Phineas Upham, "Innovation and the Interrelatedness of Core Competencies: How Taiwan's Giant Bicycles Broke into the US Bicycle Market," *Managing Global Transitions* 4, no. 1 (2006): 23.
5. Mei-Chih Hu and Ching-Yan Wu, "Giant Bicycle and King Liu," in *Handbook of East Asian Entrepreneurship*, ed. Fu-Lai Tony Yu and Ho-Don Yan (Abingdon, UK: Routledge, 2014), 291–292, 294–295; Fu-Lai Tony Yu, "Giants: Taiwan's World Brand Bicycle," in *Entrepreneurship and Taiwan's Economic Dynamics*, ed. Fu-Lai Tony Yu (Berlin: Springer, 2012), 91–92; "9921:Taiwan Stock Quote—Giant Manufacturing Co Ltd.," Bloomberg.com, https://www.bloomberg.com/quote/9921:TT, accessed November 25, 2019.
6. R. H. Coase, "The Nature of the Firm," *Economica* 4, no. 16 (1937): 396–397; O. E. Williamson, "Managerial Discretion, Organization Form, and the Multi-division Hypothesis," in *The Corporate Economy*, ed. Robin Marris and Adrian Wood (London: Palgrave Macmillan, 1971), 351–352.
7. Timothy J. Sturgeon, "Modular Production Networks: A New American Model of Industrial Organization," *Industrial and Corporate Change* 11, no. 3 (2002): 476–477; Richard N. Langlois, "Transaction-Cost Economics in Real Time," *Industrial and*

Corporate Change 1, no. 1 (1992): 109, 122; Richard N. Langlois and Paul L. Robertson, "Networks and Innovation in a Modular System: Lessons from the Microcomputer and Stereo Component Industries," *Research Policy* 21, no. 4 (1992): 301–302; Gary Gereffi, "Global Commodity Chains: New Forms of Coordination and Control among Nations and Firms in International Industries," *Competition & Change* 1, no. 4 (1996): 429–431.

8. Dan Breznitz, *Innovation and the State: Political Choice and Strategies for Growth in Israel, Taiwan, and Ireland* (New Haven, CT: Yale University Press, 2007), 23–24.

9. Breznitz, *Innovation and the State*, 23–24.

10. Breznitz, *Innovation and the State*, 23–24.

11. Langlois and Robertson, "Networks and Innovation in a Modular System," 301–302; Timothy Sturgeon, Johannes Van Biesebroeck, and Gary Gereffi, "Value Chains, Networks and Clusters: Reframing the Global Automotive Industry," *Journal of Economic Geography* 8, no. 3 (2008): 305–307; Gary Gereffi, John Humphrey, and Timothy Sturgeon, "The Governance of Global Value Chains," *Review of International Political Economy* 12, no. 1 (2005): 90–91, 94–96; Gereffi, "Global Commodity Chains, 430.

12. Breznitz, *Innovation and the State*, 23–24; Sturgeon, "Modular Production Networks, 476–477.

13. Dan Breznitz and Michael Murphree, *Run of the Red Queen: Government, Innovation, Globalization, and Economic Growth in China* (New Haven, CT: Yale University Press, 2011), 15–16.

14. Suma S. Athreye, "The Indian Software Industry," in *From Underdogs to Tigers: The Rise and Growth of the Software Industry in Brazil, China, India, Ireland, and Israel*, ed. Ashish Arora and Alfonso Gambardella (Oxford: Oxford University Press, 2005), 35–36; Rafiq Dossani and Martin Kenney, "Software Engineering: Globalization and Its Implications," paper presented at the National Academy of Engineering Workshop on the Offshoring of Engineering: Facts, Myths, Unknowns, and Implications, in (Washington, DC:, October 24–25, 2006), 9–10.

15. Kenji E. Kushida and John Zysman, "The Services Transformation and Network Policy: The New Logic of Value Creation 1," *Review of Policy Research* 26 no. 1–2 (2009): 174, 177; Martin Kenney and John Zysman, "The Rise of the Platform Economy," *Issues in Science and Technology* 32, no. 3 (2016): 62, 66; John Zysman, Stuart Feldman, Kenji E. Kushida, Jonathan Murray, and Niels Christian Nielsen, "Services with Everything: The ICT-Enabled Digital Transformation of Services," in *The Third Globalization: Can Wealthy Nations Stay Rich in the Twenty-First Century?*, ed. Dan Breznitz and John Zysman (Oxford: Oxford University Press, 2013), 100–102, 114.

16. Erik Brynjolfsson and Tom Mitchell, "What Can Machine Learning Do? Workforce Implications," *Science* 358, no. 6370 (2017): 1533–1534; Hal R. Varian, *Intermediate Microeconomics: A Modern Approach*, 9th ed. (New York: W. W. Norton, 2014), 276.

17. Dan Breznitz, "Why Germany Dominates the U.S. in Innovation," *Harvard Business Review*, May 27, 2014.

18. Breznitz, "Why Germany Dominates the U.S. in Innovation."; Breznitz and Murphree, *Run of the Red Queen*, 195–196.

19. Mark Huberty, "Energy Systems Transformation: State Choices at the Intersection of Sustainability and Growth," in *The Third Globalization: Can Wealthy Nations Stay Rich in the Twenty-First Century?*, ed. Dan Breznitz and John Zysman (Oxford: Oxford University Press, 2013), 8; Mariana Mazzucato, *The Entrepreneurial State: Debunking Public vs. Private Sector Myths* (London: Anthem Press, 2015), 62–71.

20. Ann Markusen, "Sticky Places in Slippery Space: A Typology of Industrial Districts," *Economic Geography* 72, no. 3 (1996): 294.

21. Daron Acemoglu, "Technical Change, Inequality, and the Labor Market," *Journal of Economic Literature* 40, no. 1 (2002): 46–56; Tina C. Ambos, Björn Ambos, and Bodo B. Schlegelmilch, "Learning from Foreign Subsidiaries: An Empirical Investigation of Headquarters' Benefits from Reverse Knowledge Transfers," *International Business Review* 15, no. 3 (2006): 304–305; Susan E. Cozzens, Kamau Bobb, Kendall Deas, Sonia Gatchair, Albert George, and Gonzalo Ordonez, "Distributional Effects of Science and Technology-Based Economic Development Strategies at State Level in the United States," *Science and Public Policy* 32, no. 1 (2005): 33–34.

22. Dan Breznitz, "Industrial R&D as a National Policy: Horizontal Technology Policies and Industry-State Co-evolution in the Growth of the Israeli Software Industry," *Research Policy* 36, no. 9 (2007): 1468, 1471–1472; Daniel Felsenstein, "The Making of a High Technology Node: Foreign-Owned Companies in Israeli High Technology," *Regional Studies* 31 (1997): 377.

23. Daniel Isenberg and Vincent Onyemah, "Fostering Scaleup Ecosystems for Regional Economic Growth (Innovations Case Narrative: Manizales-Mas and Scale Up Milwaukee)," *Innovations: Technology, Governance, Globalization* 11, no. 1–2 (2016): 64, 72; Daniel Isenberg, "Focus Entrepreneurship Policy on Scale-Up, Not Start-Up," *Harvard Business Review*, November 30, 2012; Daniel Isenberg and Vincent Onyemah, "Midsize Cities Are Entrepreneurship's Real Test," *Harvard Business Review*, January 24, 2017; World Economic Forum, "Start-Ups Won't Save the Economy. But 'Scale Ups' Could" (Cologny, Switzerland: World Economic Forum, March 28, 2017), https://www.weforum.org/agenda/2017/03/start-ups-entrepreneurship-scale-ups-latin-america/.

24. Breznitz, *Innovation and the State*, 113–114; Dan Breznitz, "Development, Flexibility, and R&D Performance in the Taiwanese IT Industry—Capability Creation and the Effects of State-Industry Co-evolution," *Industrial and Corporate Change* 14, no. 1 (2005): 153–187.

25. Giulio Buciuni and Dan Breznitz, "Keeping Up in an Era of Global Specialization," in *The Oxford Handbook of Local Competitiveness*, ed. David B. Audretsch, Albert N. Link, and Mary Walshok (Oxford: Oxford University Press, 2015), 15–17.

26. G. E. Moore, "Cramming More Components onto Integrated Circuits," *Proceedings of the IEEE* 86, no. 1 (1998): 83; Nathan Rosenberg, "Problems in the Economist's Conceptualization of Technological Innovation," *History of Political Economy* 7, no. 4 (1975): 473; Nathan Rosenberg and W. Edward Steinmueller, "Why Are Americans Such Poor Imitators?" *American Economic Review* 78, no. 2 (1988): 230;

James M. Utterback and William J. Abernathy, "A Dynamic Model of Process and Product Innovation," *Omega* 3, no. 6 (1975): 645; Nathan Rosenberg, *Inside the Black Box: Technology and Economics* (Cambridge: Cambridge University Press, 1982), 62–70; Nathan Rosenberg and L. E. Birdzell, *How the West Grew Rich: The Economic Transformation of the Industrial World* (New York: Basic Books, 1986), 20, 26–27.

27. Breznitz, "Why Germany Dominates the U.S. in Innovation."
28. Michael Murphree, Li Tang, and Dan Breznitz, "Tacit Local Alliance and SME Innovation in China," *International Journal of Innovation and Regional Development* 7, no. 3 (2016): 13–14.
29. Dan Breznitz, *Innovation and the State*, 117.
30. Li Tang, Michael Murphree, and Dan Breznitz, "Structured Uncertainty: A Pilot Study on Innovation in China's Mobile Phone Handset Industry," *Journal of Technology Transfer* 41, no. 5 (2016): 1181–1184.
31. Breznitz and Murphree, *Run of the Red Queen*, 180–181, 183–184.
32. Breznitz and Murphree, *Run of the Red Queen*, 15–16.

Chapter 2

1. Naomi R. Lamoreaux, Margaret Levenstein, and Kenneth L. Sokoloff, "Mobilizing Venture Capital during the Second Industrial Revolution: Cleveland, Ohio, 1870–1920," *Capitalism and Society* 1, no. 3 (2006): 3.
2. Naomi R. Lamoreaux and Kenneth Lee Sokoloff, "Financing Invention during the Second Industrial Revolution: Cleveland, Ohio, 1870–1920," in *Financing Innovation in the United States, 1870 to the Present*, ed. Naomi R. Lamoreaux and Kenneth L. Sokoloff (Cambridge, MA: MIT Press, 2007), 46.
3. Lamoreaux and Sokoloff, "Financing Invention during the Second Industrial Revolution," 48, 49–50, 58.
4. Lamoreaux, Levenstein, and Sokoloff, "Mobilizing Venture Capital during the Second Industrial Revolution," 7. Other corporations traded at the CSE include the Eaton Manufacturing Company, Dow Chemical Company, Firestone Tire and Rubber Company, Goodyear Tire and Rubber Company, Otis Steel Company, Packer Corporation, Peerless Motor Car Corporation, Standard Oil of Ohio (and New Jersey), Timken Roller Bearing Company, United States Steel Corporation, and Vlchek Tool Company.
5. The two universities eventually merged in 1967 to form Case Western Reserve University.
6. Michael S. Fogarty, Gasper S. Garofalo, and David C. Hammack, *Cleveland from Startup to the Present: Innovation and Entrepreneurship in the 19th and Early 20th Centuries* (Cleveland: Center for Regional Economic Issues, Weatherhead School of Management, Case Western Reserve University, 2002), 22, 30–35, 43.
7. William Dennis Keating, Norman Krumholz, and David C. Perry, *Cleveland: A Metropolitan Reader* (Kent, OH: Kent State University Press, 1995), 46; David Stradling and Richard Stradling, "Perceptions of the Burning River: Deindustrialization and

Cleveland's Cuyahoga River," *Environmental History* 13, no. 3 (2008): 517; Case Western Reserve University, "ECONOMY," *Encyclopedia of Cleveland History*, May 28, 2018; "Cleveland, Ohio Population History, 1840 – 2017," Cleveland Ohio, City, BiggestUSCities.com, accessed 13 December 2019.

8. Keating, Krumholz, and Perry, *Cleveland: A Metropolitan Reader*, 45; Case Western Reserve University, "Cleveland Tomorrow," *Encyclopedia of Cleveland History*; Ben (Ben David) Armstrong, "Brass Cities: Innovation Policy and Local Economic Transformation" (PhD. diss, Massachusetts Institute of Technology, 2019), 114.

9. Paul Krugman, "Increasing Returns and Economic Geography," *Journal of Political Economy* 99, no. 3 (1991): 494–498; Michael E. Porter, "Clusters and the New Economics of Competition," *Harvard Business Review* 76, no. 6 (1998): 80–84; Masahisa Fujita and Jacques-François Thisse, "Economics of Agglomeration," *Journal of the Japanese and International Economies* 10, no. 4 (1996): 348; Clayton M. Christensen, *The Innovator's Dilemma: When New Technologies Cause Great Firms to Fail* (Cambridge, MA: Harvard Business Review Press, 2013), 10–12; Michael E. Porter, *The Competitive Advantage of Nations: With a New Introduction* (New York: Free Press, 1998), 71–73, 148–149.

10. Dan Breznitz and Mollie Taylor, "The Communal Roots of Entrepreneurial-Technological Growth—Social Fragmentation and Stagnation: Reflection on Atlanta's Technology Cluster," *Entrepreneurship & Regional Development* 26, no. 3–4 (2014): 382.

11. Breznitz and Taylor, "Communal Roots of Entrepreneurial-Technological Growth," 382.

12. Breznitz and Taylor, "Communal Roots of Entrepreneurial-Technological Growth," 382; T. R. Reid, "'Crosstalk' Gets Caught in Crossfire of Competition," *Washington Post*, April 14, 1986.

13. Breznitz and Taylor, "Communal Roots of Entrepreneurial-Technological Growth," 385. Richard L. Florida, *The Rise of the Creative Class: And How It's Transforming Work, Leisure, Community and Everyday Life* (New York: Basic Books, 2002).

14. Breznitz and Taylor, "Communal Roots of Entrepreneurial-Technological Growth," 385.

15. "Company Timeline," About Us, ISS, web.archive, April 20, 2007, accessed July 24, 2019.

16. "Appcelerator Secures $4.1 Million in Series A Venture Funding," PR Newswire, December 9, 2008 . Scott Burkett, "Standing at the Crossroads in the ATL," Scott Burkett's Pothole on the Infobahn (blog), August 2, 2008, http://www.scottburkett.com/atlanta-business-scene/standing-at-the-crossroads-in-the-atl-794.html.

17. Jeff Haynie, "What's Wrong with the Atlanta Startup Ecosystem and How to Fix It," accessed February 16, 2014.

18. "Atlanta's Tech Industry Boom Began in 1970s," *Atlanta Business Chronicle*, April 14, 2008.

19. "Scientific-Atlanta Now Part of Cisco," *Atlanta Business Chronicle*, February 27, 2006.

20. "Appcelerator Secures $4.1 Million in Series A Venture Funding," PR Newswire, December 9, 2008.

21. Breznitz and Taylor, "Communal Roots of Entrepreneurial-Technological Growth," 387–392.

22. Steven Casper, "How Do Technology Clusters Emerge and Become Sustainable?: Social Network Formation and Inter-Firm Mobility within the San Diego Biotechnology Cluster," *Research Policy* 36, no. 4 (2007): 440–441; Anna Lee Saxenian, *Regional Advantage: Culture and Competition in Silicon Valley and Route 128* (Cambridge, MA: Harvard University Press, 1994), 32–33, 34–37; Homa Bahrami and Stuart Evans, "Flexible Re-cycling and High-Technology Entrepreneurship," *California Management Review* 37, no. 3 (1995): 71–72; Mark S. Granovetter, "The Strength of Weak Ties," *American Journal of Sociology* 78, no. 6 (1973): 1363–1365; Mark Granovetter, "The Impact of Social Structure on Economic Outcomes," *Journal of Economic Perspectives* 19, no. 1 (2005): 36–37.

23. Breznitz and Taylor, "Communal Roots of Entrepreneurial-Technological Growth," 387, 390.

24. Michel Ferrary and Mark Granovetter, "The Role of Venture Capital Firms in Silicon Valley's Complex Innovation Network," *Economy and Society* 38, no. 2 (2009): 341–353; Mark Granovetter, Emilio Castilla, Hokyu Hwang, and Ellen Granovetter, "Social Networks in Silicon Valley," in *The Silicon Valley Edge*, ed. Chong-Moon Lee (Stanford, CA: Stanford University Press, 2000), 239–241; Paul A. Gompers and Joshua Lerner, *The Venture Capital Cycle* (Cambridge, MA: MIT Press, 1999), 181, 183.

25. "PwC/CB Insights MoneyTree Explorer," PricewaterhouseCoopers, accessed November 24, 2019.

26. Breznitz and Taylor, "Communal Roots of Entrepreneurial-Technological Growth," 383–384.

27. "A Cambrian Moment," *Economist*, January 16, 2014; Dan Breznitz, "Startups Are a Great Start, but Not the Goal," *Economist*, April 4, 2014.

28. "Chronology of Automobiles," Diatto, http://www.diatto.com/EN/pagine/chronology.html.

29. Joseph Schumpeter, *Capitalism, Socialism and Democracy* (London: Routledge, 1976), 83–84.

Chapter 3

1. David Champion and Nicholas G. Carr, "Starting Up in High Gear," *Harvard Business Review*, July-August 2000, https://hbr.org/2000/07/starting-up-in-high-gear.

2. Alastair Sweeney, *BlackBerry Planet: The Story of Research in Motion and the Little Device That Took the World by Storm* (Hoboken, NJ: John Wiley & Sons, 2009), 76,77.

3. "Shopify Announces $7 Million Series A Funding from Bessemer, FirstMark, and Felicis," *Plus NEWS*, December 15, 2010; Shopify Inc, "Form F-1 Registration Statement" (Securities and Exchange Commission, April 14, 2015), from SEC EDGAR database, accessed July 12, 2019.

4. Bob Zider, "How Venture Capital Works," *Harvard Business Review*, November 1, 1998; Dan Breznitz, Chris Forman, and Wen Wen, "The Role of Venture Capital in the Formation of a New Technological Ecosystem: Evidence from the Cloud," *MIS Quarterly* 42, no. 4 (2018): 1147.

5. Yves Smith, "Fake 'Unicorns' Are Running Roughshod Over the Venture Capital Industry," Intelligencer, *New York Magazine*, November 14, 2018; Will Gornall and Ilya A. Strebulaev, "Squaring Venture Capital Valuations with Reality," *Journal of Financial Economics* 135, no. 1 (2020): 135, 140, 142; Martin Kenney and John Zysman, "Unicorns, Cheshire Cats, and the New Dilemmas of Entrepreneurial Finance," *Venture Capital* 21, no. 1 (2019): 42–43; Andrew B. Hargadon and Martin Kenney, "Misguided Policy? Following Venture Capital into Clean Technology," *California Management Review* 54, no. 2 (2012): 128–129.

6. Hyman Minsky, Irwin Friend, and Victor Andrews, "Financial Crisis, Financial Systems, and the Performance of the Economy," Private Capital Markets; A Series of Research Studies Prepared for the Commission on Money and Credit, *Hyman P. Minsky Archive*, Paper 232 (1960): 175–177; Hyman Minsky, "The Financial-Instability Hypothesis: Capitalist Processes and the Behavior of the Economy," in *Financial Crises: Theory, History, and Policy*, ed. Charles P. Kindleberger and Jean-Pierre Laffargue (Cambridge: Cambridge University Press, 1982), 24–26, 30–33; Hyman Minsky, "A Theory of Systemic Fragility," in *Financial Crises: Institutions and Markets in a Fragile Environment*, ed. E. D. Altman and A. W. Sametz (New York: John Wiley & Sons, 1977), 145–147.

7. Dan Breznitz, "Industrial R&D as a National Policy: Horizontal Technology Policies and Industry-State Co-evolution in the Growth of the Israeli Software Industry," *Research Policy* 36, no. 9 (2007): 1465–1466; Breznitz, Forman, and Wen, "The Role of Venture Capital," 1157,1165; Dan Breznitz, *Innovation and the State: Political Choice and Strategies for Growth in Israel, Taiwan, and Ireland* (New Haven, CT: Yale University Press, 2007), 62–96.

8. Breznitz, *Innovation and the State*, 42, 197, 218.

9. Dan Senor and Saul Singer, *Start-Up Nation: The Story of Israel's Economic Miracle* (New York: Random House Digital, 2011).

10. OECD, *OECD Economic Surveys: Israel 2018* (Paris: OECD Publishing, 2018), 8; Gil Avnimelech and Morris Teubal, "Strength of Market Forces and the Successful Emergence of Israel's Venture Capital Industry: Insights from a Policy-Led Case of Structural Change," *Revue économique* 55, no. 6 (2004): 1274.

11. OECD, *OECD Economic Surveys: Israel 2018*, 15, 39–40.

12. William A Sahlmann, "The Structure and Governance of Venture-Capital Organizations," *Journal of Financial Economics* 27, no. 2 (1990): 487, 490; Marco Da Rin, Thomas Hellmann, and Manju Puri, "A Survey of Venture Capital Research," in *Handbook of the Economics of Finance*, ed. George M. Constantinides, Milton Harris, and Rene M. Stulz (Amsterdam: Elsevier, 2013), 575.

13. Sahlman, "The Structure and Governance of Venture-Capital Organizations," 491; Breznitz, Forman, and Wen, "The Role of Venture Capital," 1147.

14. Peter A. Thiel and Blake Masters, *Zero to One: Notes on Startups, or How to Build the Future* (New York: Crown Business, 2014), 83–87; Breznitz, Forman, and Wen, "The Role of Venture Capital," 1147–1148.

15. Breznitz, Forman, and Wen, "The Role of Venture Capital," 1148.

16. Diane Mulcahy, "Venture Capitalists Get Paid Well to Lose Money," *Harvard Business Review*, August 5, 2014.

17. William H. Janeway, *Doing Capitalism in the Innovation Economy: Reconfiguring the Three-Player Game between Markets, Speculators and the State* (Cambridge: Cambridge University Press, 2018), 181–182, 203–208.

18. Martin Kenney, and Andrew Hargadon, "Venture Capital and Clean Technology," in *Can Green Sustain Growth?: From the Religion to the Reality of Sustainable Prosperity*, ed. John Zysman and Mark Huberty (Stanford, CA: Stanford University Press, 2014), 68–70; Hargadon and Kenney, "Misguided Policy?," 123, 125–129; Richard L. Florida and Martin Kenney, "Venture Capital-Financed Innovation and Technological Change in the USA," *Research Policy* 17, no. 3 (1988): 120–121, 127–129.

Chapter 4

1. Martin K. Perry, "Vertical Integration: Determinants and Effects," *Handbook of Industrial Organization* 1 (1989): 185–187; Eva Flügge, "Possibilities and Problems of Integration in the Automobile Industry," *Journal of Political Economy* 37, no. 2 (1929): 165–166; Ray T. Bohacz, "The River Runs through It," *Hemmings Motor News*, February 1, 2005; Joseph A. Russell, "Fordlandia and Belterra, Rubber Plantations on the Tapajos River, Brazil," *Economic Geography* 18, no. 2 (1942): 125–145; Koichi Shimokawa, "From the Ford System to the Just-in-Time Production System," *Japanese Yearbook on Business History* 10 (1994): 95; David Hounshell, *From the American System to Mass Production, 1800–1932: The Development of Manufacturing Technology in the United States* (Baltimore: Johns Hopkins University Press, 1985), 267–268; "Henry Ford's Bid to Buy-Up America's Mines," *Global Mining Observer*, October 5, 2018,

2. Robert Hessen, "The Transformation of Bethlehem Steel, 1904–1909," *Business History Review* 46, no. 3 (1972): 346–347; William Sisson, "A Revolution in Steel: Mass Production in Pennsylvania, 1867–1901," *IA: The Journal of the Society for Industrial Archeology* (1992): 88–89.

3. "Al Qaeda Forces in Standoff With Pakistanis; Iraq One Year Later," CNN WOLF BLITZER REPORTS (CNN, March 19, 2004), http://www.cnn.com/TRANSCRIPTS/0403/19/wbr.00.html.

4. After he became the 45th president, the Wharton School seems to be distancing itself from Trump. Nonetheless, in the past Wharton was very proud of its 1968 alumnus. In 1984 Trump was given Wharton Entrepreneurial Club's first annual "Entrepreneur of the Year" award, in 1987 he was elected to Wharton's Board of Overseers, and in 2006–2007 he was featured in Wharton's alumni magazine's list of 125 influential people and ideas, celebrating Wharton's 125th anniversary.

5. Frederick Winslow Taylor, *The Principles of Scientific Management* (New York: Harper & Brothers, 1919), 37–39; Horace Bookwalter Drury, *Scientific Management: A History and Criticism*, Studies in History, Economics and Public Law, edited by the Faculty of Political Science of Columbia University, vol. 65, no. 2; whole no. 157 (New York: Columbia University, 1915), 100; Henry Rand Hatfield, "The Taylor White Process for Tool Steel," *Journal of Political Economy* 8, no. 4 (1900): 538–539.

6. Marcelo Prince and Willa Plank, "A Short History of Apple's Manufacturing in the U.S.," *Wall Street Journal*, December 6, 2012.

7. Donald L. Barlett and James B. Steele, "Apple's American Job Disaster," *Philadelphia Inquirer*, November 20, 2011.

8. "Apple Will Buy Colorado Plant," *New York Times*, March 21, 1991, sec. Business Day.

9. Prince and Plank, "A Short History"; Patrick Moorhead, "Who Are Apple's IPhone Contract Manufacturers?" *Forbes*, April 13, 2019.

10. Paul Krugman, "Paul Krugman Explains Trade and Tariffs," *New York Times*, March 15, 2018, sec. Opinion.

11. Charles Duhigg and Keith Bradsher, "Apple, America and a Squeezed Middle Class," *New York Times*, January 21, 2012, sec. Business Day.

12. Nathan Rosenberg, *Inside the Black Box: Technology and Economics* (Cambridge: Cambridge University Press, 1983), 3–4.

13. Amie Tsang and Adam Satariano, "Apple to Add $1 Billion Campus in Austin, Tex., in Broad U.S. Hiring Push," *New York Times*, December 13, 2018, sec. Technology; Jack Nicas, "A Tiny Screw Shows Why IPhones Won't Be 'Assembled in U.S.A,'" *New York Times*, January 28, 2019, sec. Technology.

14. Dan Breznitz and Michael Murphree, *Run of the Red Queen: Government, Innovation, Globalization, and Economic Growth in China* (New Haven: Yale University Press, 2011), 35.

Chapter 5

1. OECD, *Education Policy Outlook 2018: Putting Student Learning at the Centre* (Paris: OECD, 2018), 195; "World University Rankings," *Times Higher Education*, August 20, 2019; Author's own calculations; Clarivate Analytics and Thomson Reuters, "InCites Dataset," in *InCites: Calibrate Your Strategic Research Vision* (November 26, 2019), distributed by Thomson Reuters, can also be found at https://incites.clarivate.com

2. Authors own calculations.

3. "World University Rankings," *Times Higher Education*, September 26, 2018.

4. Chalmers Johnson, "Introduction: The Idea of Industrial Policy," in *The Industrial Policy Debate*, ed. Chalmer Johnson (San Francisco: ICS Press, 1984), 3–26; J. K. Arrow, "Economic Welfare and the Allocation of Resources for Invention," in *The Rate and Direction of Inventive Activity: Economic and Social Factors*, ed. R. R. Nelson (Princeton, NJ: Princeton University Press, 1962), 609–626.

5. John Zysman, "How Institutions Create Historically Rooted Trajectories of Growth," *Industrial and Corporate Change* 3, no. 1 (1994): 265–268, 279–280; John Zysman, *Governments, Markets, and Growth: Financial Systems and the Politics of Industrial Change*, vol. 15 (Ithaca, NY: Cornell University Press, 1984), 69–73, 80–81, 285–287, 303–305; Dan Breznitz and John Zysman, "Conclusion: A Third Globalization, Lessons for Sustained Growth?," in *The Third Globalization: Can Wealthy Nations Stay Rich in the Twenty-First Century?*, ed. Dan Breznitz and John Zysman (New York: Oxford University Press, 2013), 375, 383; John Zysman and Dan Breznitz, "Double Bind: Governing the Economy in an ICT Era," *Governance* 25, no. 1 (2012): 130–131, 144–146.

6. Dan Breznitz and Peter Cowhey, "America's Two Systems of Innovation: Innovation for Production in Fostering US Growth," *Innovations: Technology, Governance, Globalization* 7, no. 3 (2012): 127–154; Dan Breznitz and Guilio Buciuni, "Keeping Up in an Era of Global Specialization: Semi-public Goods and the Competitiveness of Integrated Manufacturing Districts," in *The Oxford Handbook of Local Competitiveness* (Oxford: Oxford University Press, 2015): 102–125; Dan Breznitz and Michael Murphree, "China's Run—Economic Growth, Policy, Interdependencies, and Implications for Diverse Innovation Policies in a World of Fragmented Production," in *The Third Globalization: Can Wealthy Nations Stay Rich in the Twenty-First Century*, ed. Dan Breznitz and John Zysman (Oxford: Oxford University Press, 2013), 35–56.

7. Harald Bathelt, Anders Malmberg, and Peter Maskell, "Clusters and Knowledge: Local Buzz, Global Pipelines and the Process of Knowledge Creation," *Progress in Human Geography* 28, no. 1 (2004): 45–47; Neil M Coe, Peter Dicken, and Martin Hess, "Global Production Networks: Realizing the Potential," *Journal of Economic Geography* 8, no. 3 (2008): 272–274; Peter Maskell and Anders Malmberg, "Myopia, Knowledge Development and Cluster Evolution," *Journal of Economic Geography* 7, no. 5 (2007): 612–613; Harald Bathelt, Francesca Golfetto, and Diego Rinallo, *Trade Shows in the Globalizing Knowledge Economy* (Oxford: Oxford University Press, 2014), 55; Henry Wai-chung Yeung, *Strategic Coupling: East Asian Industrial Transformation in the New Global Economy* (Ithaca, NY: Cornell University Press, 2016), 4, 54–56.

8. Dan Breznitz, "Collaborative Public Space in a National Innovation System: A Case Study of the Israeli Military's Impact on the Software Industry," *Industry & Innovation* 12, no. 1 (2005): 37–38; Breznitz and Cowhey, "America's Two Systems of Innovation," 134; D. P. Angel, "High-Technology Agglomeration and the Labor Market: The Case of Silicon Valley," *Environment and Planning A: Economy and Space* 23, no. 10 (October 1991): 1507–1508.

9. Michael J, Piore and Andrew Schrank, *Root-Cause Regulation: Protecting Work and Workers in the Twenty-first Century* (Cambridge, MA: Harvard University Press, 2018), 30–35, 50, 75–76.

10. Erik Roth, Jeongmin Seong, and Jonathan Woetzel, "Gauging the Strength of Chinese Innovation," (Washington, DC: McKinsey Global Institute, 2015), https://www.mckinsey.com/business-functions/strategy-and-corporate-finance/our-insights/gauging-the-strength-of-chinese-innovation; Juro Osawa, "The Rise of China's Innovation Machine," *Wall Street Journal*, January 16, 2014; Dan Prud'homme

and Max von Zedtwitz, "The Changing Face of Innovation in China," *MIT Sloan Management Review* 59, no. 3 (2018): 24–32.

11. Dan Breznitz and Michael Murphree, *Run of the Red Queen: Government, Innovation, Globalization, and Economic Growth in China* (New Haven: Yale University Press, 2011), 161; Hsien-che Lai, Yi-Chia Chiu, and Horng-der Leu, "Innovation Capacity Comparison of China's Information Technology Industrial Clusters: The Case of Shanghai, Kunshan, Shenzhen and Dongguan," *Technology Analysis & Strategic Management* 17, no. 3 (2005): 304–306; Hongbin Li, Lei Li, Binzhen Wu, and Yanyan Xiong, "The End of Cheap Chinese Labor," *Journal of Economic Perspectives* 26, no. 4 (2012): 57–74; Adam Segal, *Digital Dragon: High-Technology Enterprises in China* (Ithaca, NY: Cornell University Press, 2003), 121–122.

12. Douglas Zhihua Zeng, "How Do Special Economic Zones and Industrial Clusters Drive China's Rapid Development?," in *Building Engines for Growth and Competitiveness in China: Experience with Special Economic Zones and Industrial Clusters,* ed. Douglas Zhihua Zeng (Washington, DC: World Bank, 2010), 8–9; Yiming Yuan, Hongyi Guo, Hongfei Xu, Weiqi Li, Shanshan Luo, Haiqing Lin, and Yuan, "China's First Special Economic Zone: The Case of Shenzhen," in *Building Engines for Growth and Competitiveness in China: Experience with Special Economic Zones and Industrial Clusters,* ed. Douglas Zhihua Zeng (Washington, DC: World Bank, 2010), 56–57; Wei Ge, *Special Economic Zones and the Economic Transition in China,* Economic Ideas Leading to the 21st Century, vol. 5 (River Edge, NJ: World Scientific, 1999), 46.

13. Fu Jing, "Shenzhen Zen: Fishing Village Turned Boomtown," *China Daily,* August 4, 2008; Yuan et al., "China's First Special Economic Zone," 56; Wanda Guo and Yueqiu Feng, "Special Economic Zones and Competitiveness: A Case Study of Shenzhen, the People's Republic of China," PRM Policy Note, series no. 2 (Islamabad: Pakistan Resident Mission, Asian Development Bank, 2007); University of Michigan and Beijing Hua tong ren shi chang xin xi you xian ze ren gong si, *China data online = Zhongguo shu ju zai xian* (2002), distributed by All China Marketing Research Co.

14. The next section draws heavily on the research and knowledge of my friend and co-author Michael Murphree. I would strongly urge anyone who wants to understand the reality of production and innovation in the Shenzhen-Dongguan area from the micro-level up to read his work: Michael Murphree, Li Tang, and Dan Breznitz, "Tacit Local Alliance and SME Innovation in China," *International Journal of Innovation and Regional Development* 7, no. 3, (2016): 184–202; Li Tang, Michael Murphree, and Dan Breznitz, "Structured Uncertainty: A Pilot Study on Innovation in China's Mobile Phone Handset Industry," *Journal of Technology Transfer* 41, no. 5 (2016): 1168–1194.

15. Cai Fang and D. U. Yang, "Wage Increases, Wage Convergence, and the Lewis Turning Point in China," *China Economic Review* 22, no. 4 (2011): 601–610; Sophia Yan, "'Made in China' Isn't So Cheap Anymore, and That Could Spell Headache for Beijing," CNBC (online), February 27, 2017; W. Raphael Lam, Xiaoguang Liu, and Alfred Schipke, "China's Labor Market in the 'New Normal,'" IMF Working Papers

(Washington, DC: International Monetary Fund, 2015), 5–6; Wu Yan, "China's Labor Market: Shrinking Workforce, Rising Wages," *China Daily*, November 21, 2016.

16. Muhammad Shiraz, Md Whaiduzzaman, and Abdullah Gani, "A Study on Anatomy of Smartphone," *Computer Communication & Collaboration* 1, no. 1 (2013): 24–31.

17. Jici Wang and John H. Bradbury, "The Changing Industrial Geography of the Chinese Special Economic Zones," *Economic Geography* 62, no. 4 (1986): 314–318; Bi-Huei Tsai and Yiming Li, "Cluster Evolution of IC Industry from Taiwan to China," *Technological Forecasting and Social Change* 76, no. 8 (2009): 1093; Chun Yang and Haifeng Liao, "Backward Linkages of Cross-border Production Networks of Taiwanese PC Investment in the Pearl River Delta, China," *Tijdschrift voor economische en sociale geografie* 101, no. 2 (2010): 205–206; Dan Breznitz and Michael Murphree, "China's Run—Economic Growth, Policy, Interdependencies, and Implications for Diverse Innovation Policies in a World of Fragmented Production," in *The Third Globalization: Can Wealthy Nations Stay Rich in the Twenty-First Century* (Oxford: Oxford University Press, 2013), 45; Michael Murphree and Dan Breznitz, "Collaborative Public Spaces and Upgrading through Global Value Chains: The Case of Dongguan, China," *Global Strategy Journal* 10, no. 3 (2020): 556–584.

18. Tang, Murphree, and Breznitz, "Structured Uncertainty," 1181–1184; Ming Dong and Stephen Flowers, "Exploring Innovation in Shanzhai: The Case of Mobile Phones," *Asian Journal of Technology Innovation* 24, no. 2 (2016): 238–242.

19. Claudio Giachetti and Gianluca Marchi, "Evolution of Firms' Product Strategy Over the Life Cycle of Technology-Based Industries: A Case Study of the Global Mobile Phone Industry, 1980–2009," *Business History* 52, no. 7 (2010): 1138, 1147; Grazia Cecere, Nicoletta Corrocher, and Riccardo David Battaglia, "Innovation and Competition in the Smartphone Industry: Is There a Dominant Design?," *Telecommunications Policy* 39, no. 3–4 (2015): 172; Adam Satariano and Jack Nicas, "E.U. Fines Google $5.1 Billion in Android Antitrust Case," *New York Times*, July 18, 2018, sec. Technology; Angela Daly, "Recent Issues for Competition on the Internet: Google's Search and Advertising, the Apple App Store, and the AOL Huffington Post Merger," Paper presented at the 5th Competition Law and Economics European Network (CLEEN) Workshop, European University Institute, 2011, 3–9.

20. Tang, Murphree, and Breznitz, "Structured Uncertainty," 1184–1185, 1188; Paul Mozur, "U.S. Restricts Sales to ZTE, Saying It Breached Sanctions," *New York Times*, March 7, 2016; Karen Freifeld, "U.S. Lifts Ban on Suppliers Selling to China's ZTE," Reuters, July 13, 2018.

21. Breznitz and Murphree, *Run of the Red Queen*, 170–171; Murphree and Breznitz, "Collaborative Public Spaces and Upgrading," 23–24.

22. Breznitz and Murphree. *Run of the Red Queen* , 190; Wage Indicator, "Minimum Wage–Guangdong," *WageIndicator.org*, accessed November 14, 2019.

23. Breznitz and Murphree. *Run of the Red Queen*, 190–191.

24. Breznitz and Murphree, *Run of the Red Queen* , 191–192; Nanfang Ribao, "*Xiao Qi Lian Yin Ji Huo Chan Ye Chuang Xin Ji Yin*" [School-Business Marriage Enlivens Industry Innovation Gene], Nanfang Ribao, June 28, 2007.

Chapter 6

1. William J. Baumol, *The Free-Market Innovation Machine: Analyzing the Growth Miracle of Capitalism* (Princeton, NJ: Princeton University Press, 2002), 51–53; Nathan Rosenberg, *Exploring the Black Box: Technology, Economics, and History* (Cambridge: Cambridge University Press, 1994), 130; Nathan Rosenberg and L. E. Birdzell, *How the West Grew Rich: The Economic Transformation of the Industrial World* (New York: Basic Books, 1986), 20, 26–27.

2. Ingrid Lunden, "Google Takes 6.3% Stake In Google Glass Tech Supplier Himax Display as It Preps to Ramp Up Production," *TechCrunch* (blog), July 22, 2013; "'Microdisplay Products,' Himax Technologies, Inc.," himax.com, accessed 31 January 2020.

3. Liz Gannes, "The Backstory on Google's Investment in Google Glass Micro-Display Supplier Himax," *AllThingsD* (blog), July 23, 2013; Mark Gomes, "Google Glass Coming Early—Shares of Himax Are Poised to Triple," *Seeking Alpha*, March 5, 2013.

4. Otto Chui Chao Lin, *Innovation and Entrepreneurship: Choice and Challenge* (Singapore: World Scientific Publishing, 2018), 149–152.

5. Dan Breznitz, *Innovation and the State: Political Choice and Strategies for Growth in Israel, Taiwan, and Ireland* (New Haven, CT: Yale University Press, 2007), 104.

6. Breznitz, *Innovation and the State*, 104; Constance Squires Meaney, "State Policy and the Development of Taiwan's Semiconductor Industry," in *The Role of the State in Taiwan's Development*, ed. Joel D. Aberbach, David Dollar, and Kenneth L. Sokoloff (Armonk, NY : M.E. Sharpe, 1994), 175; Robert Wade, *Governing the Market: Economic Theory and the Role of Government in East Asian Industrialization* (Princeton, NJ: Princeton University Press, 2004), 98; S. G. Hong, *The Political Economy of Industrial Policy in East Asia: The Semiconductor Industry in Taiwan and South Korea* (Cambridge: Edward Elgar, 1997), 49.

   The similarities in names with the famous mainland universities are not accidental: Tsing Hua is the recreation in exile of Tsinghua University in Beijing, and Chiao Tung sees itself as the recreation of Jiao Tong of Shanghai, with both of them claiming to be the rightful successors of the Nanyang Public School.

7. Breznitz, *Innovation and the State*, 105; Douglas Fuller, Akintunde Akinwande, and Charles Sodini, "Leading, Following or Cooked Goose? Innovation Successes and Failures in Taiwan's Electronics Industry," *Industry and Innovation* 10, no. 2 (2003): 181–182; Wade, *Governing the Market*, 104.

8. Breznitz, *Innovation and the State*, 105; Wade, *Governing the Market*, 103–104.

   Now, partly thanks to the catchy nickname—Silicon Valley—and the idolization of veteran industry leaders such as Steve Jobs, Gordon Moore, Andy Grove, and Larry Allison, most people think that semiconductors and computing has always been a West Coast–based industry. The truth is that until the 1980s it was the East Coast that led the industry, with such companies as IBM, RCA, Digital (DEC), and NCR, and those of us who were computer enthusiasts (aka awkward geeks) in the beginning of the 1980s share the loving memory of Commodore, the greatest Canadian company in computing history (at least for anyone who was a kid in 1982), which ended up producing the bestselling home computer of all time—the Commodore 64.

9. Breznitz, *Innovation and the State*, 105–106; Meaney, "State Policy and the Development of Taiwan's Semiconductor Industry," 176; Fuller, Akinwande, and Sodini, "Leading, Following or Cooked Goose?," 181.

10. Breznitz, *Innovation and the State*, 106.

11. Hong, *The Political Economy of Industrial Policy in East Asia*, 53; Y. D. Hwang, *A Rise of a New World Economic Power: Postwar Taiwan* (New York: Greenwood Press, 1991), 81. At the time, advancement to the higher administrative positions in Taiwanese universities was political; hence, S. S. Hsu, the president of Taiwan's leading technical university, wielded considerable political power within the KMT.

12. Wen-Hsiung Lee and Wei-Tzen Yang, "The Cradle of Taiwan High Technology Industry Development—Hsinchu Science Park (HSP)," *Technovation* 20, no. 1 (2000): 55; John A. Mathews and Tong-sŏng Cho, *Tiger Technology: The Creation of a Semiconductor Industry in East Asia* (Cambridge: Cambridge University Press, 2000), 160, 166–168, 186, 191–192.

13. Breznitz, *Innovation and the State*, 106–107; Hong, *The Political Economy of Industrial Policy in East Asia*, 53–55; Mathews and Cho, *Tiger Technology*, 165, 167.

14. As with many other records and statistical data regarding the IT industry in Taiwan, there seems to be a slight disagreement between different researchers and official statements. For two different cost statements, see Hong, *The Political Economy of Industrial Policy in East Asia*; Mathews and Cho, *Tiger Technology*.

15. Martin Kenney, Dan Breznitz, and Michael Murphree, "Coming Back Home after the Sun Rises: Returnee Entrepreneurs and Growth of High Tech Industries," *Research Policy* 42, no. 2 (2013): 398–399; Wade, *Governing the Market*, 104; Breznitz, *Innovation and the State*, 107.

16. Breznitz, *Innovation and the State*, 223.

17. Jeorge S. Hurtarte, Evert A. Wolsheimer, and Lisa M. Tafoya, *Understanding Fabless IC Technology* (Amsterdam: Elsevier/Newnes, 2007), xvii, 7–8; Fuller, Akinwande, and Sodini, "Leading, Following or Cooked Goose?," 181; Dan Breznitz, "Development, Flexibility and R&D Performance in the Taiwanese IT Industry: Capability Creation and the Effects of State-Industry Coevolution," *Industrial and Corporate Change* 14, no. 1 (2005): 160–161.

18. Hurtarte, Wolsheimer, and Tafoya, *Understanding Fabless IC Technology*, 11; Fuller, Akinwande, and Sodini, "Leading, Following or Cooked Goose?," 182.

19. Breznitz, *Innovation and the State*, 112.

20. Lin, *Innovation and Entrepreneurship*, 165, 167.

21. John A. Mathews, "The Origins and Dynamics of Taiwan's R&D Consortia," *Research Policy* 31, no. 4 (2002): 638–639.

22. Mathews, "Origins and Dynamics of Taiwan's R&D Consortia," 638–639; Gregory W. Noble, *Collective Action in East Asia: How Ruling Parties Shape Industrial Policy* (Ithaca: Cornell University Press, 1998), 137.

Because US IP protection laws were revised to include computer codes only in 1980, Apple's lawsuit was one of the first of such suits worldwide. The best analysis, by far, of ITRI's consortia is Noble's *Collective Action in East Asia* (1998), a book that I highly recommend for anyone who wants to understand the origin of Asia's economic growth.

23. Noble, *Collective Action in East Asia*, 138–139. The BIOS system was the main, if not the sole, subsystem that IBM uniquely developed for its PC. Most of the rest of the PC was developed on the basis of open-system from standardized components that could be bought in the market.

24. Noble, *Collective Action in East Asia*, 138–139; Mathews, "Origins and Dynamics of Taiwan's R&D Consortia,"639; Pao-Long Chang, Chiung-Wen Hsu, and Chien-Tzu Tsai, "A Stage Approach for Industrial Technology Development and Implementation—The Case of Taiwan's Computer Industry," *Technovation* 19, no. 4 (1999): 237.

25. Lin, *Innovation and Entrepreneurship*, 151–152, 155–159, 195–196. Each Fraunhofer institute is devoted to specific technologies, which are key to the industries in the locality in which it is situated.

26. Breznitz, *Innovation and the State*, 118–119.

27. Reuters, "Company News; VIA Technologies is Sued for Patent Infringement," *New York Times*, September 8, 2001; "Intel and VIA Technologies, Inc. Settle Patent Infringement Cases," *Business Wire*, April 7, 2003; VIA Technologies, Inc. and Subsidiaries, *Consolidated Financial Statements for the Years Ended December31, 2001 and 2000 and Independent Auditors' Report*, 2002; VIA Technologies, Inc. and Subsidiaries, *Consolidated Financial Statements for the Years Ended December31, 2017 and 2016 and Independent Auditors' Report*, March 2018, 6.

28. Interviews with Intel, VIA, and FIC executives (1/17/2000, 3/24/1999).

29. P. R. Bhatt, "HTC Corporation: A Different Kind of Leadership of Cher Wang," *South Asian Journal of Business and Management Cases* 2, no. 2 (2013): 217–228; David B. Yoffie and Renee Kim, "HTC Corp. in 2009," *Harvard Business School Case 709-466* (Revised 2010): 2–3.

30. Business Wire, "HTC Touch(TM) Delivers New Touch Screen Experience," businesswire.com, June 5, 2007; "T-Mobile Officially Announces the G1 Android Phone," *TechCrunch* (blog), September 23, 2008; Yoffie and Kim, "HTC Corp. in 2009," 3, 11–13.

31. Tim Culpan and Hugo Miller, "HTC Takes Lead in U.S. Smartphone Market as Apple, RIM Decline," Bloomberg.com, November 2, 2011; Brad Stone, "Apple Sues Nexus One Maker HTC," *New York Times*, March 2, 2010; David B. Yoffie, Juan Alcacer, and Renee Kim, "HTC Corp. in 2012," *Harvard Business School Case 712-423*, May 2012 (Revised September 2012): 9–10.

32. Dante D'Orazio, "Valve's VR Headset Is Called the Vive and It's Made by HTC," *The Verge*, March 1, 2015; Paul Lamkin, "HTC Vive VR Headset Sales Revealed," *Forbes*, October 21, 2016; Mark Bergen et al., "Google Buys HTC Talent for $1.1 Billion to Spur Devices Push," Bloomberg.com, September 21, 2017; HTC, *HTC 2015 Annual Report*, April 2016, 19, 27–29, 45–46; HTC, *2018 HTC Annual Report*, 2019, 79 197, 237.

33. Robyn Klingler-Vidra, "Diffusion and Adaptation: Why Even the Silicon Valley Model Is Adapted as It Diffuses to East Asia," *Pacific Review* 29, no. 5 (2016): 770–771; Martin Kenney, Kyonghee Han, and Shoko Tanaka, "Scattering Geese: The Venture Capital Industries of East Asia: A Report to the World Bank," BRIE Working Paper, UCAIS Berkeley Roundtable on the International Economy, Working Paper Series (Berkeley: University of California, March 1, 2002), 36; Robyn Klingler-Vidra, Martin Kenney, and Dan Breznitz, "Policies for Financing Entrepreneurship through Venture Capital: Learning from the Successes of Israel and Taiwan," *International Journal of Innovation and Regional Development* 7, no. 3 (2016): 213.

34. Kenney, Han, and Tanaka, "Scattering Geese," 37. Lee-Rong Wang, "Taiwan's Venture Capital," *Journal of Industry Studies* 2, no. 1 (August 1, 1995): 89; Robyn Klingler-Vidra, *The Venture Capital State: The Silicon Valley Model in East Asia*, The Venture Capital State (Ithaca, NY: Cornell University Press, 2018), 84.

    The tax credit required that investors maintain their commitment for a minimum of two years. Taiwan's tax credit was expanded to include corporations investing in VC funds in 1991 (Kenney, Han, and Tanaka, "Scattering Geese"). Tax exemptions were also offered on the capital gains earned by VC managers investing in high-technology start-ups (Wang 1995) and for earnings from VC monies that were reinvested (Koh and Wong 2005, 26).

35. Thomas M. F. Yeh, "Venture Capital Industry Development in Taiwan," in *Fourteenth Conference on Pacific Basin Finance, Economics and Accounting*, July 14, 2006. Robyn Klingler-Vidra, *The Venture Capital State: The Silicon Valley Model in East Asia*, The Venture Capital State (Ithaca, NY: Cornell University Press, 2018), 82–83; 85–86.

36. Interestingly when I interviewed the same Taiwanese VCs about their investment in the United States, they were quite blunt about the fact that different financial and ecosystem regulations mean that they look for very different business models in the two places. They were all quite adamant that the same individuals will be given money to start companies based on very different business models (stage 1 versus stage 3 innovation), depending on the location in which they aim to start their company, Silicon Valley or Taiwan. One even gave an example of his long relationship with a Taiwanese serial entrepreneur, who after several successful financial exits in Silicon Valley, backed partly by the Taiwanese VC, decided he wanted to go back home and raise his family in Taiwan. To do so he had to change his business plan to those of an ODM/2nd generation IC component business, which was the demand of the VC as a condition of investing in a company based in Hsinchu Park. See Christopher Gulinello, "Engineering a Venture Capital Market and the Effects of Government Control on Private Ordering: Lessons from the Taiwan Experience," *George Washington International Law Review* 37, no. 4 (2005): 848.

37. A few examples out of the many are: Stefan Thomke and Ashok Nimgade, "IDEO," *Harvard Business School Case 600-143* (Cambridge, MA: Harvard Business School, 2000) (Revised October 2017); Ryan W. Buell and Andrew Otazo, "IDEO: Human-Centered Service Design," *Harvard Business School Case 615-022*, October 2014 (Revised January 2016); Tim Brown, "Design Thinking," *Harvard Business Review* 86, no. 6 (2008): 8; Teresa Amabile Brown, Colin M. Fisher, and Julianna Pillemer,

"IDEO's Culture of Helping," *Harvard Business Review* 92, no. 1 (2014): 54–61; Tom Kelley and Jonathan Littman, *The Art of Innovation: Lessons in Creativity from IDEO, America's Leading Design Firm* (New York: Currency/Doubleday, 2001); Bruce Nussbaum, "The Power of Design," *BusinessWeek*, May 17, 2004.

38. "Creating the First Usable Mouse," Work, IDEO, accessed 31 January 2020; Ryan W. Buell and Andrew Otazo, "IDEO: Human-Centered Service Design," *Harvard Business School Case 615-022*, October 2014 (Revised January 2016), 2, 6; Brown, "Design Thinking," 8; *ABC Nightline*, "IDEO Redesigns the Shopping Cart," in *The Deep Dive: One Company's Secret Weapon for Innovation* (New York: Films Media Group, 1999).

39. Ron Martin, Peter Sunley, Ben Gardiner, and Peter Tyler, "How Regions React to Recessions: Resilience and the Role of Economic Structure," *Regional Studies* 50, no. 4 (2016): 561–585; James Simmie and Ron Martin, "The Economic Resilience of Regions: Towards an Evolutionary Approach," *Cambridge Journal of Regions, Economy and Society* 3, no. 1 (2010): 27–43; Ron Martin and Peter Sunley, "On the Notion of Regional Economic Resilience: Conceptualization and Explanation," *Journal of Economic Geography* 15, no. 1 (2015): 1–42.

While resiliency is a useful concept, and indeed shows how the current is based on the past and how that past can be used to imagine the future, it misses too much of the contours of the evolutionary process. Evolution is a process of coming with workable new solutions that allow already existing organisms (in the case of economics, social systems) to survive, adapt, and prosper in a changed/changing environment. Our role as social scientists should not be only to celebrate continuity, but to explain how the new models are different from the past, and why.

40. Giulio Buciuni and Gary Pisano, "Knowledge Integrators and the Survival of Manufacturing Clusters," *Journal of Economic Geography* 18, no. 5 (2018): 1069–1089; Giulio Buciuni, Giancarlo Coro, and Stefano Micelli, "Rethinking the Role of Manufacturing in Global Value Chains: An International Comparative Study in the Furniture Industry," *Industrial and Corporate Change* 23, no. 4 (2013): 967–996; Giulio Buciuni and Vladi Finotto, "Innovation in Global Value Chains: Co-location of Production and Development in Italian Low-Tech Industries," Regional Studies 50, no. 12 (2016): 2010–2023; Dan Breznitz and Giulio Buciuni, "Keeping Up in an Era of Global Specialization: Semi-Public Goods and the Competitiveness of Integrated Manufacturing Districts," in *The Oxford Handbook of Local Competitiveness*, ed. David B. Audretsch, Albert N. Link, and Mary Walshok (Oxford: Oxford University Press, 2015), 102–125.

41. Buciuni and Pisano, "Knowledge Integrators," 1075.

42. Alessandro Brun, Federico Caniato, Maria Caridi, Cecilia Castelli, Giovanni Miragliotta, Stefano Ronchi, Andrea Sianesi, and Gianluca Spina, "Logistics and Supply Chain Management in Luxury Fashion Retail: Empirical Investigation of Italian Firms," *International Journal of Production Economics* 114, no. 2 (2008): 463; Romeo Bandinelli and Sergio Terzi, "An Exploratory Study on Product Lifecycle Management in the Fashion Chain: Evidences from the Italian Leather Luxury Industry," in *Industrial Engineering: Concepts, Methodologies, Tools, and Applications,*

ed. Information Resources Management Association (Hershey, PA: Engineering Science Reference, 2013) 1406.

43. Alessia Amighini and Roberta Rabellotti, "How Do Italian Footwear Industrial Districts Face Globalization?," *European Planning Studies* 14, no. 4 (2006): 497–498; Buciuni and Pisano, "Knowledge Integrators," 1069–1089; Buciuni and Finotto, "Innovation in Global Value Chains," 2010–2023; Breznitz and Buciuni, "Keeping Up in an Era of Global Specialization," 102–125.

44. Amighini and Rabellotti, "How Do Italian Footwear Industrial Districts Face Globalization?," 497; Roberta Rabellotti, "How Globalization Affects Italian Industrial Districts: The Case of Brenta," in *Local Enterprises in the Global Economy: Issues of Governance and Upgrading*, ed. Hubert Schmitz (Cheltenham, UK: Edward Elgar Publishing, 2004), 143; Buciuni and Pisano, "Knowledge Integrators," 1076–1077; Buciuni and Finotto, "Innovation in Global Value Chains," 2018–2019.

45. Rabellotti, "How Globalization Affects Italian Industrial Districts," 152–154; Amighini and Rabellotti, "How Do Italian Footwear Industrial Districts Face Globalization?," 497.

46. Buciuni and Finotto, "Innovation in Global Value Chains," 2018.

47. Giulio Buciuni and Gary Paul Pisano, "Can Marshall's Clusters Survive Globalization?," Harvard Business School Working Paper no. 15-088 (Cambridge, MA: Harvard Business School, May 13, 2015.

48. Gary P. Pisano and Willy C. Shih, *Producing Prosperity: Why America Needs a Manufacturing Renaissance* (Boston: Harvard Business Review Press, 2012), 56.

49. Breznitz and Buciuni, "Keeping Up in an Era of Global Specialization," 115–116.

50. A.C.Ri.B—Associazione Calzaturifici della Riviera del Brenta, "ACRIB System," *acrib. it*, accessed October 3, 2019.

51. Breznitz and Buciuni, "Keeping Up in an Era of Global Specialization," 116.

52. Breznitz and Buciuni, "Keeping Up in an Era of Global Specialization," 116.

Chapter 7

1. For more on the early history of the ICT industry in Israel, see: Teubal Morris, "The R&D Performance through Time of Young, High-Technology Firms: Methodology and an Illustration, " *Research Policy* 11, no. 6 (1982): 333–346; Gil Avnimelech and Morris Teubal, "Venture Capital Start-Up Co-evolution and the Emergence and Development of Israel's New High Tech Cluster: Part 1: Macro-Background and Industry Analysis," *Economics of Innovation and New Technology* 13, no. 1 (2004): 33–60; Dan Breznitz, "Innovation-Based Industrial Policy in Emerging Economies? The Case of Israel's IT Industry," *Business and Politics* 8, no. 3 (2006): 1–35; Dan Breznitz, *Innovation and the State: Political Choice and Strategies for Growth in Israel, Taiwan, and Ireland* (New Haven, CT: Yale University Press, 2007); Morris Teubal and Pablo T. Spiller, "Analysis of R&D Failure," *Research Policy* 6, no. 3 (1977): 254–275.

2. Efriam Katchalski, *The Report of the Committee to Inquire into the Organization of Governmental Research and Its Management* (Jerusalem: Office of the Prime Minister, 1968), in Hebrew.

3. Dan Breznitz and Darius Ornston, "The Revolutionary Power of Peripheral Agencies: Explaining Radical Policy Innovation in Finland and Israel," *Comparative Political Studies* 46, no. 10 (October 2013): 1231; Dan Breznitz, "Industrial R&D as a National Policy: Horizontal Technology Policies and Industry-State Co-evolution in the Growth of the Israeli Software Industry," *Research Policy* 36, no. 9 (2007): 1465–1471. France was Israel's main source of armaments and research collaboration until de Gaulle became president. Israel's supposedly historic alliance with the United States did not fully commence until the 1973 war. For more, see Breznitz, *Innovation and the State*, 41–96.

4. Breznitz, *Innovation and the State*, 51–53; Authors' Interview, United States, September 28, 2000. The view at the time was that industrial R&D was the domain of the public research institutions. Indeed, the official mission of the Katchalski committee, which is credited with creating the OCS, was to improve those institutions.

5. Morris Teubal, "A Catalytic and Evolutionary Approach to Horizontal Technology Policies (HTPs)," *Research Policy* 25, no. 8 (1997): 1163, 1165–1166; Breznitz, *Innovation and the State*, 54.

   Yaakov was also a protégé of Katchalski, who was then serving as the president of Israel. After leaving the OCS, Yaakov served as a special advisor for the World Bank to Taiwan and South Korea at the time they went through their rapid high-technology industrialization period.

   While for all intents and purposes the tool is one of conditionally repayable loans, officially those are designated as grants for accounting purposes. Otherwise they will have to be counted as a financial liability, causing more damage than good to the SMEs that receives them.

6. Authors' Interview, United States, September 28, 2000.

7. Authors' Interview, Israel, May 2, 2002.

8. Breznitz and Ornstein, "The Revolutionary Power of Peripheral Agencies," 15; Breznitz, *Innovation and the State*, 63–64; Stanley Fischer, Ratna Sahay, and Carlos A. Végh, "Modern Hyper- and High Inflations," *Journal of Economic Literature* 40, no. 3 (2002): 874.

9. Manuel Trajtenberg, "Innovation in Israel 1968–1997: A Comparative Analysis Using Patent Data," *Research Policy* 30, no. 3 (2001): 367; Breznitz, "Industrial R&D as a National Policy," 1468–1469; Breznitz, *Innovation and the State*, 84–85.

10. Breznitz, *Innovation and the State*, 62, 68.

11. Daron Acemoglu, "Technical Change, Inequality, and the Labor Market," *Journal of Economic Literature* 40, no. 1 (2002): 41; Sarit Cohen Goldner, Zvi Eckstein, and Yoram Weiss, *Immigration and Labor Market Mobility in Israel, 1990 to 2009* (Cambridge, MA: MIT Press, 2012), 1–3; Breznitz, *Innovation and the State*, 77; Breznitz, "Industrial R&D as a National Policy," 1477.

   While the wave of immigration from the former USSR created the pretext with which the OCS was able to secure finance and political agreement to start these four

programs, the Russian immigrants themselves have not become successful technological entrepreneurs, and seem to play the important but more minor role of providing highly skilled labor. However, their children, educated at least partly in Israel,
have become part and parcel of the Israeli high-tech industry. See Mark Feldman
and Michal Abouganem, "Development of the High-Tech Industry in Israel, 1995-
1999: Labour Force and Wages," Working Paper Series 1, (Jerusalem: Central Bureau
of Statistics, 2002), 27–28; Breznitz, *Innovation and the State*.

12. David Brodet, Moshe Justman, and Morris Teubal, eds., *Industrial-Technological
Policy for Israel* (Jerusalem, Jerusalem Institute for Israel Studies, 1990), in Hebrew;
Breznitz and Ornstein, "The Revolutionary Power of Peripheral Agencies," 14, 16.

13. Breznitz, *Innovation and the State*, 78; Economics, E. G. P. A. "The operational
achievements of the Israeli technology incubators program," *Report for the Technology
Incubators Administration, the Office of the Chief Scientist in the Ministry of Trade and
Industry, Israel* (2001); Interview with the Director of the Incubators Program (Israel,
February 8, 2000); Manuel Trajtenberg, "'R&D Policy in Israel: An Overview and
Reassessment," NBER Working Paper no. 7930 (Cambridge, MA: National Bureau
of Economic Research, 2000), 10–11; Tzamaret Rubin, Tor Helge Aas, and Andrew
Stead, "Knowledge Flow in Technological Business Incubators: Evidence from
Australia and Israel," *Technovation* 41 (2015):15; Gil Avnimelech, Dafna Schwartz,
and Raphael Bar-El, "Entrepreneurial High-Tech Cluster Development: Israel's
Experience with Venture Capital and Technological Incubators," *European Planning
Studies* 15, no. 9 (2007): 1188.

For two thorough reviews of the Israeli incubator program, see Economics, 2001;
Daniel Shefer and Amnon Frenkel, "For the Support of Entrepreneurship," Israeli
Financing Instruments for the Support of Entrepreneurship (Haifa, Israel: Samuel
Neaman Institute, 2002). Currently the incubators are semi-privatized, where man-
agement is now private but the R&D support to approved firms is still public and
comes from the IIA budget.

14. Robyn Klingler-Vidra, Martin Kenney, and Dan Breznitz, "Policies for Financing
Entrepreneurship through Venture Capital: Learning from the Successes of Israel
and Taiwan," *International Journal of Innovation and Regional Development* 7, no. 3
(2016): 210–211; Breznitz, *Innovation and the State*, 80. The first Israeli ICT company
to be listed on NASDAQ, Elscient, did it as early as 1972, one year after NASDAQ was
established. By 1993 there were already more than a score of IPO events involving
Israeli companies on NASDAQ (Breznitz, "Industrial R&D as a National Policy," 53,
79–80).

15. Breznitz, *Innovation and the State*, 83.

16. Klingler-Vidra, Kenney, and Breznitz, "Policies for Financing Entrepreneurship,"
210–211, 212–214.

17. For more on Yozma and the growth of the Israeli VC industry, see Avnimelech and
Teubal, "Venture Capital Start-Up Co-evolution," 33–60; Gil Avnimelech and Morris
Teubal, "Creating Venture Capital Industries That Co-evolve with High Tech: Insights
from an Extended Industry Life Cycle Perspective of the Israeli Experience," *Research
Policy* 35, no. 10 (2006): 1477–1498; Dan Breznitz and Amos Zehavi, "The Limits of

Capital: Transcending the Public Financer–Private Producer Split in Industrial R&D," *Research Policy* 39, no. 2 (2010): 301–312.

18. OECD (Organisation for Economic Co-operation and Development), *OECD Economic Surveys: Israel 2018* (Paris: OECD Publishing, 2018), 15, 18, 27, 37–38.

19. Breznitz, *Innovation and the State*, 91; Daniel Felsenstein, "The Making of a High Technology Node: Foreign-Owned Companies in Israeli High Technology," *Regional Studies* 31, no. 4 (1997): 377.

20. Breznitz, *Innovation and the State*, 67; Maria Fakhruddin, Pratique Kain, and Chenping Wang, *Economic Assessment Framework for Post BEPS Israel* (Toronto: Munk School of Global Affairs and Public Policy, 2017), 7–8.

21. Interviews with IIA officials in Toronto and Tel Aviv, 2018 and 2019.

22. OECD, *OECD Economic Surveys: Israel 2018*, 15, 39–40, 45; Harriet Sherwood, "Israeli Protests: 430,000 Take to Streets to Demand Social Justice," *Guardian*, September 4, 2011; Moshie Lichtman and Adrian Filut, "Build Smaller Apartments, Fines for Empty Homes," *Globes*, September 25, 2011, 2020; Timothy F. Bresnahan and Manuel Trajtenberg, "General Purpose Technologies 'Engines of Growth'?," *Journal of Econometrics* 65, no. 1 (1995): 83–108; Elhanan Helpman and Manuel Trajtenberg, "Diffusion of General Purpose Technologies," NBER Working Paper no. 5773 (Cambridge, MA: National Bureau of Economic Research, 1996). Israel Prime Minister's Office, "Cabinet Approves Trajtenberg Report," press release, October 9, 2011.

23. Amos Zehavi and Dan Breznitz, "Distribution Sensitive Innovation Policies: Conceptualization and Empirical Examples," *Research Policy* 46, no. 1 (2017): 330; OCS–Office of the Chief Scientist, "R&D Incentive Programs" (Jerusalem: Office of Chief Scientist, Ministry of Economy, State of Israel, 2014), 8.

24. Israel Ministry of Foreign Affairs, "Government Approves National Authority for Technology and Innovation," press release, June 21 2015.

25. Daanish Hussain, Travis Southin, and Christopher Villegas-Cho, "From Exit Nation to Startup Nation," White Paper (Toronto: Munk School of Global Affairs and Public Policy, 2016), 6–7.

26. CBC News, "McMaster-Based Company Nabs over $140M in Financing for Cancer Research," CBC News, April 3, 2019; Tom Hogue, "The Forge and Innovation Factory: Innovation and Incubation Work Well Together in Hamilton," *Hamilton Spectator*, November 7, 2019.

27. Harold Bloom, "Emergence of the Modern City: Hamilton, 1891–1950," in *Steel City: Hamilton and Region*, ed. Michael J. Dear, John Julian Drake, and Lloyd George Reeds (Toronto: University of Toronto Press, 1987), 122–123; W. P. Anderson, "The Changing Competitive Position of the Hamilton Steel Industry," in *Steel City: Hamilton and Region*, ed. Michael J. Dear, John Julian Drake, and Lloyd George Reeds (Toronto: University of Toronto Press, 1987), 209–210, 215–216; Peter Warrian, "Biotech and Lunch Buckets: The Curious Knowledge Networks of Steel Town," Innovations Systems Research Network (ISRN) Working Paper (Toronto: University of Toronto, June 2011), 7–8; "1930: McMaster University Moves to Hamilton from Toronto," *Hamilton Spectator*, September 23, 2016; Peter Warrian,

Canadian Metallurgy, Its Benefits and Contribution to the Economy and Society (Ottawa: Ingentium, 2020).

28. David Livingstone, "Melting the Core Steel Workforce: 1981–2003," in *Manufacturing Meltdown: Reshaping Steel Work*, ed. David Livingstone, Dorothy Smith, and Warren E. Smith (Peterborough ON: Fernwood, 2011), 9–71; "Innovation Policy Lab Database," Innovation Policy Lab, 2019.

Stelco—the Steel Company of Canada—was established in 1910 and had a successful phase as a leading global steel company until 2004, when it sought bankruptcy protection, from which it emerged in 2006. In August 2007 it was bought by US Steel, which renamed it US Steel Canada Inc. and delisted it from the Toronto Stock Exchange. US Steel itself then went into financial difficulties and bankruptcy protection, with most of the Hamilton activities.

29. Eric von Hippel, *Free Innovation* (Cambridge, MA: MIT Press, 2017), 144; Eric von Hippel, "The Dominant Role of Users in the Scientific Instrument Innovation Process," *Research Policy* 5, no. 3 (July 1, 1976): 213, 220–224, 231–232; Eric von Hippel, "Lead Users: A Source of Novel Product Concepts," *Management Science* 32, no. 7 (July 1, 1986): 796–797; Eric von Hippel, *Democratizing Innovation* (Cambridge, MA: MIT Press, 2005), 1–2, 4–5.

30. Peter Warrian and Allison Bramwell, "Innovation in an Industrial City: Economic Transformation in Hamilton," in *Growing Urban Economies: Innovation, Creativity and Governance in Canadian City-Regions*, ed. David Wolfe and Meric Gertler (Toronto: University of Toronto Press, 2016), 187–189; Warrian, "Biotech and Lunch Buckets," 17–18.

31. Warrian, "Biotech and Lunch Buckets," 18; Warrian and Bramwell, "Innovation in an Industrial City," 187–189; "Hospital History: The Beginning of Health Care in Hamilton," *Hamilton Health Sciences* (blog), July 7, 2016.

32. Interviews in Hamilton, July 2019.

33. Howard S. Barrows and Robyn M. Tamblyn, *Problem-Based Learning: An Approach to Medical Education*, Springer Series on Medical Education 1 (New York: Springer, 1980), 12–13; V. R. Neufeld and H. S. Barrows, "The 'McMaster Philosophy': An Approach to Medical Education," *Academic Medicine* 49, no. 11 (November 1974): 1042–1045; Howard S. Barrows, "Problem-Based Learning in Medicine and Beyond: A Brief Overview," *New Directions for Teaching and Learning* 1996, no. 68 (1996): 3–6.

34. David Sackett, "How to Read Clinical Journals: I. Why to Read Them and How to Start Reading Them Critically," *Canadian Medical Association Journal* 124, no. 5 (March 1, 1981): 555–558; David L. Sackett, "Tracking Down the Evidence to Solve Clinical Problems," in *Clinical Epidemiology: A Basic Science for Clinical Medicine*, 2nd ed. (Boston: Little, Brown, 1991), 335–354; David L. Sackett, "Surveying the Medical Literature to Keep Up to Date," in *Clinical Epidemiology: A Basic Science for Clinical Medicine*, 2nd ed. (Boston: Little, Brown, 1991), 359–376; Andrew D. Oxman et al., "Users' Guides to the Medical Literature: I. How to Get Started," *JAMA* 270, no. 17 (November 3, 1993): 2093–95.

35. Roger L. Sur and Philipp Dahm, "History of Evidence-Based Medicine," *Indian Journal of Urology* 27, no. 4 (2011): 487–489; David L. Sackett, "Evidence-Based Medicine," in "Fatal and Neonatal Hematology for the 21st Century," special issue, *Seminars in Perinatology* 21, no. 1 (February 1, 1997): 3–5; John A. Cairns et al., "Aspirin, Sulfinpyrazone, or Both in Unstable Angina," *New England Journal of Medicine* 313, no. 22 (November 28, 1985): 1369–1375; Gordon Guyatt et al., "Evidence-Based Medicine: A New Approach to Teaching the Practice of Medicine," *JAMA* 268, no. 17 (November 4, 1992): 2420–2425; "Medical Milestones," *The BMJ*, https://www.bmj.com/content/medical-milestones, accessed September 28, 2020.

36. Guyatt et al., "Evidence-Based Medicine," 2421–2422; David L. Sackett et al., "Evidence Based Medicine: What It Is and What It Isn't," *BMJ* 312, no. 7023 (January 13, 1996): 71–72.

37. "Partners," Centre for Probe Development and Commercialization, accessed January 21, 2020. https://www.imagingprobes.ca/partners/; "Governance Management," (Hamilton, ON: Population Health Research Institute), phri.ca, accessed January 21, 2020; "McMaster Opens $33M Biomedical Engineering and Advanced Manufacturing Research Centre," (Hamilton, ON: McMaster University, March 7, 2018), https://brighterworld.mcmaster.ca/articles/mcmaster-opens-33m-biomedical-engineering-and-advanced-manufacturing-research-centre/.

   Evan's continued to play and important role in the transformation of medical teaching and research, especially in population health. After McMaster he become the president of the University of Toronto (1972–1978), then the founding director of the Population, Health and Nutrition Department of the World Bank, before he became the first Canadian to be elected as the chair of the Rockefeller Foundation.

38. "Targeted Alpha Therapeutics," Technology, Fusion Pharma (website), https://fusionpharma.com/targeted-alpha-therapeutics/, accessed September 24, 2019; Centre for Probe Development and Commercialization (CPDC), Funded Networks and Centres, Networks of Centres of Excellence of Canada, June 28, 2016, https://nce-rce.gc.ca/NetworksCentres-CentresReseaux/CECR-CECR/CPDC-CDCT_eng.asp; "McMaster-Based Company Nabs over $140M in Financing for Cancer Research," CBC News, April 3, 2019, https://www.cbc.ca/news/canada/hamilton/research-announcement-1.5082767.

39. "Adapsyn Signs $162M Microbe-Mining Deal with Pfizer," FierceBiotech (website), January 10, 2018, https://www.fiercebiotech.com/biotech/adapsyn-signs-162m-microbe-mining-deal-pfizer; "Probing Genomes to Unearth New Uses for Old Drugs" (Ottawa: Chemical Institute of Canada, March 1, 2016.

40. "Technology & Science," Triumvira Immunologics (website), https://triumvira.com/technology-science/, accessed September 24, 2019.

41. Jack Miller, "Cap for Tooth Ready in Minutes, Thanks to Computer [HO2 Edition]," *Toronto Star*, October 13, 1986; Rick Weiss, "Chips, Bytes and New Technology; Computers Can Design Bridges and Crowns—But Are They Better Than the Old-Fashioned Kind?," *Washington Post*, January 10, 1989; Warrian, "Biotech and Lunch Buckets," 18–19; Warrian and Bramwell, "Innovation in an Industrial," 188.

42. "Our Story," Genesis Pain Relief Light (website), https://genesishealthlight.com/our-story/, accessed 21 January 2020; "Photodynamic Therapy: How Does It Work?," Illumacell Inc. (website), https://www.illumacell.com/how.html, accessed January 21, 2020.

Chapter 8

1. Shiri M. Breznitz, *The Fountain of Knowledge: The Role of Universities in Economic Development*, Innovation and Technology in the World Economy (Stanford, CA: Stanford Business Books, 2014), 69, 71–72, 76, 79.

2. Joshua Lerner, *Boulevard of Broken Dreams: Why Public Efforts to Boost Entrepreneurship and Venture Capital Have Failed and What to Do about It*, The Kauffman Foundation Series on Innovation and Entrepreneurship (Princeton, NJ: Princeton University Press, 2009), 10–14.

3. Dan Breznitz, Darius Ornston, and Steven Samford, "Mission Critical: The Ends, Means, and Design of Innovation Agencies," *Industrial and Corporate Change* 27, no. 5 (October 1, 2018): 883–896; Dan Breznitz and Darius Ornston, "The Politics of Partial Success: Fostering Innovation in Innovation Policy in an Era of Heightened Public Scrutiny," *Socio-Economic Review* 16, no. 4 (October 1, 2018): 721–741; Dan Breznitz and Darius Ornston, "The Revolutionary Power of Peripheral Agencies: Explaining Radical Policy Innovation in Finland and Israel," *Comparative Political Studies* 46, no. 10 (October 1, 2013): 1219–1245; Dan Breznitz and Darius Ornston, "Scaling Up and Sustaining Experimental Innovation Policies with Limited Resources: Peripheral Schumpeterian Development Agencies," in *Making Innovation Policy Work: Learning from Experimentation*, ed. Mark A. Dutz et al. (Paris: OECD, 2014), 247–284; Erkki Karo and Rainer Kattel, "How to Organize for Innovation: Entrepreneurial State and Organizational Variety," Working Papers in Technology Governance and Economic Dynamics (Tallinn, Estonia: Tallinn University of Technology, 2016).

4. On large pilot agencies, see Joseph Wong, *Betting on Biotech: Innovation and the Limits of Asia's Developmental State* (Ithaca, NY: Cornell University Press, 2011). On small, lightly funded innovation agencies, see Breznitz and Ornston, "The Revolutionary Power of Peripheral Agencies," 1219–1245. For instances in which innovation agencies have clear technological objectives and conduct in-house research, see Erica R. Fuchs, "Cloning DARPA Successfully," *Issues in Science and Technology* 26, no. 1 (2009): 651–677. On innovation agencies that conduct policy insulated from political pressures, see Dan Breznitz, "Collaborative Public Space in a National Innovation System: A Case Study of the Israeli Military's Impact on the Software Industry," *Industry and Innovation* 12, no. 1 (March 1, 2005): 31–64. For innovation agencies that primarily function through embedding themselves within political and industrial structures, see Steven Samford, "Networks, Brokerage, and State-Led Technology Diffusion in Small Industry," *American Journal of Sociology* 122, no. 5 (March 1, 2017): 1339–1370.

5. Breznitz, Ornston, and Samford, "Mission Critical," 883–896.

6. Breznitz, Ornston, and Samford, "Mission Critical," 885–886.

7. Breznitz, Ornston, and Samford, "Mission Critical," 887; Håkan Gergils, *Dynamic Innovation Systems in the Nordic Countries: A Summary Analysis and Assessment* (Stockholm: SNS Förlag, 2005), 49.

8. Gergils, *Dynamic Innovation Systems in the Nordic Countries*, 49.

9. Gergils, *Dynamic Innovation Systems in the Nordic Countries*, 49–53.

10. Ash Amin and Daminan Thomas, "The Negotiated Economy: State and Civic Institutions in Denmark," *Economy and Society* 25, no. 2 (May 1, 1996): 270; Darius Ornston, *When Small States Make Big Leaps: Institutional Innovation and High-Tech Competition in Western Europe*, Cornell Studies in Political Economy (Ithaca, NY: Cornell University Press, 2012), 109–110.

11. Dan Breznitz and Steven Samford, "Innovation Agency Case Study: Canada's Industrial Research Assistance Program (NRC-IRAP)," (Washington, DC: Inter-American Development Bank, Division of Competitiveness, Technology, and Innovation, 2017), 6, 7, 10–11, 16, 20, 28–29.

12. Interview with IRAP ITA, August 2, 2016; Interview with Senior IRAP Official, July 15, 2016; Breznitz and Samford, "Innovation Agency Case Study," 6, 23–24, 26, 37; Goss Gilroy, "Evaluation of the NRC Industrial Research Assistance Program (NRC-IRAP)" (Ottawa: National Research Council, 2012) 6, 7, 16.

13. Interview with IRAP ITA, August 2, 2016; Gilroy, "Evaluation of the NRC Industrial Research Assistance Program," 23, 26; Breznitz and Samford, "Innovation Agency Case Study," 37.

14. Breznitz, Ornston, and Samford, "Mission Critical," 885–886.

15. Breznitz, Ornston, and Samford, "Mission Critical," 886; Wong, *Betting on Biotech*, 69.

16. Wong, *Betting on Biotech*, 69.

17. Wong, *Betting on Biotech*, 72–73; Breznitz and Ornston, "The Politics of Partial Success," 730.

18. Breznitz and Ornston, "The Politics of Partial Success," 730; Breznitz, Ornston, and Samford, "Mission Critical," 889; Wong, *Betting on Biotech*, 72–73.

19. Chia Yin Min, "Over $380 Million Invested in R&D, 19 Labs Set Up: A*Star," *The Straits Times*, March 19, 2015; Breznitz and Ornston, "The Politics of Partial Success," 730–731; Breznitz, Ornston, and Samford, "Mission Critical," 889.

20. Cristian Torres, "Gobierno define los siete sectores estratégicos para el desarrollo de clústers en el país," *Redbionova*, February 6, 2015; Gonzalo Rivas, "La experiencia de CORFO y la transformación productiva de Chile. Evolución, aprendizaje y lecciones de desarrollo," Serie Políticas Públicas y Transformación Productiva (Caracas: CAF, 2012); Breznitz, Ornston, and Samford, "Mission Critical," 889–890; Facundo Luna, "Ana´ Lisis de Agencias de Innovacio´n: Estudio de Caso: Corporacio´n de Fomento" [Analysis of innovation agencies: Case study: Growth Corporation of Chile]." (Washington DC: Inter-American Development Bank, 2017).

21. Paola Perez-Aleman, "Cluster Formation, Institutions and Learning: The Emergence of Clusters and Development in Chile," *Industrial and Corporate Change* 14, no. 4 (2005): 664–665, 668; OECD (Organisation for Economic Co-operation and Development), *OECD Reviews of Innovation Policy: Chile 2007* (Paris: OECD, 2007), 134, 136.

22. Breznitz, Ornston, and Samford, "Mission Critical," 889–890.

23. Breznitz, Ornston, and Samford, "Mission Critical," 888, 890.

24. Breznitz, Ornston, and Samford, "Mission Critical," 890.

25. Fuchs, "Cloning DARPA Successfully," 67; Michael J. Piore, Phech Colatat, and Elisabeth Beck, "NSF and DARPA as Models for Research Funding: An Institutional Analysis," in *The DARPA Model for Transformative Technologies: Perspectives on the U.S. Defense Advanced Research Projects Agency*, ed. William Boone Bonvillian, Richard Van Atta, and Patrick Windham (Cambridge: Open Book Publishers, 2020), 53–54; Michael J. Piore, "Beyond Markets: Sociology, Street-Level Bureaucracy, and the Management of the Public Sector," *Regulation & Governance* 5, no. 1 (2011): 149.

26. Erica R. H. Fuchs, "Rethinking the Role of the State in Technology Development: DARPA and the Case for Embedded Network Governance," *Research Policy* 39, no. 9 (November 1, 2010): 1139–1140; Piore, Colatat, and Beck, "NSF and DARPA as Models for Research Funding," 55.

27. Breznitz, "Collaborative Public Space," 36–38; Breznitz, Ornston, and Samford, "Mission Critical," 891; Steven Samford, "Innovation and Public Space: The Developmental Possibilities of Regulation in the Global South," *Regulation & Governance* 9, no. 3 (2015): 297; Fred Block, "Swimming against the Current: The Rise of a Hidden Developmental State in the United States," *Politics & Society* 36, no. 2 (June 1, 2008): 7; Michael Murphree and Dan Breznitz, "Collaborative Public Spaces and Upgrading through Global Value Chains: The Case of Dongguan, China," *Global Strategy Journal* 10, no. 3 (2020): 556–584.

28. Fuchs, "Rethinking the Role of the State," 1141, 1144; William B. Bonvillian and Richard Van Atta, "ARPA-E and DARPA: Applying the DARPA Model to Energy Innovation," *Journal of Technology Transfer* 36, no. 5 (July 19, 2011): 506–509.

29. Breznitz, Ornston, and Samford, "Mission Critical," 891.

30. Breznitz, Ornston, and Samford, "Mission Critical," 881.

31. Olli Rehn, "Corporatism and Industrial Competitiveness in Small European States : Austria, Finland and Sweden, 1945–95" (PhD diss., University of Oxford, 1996); Eli Moen and Karl Lilja, "Change in Coordinated Market Economies: The Case of Nokia and Finland," in *Changing Capitalisms: Internationalization, Institutional Change and Systems of Economic Organization*, ed. Glenn Morgan, Richard Whitley, and Eli Moen (Oxford: Oxford University Press, 2005), 369; Ornston, *When Small States Make Big Leaps*, 57, 62, 67; Breznitz, Ornston, and Samford, "Mission Critical," 892.

32. Breznitz and Ornston, "The Politics of Partial Success," 722, 725–726; Breznitz and Ornston, "The Revolutionary Power of Peripheral Agencies," 1230–1231.

33. Dan Steinbock, *The Nokia Revolution: The Story of an Extraordinary Company That Transformed an Industry* (New York: AMACOM, 2001), 28; Rehn, "Corporatism and Industrial Competitiveness," 230–231; Rehn, "Corporatism and Industrial Competitiveness," 278–282.

34. Ornston, *When Small States Make Big Leaps*; Breznitz and Ornston, "The Revolutionary Power of Peripheral Agencies," 1226; Eero Murto, Mika Niemelä, and

Tapio Laamanen, *Finnish Technology Policy from the 1960s to the Present Day: Public Sector Activities Promoting Research and Development* (Helsinki: Ministry of Trade and Industry, 2006), 31.

35. Murto, Niemelä, and Laamanen. *Finnish Technology Policy*, 31, 70.

36. Moen and Lilja, "Change in Coordinated Market Economics," 373; Ornston, *When Small States Make Big Leaps*, 36, 37; Breznitz and Ornston, "The Revolutionary Power of Peripheral Agencies," 1240; Charles Sabel and Anna Lee Saxenian, "A Fugitive Success," Sitra Reports (Helsinki: Sitra, 2008), 61; "Data Explorer," Eurostat, January 31, 2020.

    High-technology firms were still politically marginalized at this time. Indeed the motto of the main industry association was that it should export nothing "smaller than a horse."

37. Ornston, *When Small States Make Big Leaps*, 73; Darius Ornston, *Good Governance Gone Bad, How Nordic Adaptability Leads to Excess* (Ithaca, NY: Cornell University Press, 2018), 84–85; Breznitz and Ornston, "The Revolutionary Power of Peripheral Agencies," 1228;

38. Terttu Luukkonen, "Venture Capital Industry in Finland: Country Report for the Venture Fun Project," ETLA Discussion Paper (Helsinki: ETLA, 2006), 6; Ornston, *When Small States Make Big Leaps*, 74; Breznitz and Ornston, "The Revolutionary Power of Peripheral Agencies," 1228.

39. Luukkonen, "Venture Capital Industry in Finland," 9, 11; Risto Heiskala and Timo J. Hämäläinen,"Social Innovation or Hegemonic Change? Rapid Paradigm Change in Finland in the 1980s and 1990s," in *Social Innovations, Institutional Change, and Economic Performance: Making Sense of Structural Adjustment Processes in Industrial Sectors, Regions, and Societies*, ed. Timo J. Hämäläinen and Risto Heiskala (Cheltenham, UK: Edward Elgar, 2007), 84–85; Breznitz and Ornston, "The Revolutionary Power of Peripheral Agencies," 1228.

40. Breznitz and Ornston, "The Revolutionary Power of Peripheral Agencies," 1229.

41. Breznitz and Ornston, "The Revolutionary Power of Peripheral Agencies," 1230.

42. Breznitz and Ornston, "The Revolutionary Power of Peripheral Agencies," 1230.

43. Breznitz and Samford, "Innovation Agency Case Study," 37–39.

44. Block, "Swimming against the Current," 169–206; Fred Block, "Introduction," in *State of Innovation: The U.S. Government's Role in Technology Development*, ed. Fred L. Block, Matthew R. Keller, and Matthew R. Keller (London: Routledge, 2015), 4–20; John F. Sargent Jr., "The Obama Administration's Proposal to Establish a National Network for Manufacturing Innovation," CRS Report for Congress (Washington, DC: Congressional Research Service, 2012), 2–3, 4–6; Thomas A. Hemphill, "Policy Debate: The US Advanced Manufacturing Initiative: Will It Be Implemented as an Innovation—or Industrial—Policy?," *Innovation* 16, no. 1 (March 1, 2014): 67–70; William B. Bonvillian, "Advanced Manufacturing: A New Policy Challenge," *Annals of Science and Technology Policy* 1, no. 1 (March 30, 2017): 25–36, 58–70.

Chapter 9

1. Milton Friedman, *Capitalism and Freedom* (Chicago: University of Chicago Press, 1982).
2. Kenneth J. Arrow, "Economic Welfare and the Allocation of Resources of Invention," in *The Rate and Direction of Inventive Activity: Economic and Social Factors,* ed. R.R. Nelson (Princeton, NJ: Princeton University Press, 1962), 615–616.
3. Arrow, "Economic Welfare," 616; Richard R. Nelson, "The Simple Economics of Basic Scientific Research," *Journal of Political Economy* 67, no. 3 (1959): 297–306.
4. Arrow, "Economic Welfare," 616–617; Gene M. Grossman and Elhanan Helpman, *Innovation and Growth in the Global Economy* (Cambridge, MA: MIT Press, 1993), 16.
5. Marvin B. Lieberman and David B. Montgomery, "First-Mover Advantages," *Strategic Management Journal* 9, no. S1 (1988): 47–48.
6. Arrow, "Economic Welfare," 619.
7. Paul M. Romer, "Increasing Returns and Long-Run Growth," *Journal of Political Economy* 94, no. 5 (1986): 1003; Grossman and Helpman, *Innovation and Growth,* 16–17; Ivan P. Png, "Law and Innovation: Evidence from State Trade Secrets Laws," *Review of Economics and Statistics* 99, no. 1 (2017): 167, 178; Matt Marx, Jasjit Singh, and Lee Fleming, "Regional Disadvantage? Employee Non-compete Agreements and Brain Drain," *Research Policy* 44, no. 2 (2015): 54–56, 395, 403.

   Adding to the dysfunctionality of our IPR system, the latest trend in trade deals is incorporating draconian trade secrets and anti-compete laws. Our governments have been signing these trade deals, badly written by lobbyists, into effect left and right, and our children will suffer the consequences.
8. Edmund W. Kitch, "The Nature and Function of the Patent System," *Journal of Law and Economics* 20, no. 2 (1977): 266, 275–280.
9. Davis, Jacob W. Davis, Improvements in Fastening Pocket-openings, US Patent 139121A, filed August 9, 1872, and issued May 20, 1873; Carlo Saccon, "Rialto in Jeans as Venice Finds Cash for Repair," Reuters, December 14, 2012.
10. Ronald H. Coase, "The Problem of Social Cost," *Journal of Law and Economics* 56, no. 4 (2013): 843, 850–851; David J. Teece, "'Profiting from Technological Innovation: Implications for Integration, Collaboration, Licensing and Public Policy," *Research Policy* 15, no. 6 (1986): 290; Ashish Arora, Andrea Fosfuri, and Alfonso Gambardella, *Markets for Technology: The Economics of Innovation and Corporate Strategy* (Cambridge, MA: MIT Press, 2004), 117, 139–140.
11. Thanks to the pioneering work of many, but especially Bronwyn Hall, Adam Jaffe, and Manuel Trajtenberg, not only has the study of patents been systemized, but several data sets have made it a very accessible and incredibly rich source of data. (See Bronwyn H. Hall, Adam B. Jaffe, and Manuel Trajtenberg, "The NBER Patent Citation Data File: Lessons, Insights and Methodological Tools," Working Paper 8498 [Cambridge, MA: National Bureau of Economic Research, 2001].) The result has been an explosion of studies in economics, geography, business, history, and more or less anything else using patents. The study of patents now consists of a mid-sized cottage industry with multiple thousands of publications. This also led to follow-on

innovation as researchers struggle to identify key aspects in the patent data sets (for example, which John Smith is the author of which of the many patents whose author is John Smith), and the patenting of techniques to do so, some of them by my colleagues and friends, such as: John P. Walsh and Li Tang, 2014, Identification Disambiguation in Databases, US Patent 8799237B2, filed September 29, 2010, and issued August 5, 2014.

Thus, here I offer only a sample of works with regards to the findings presented out of the several tens of millions of words written about this subject: Edward J. Egan and David J. Teece, "Untangling the Patent Thicket Literature," Rice University Working Paper Series (Houston: Rice University, 2015); Carl Shapiro, "Navigating the Patent Thicket: Cross Licenses, Patent Pools, and Standard Setting, *Innovation Policy and the Economy* 1 (2000): 119–150; Heidi L. Williams, "Intellectual Property Rights and Innovation: Evidence from the Human Genome," *Journal of Political Economy* 121, no. 1 (2013): 1–27; Heidi L. Williams, "How Do Patents Affect Research Investments?," *Annual Review of Economics* 9, no. 1 (2017): 441–469; Alberto Galasso and Mark Schankerman, "Patent Thickets, Courts, and the Market for Innovation," *RAND Journal of Economics* 41, no. 3 (2010): 472–503.

In addition, two books that looks very critically at our current patent system, while having a too optimistic view of it as a whole (they mistakenly think it can be fixed), are: Adam B. Jaffe and Josh Lerner, *Innovation and its Discontents: How Our Broken Patent System Is Endangering Innovation and Progress, and What to Do about It* (Princeton, NJ: Princeton University Press, 2011); James E. Bessen and Michael James Meurer, *Patent Failure: How Judges, Bureaucrats, and Lawyers Put Innovators at Risk* (Princeton, NJ: Princeton University Press, 2008).

12. Federal Trade Commission, "Patent Assertion Entity Activity: An FTC Study," United States of America Federal Trade Commission, 2016, 15.

13. Federal Trade Commission, "Patent Assertion Entity Activity: An FTC Study," 47–48, 52; James E. Bessen, Jennifer Ford, and Michael J. Meurer, "The Private and Social Costs of Patent Trolls," *Regulation* 11 (2012): 26, 28, 31; Ira Glass, Alex Blumberg, and Laura Sydell, "When Patents Attack!," *This American Life* (podcast), July 22, 2011, MP3 audio, 58:01; *Last Week Tonight with John Oliver*, Season 2, episode 10, "Patents," aired April 19, 2015, on HBO.

14. Nancy Gallini and Adian Hollis, ""To Sell or Scale Up: Canada's Patent Strategy in a Knowledge Economy," *IRPP Study* 72 (2019): 13–16; Yuichi Furukawa, "Intellectual Property Protection and Innovation: An Inverted-U Relationship." *Economics Letters* 109, no. 2 (2010): 101; Yuichi Furukawa, "The Protection of Intellectual Property Rights and Endogenous Growth: Is Stronger Always Better?," *Journal of Economic Dynamics and Control* 31, no. 11 (2007): 3656–3657.

15. Wendy Dobson, Julia Tory, and Daniel Trefler, "NAFTA Modernization: A Canadian Perspective," in *A Path Forward for NAFTA*, ed. C. Fred Bergsten, and Monica de Bolle (Washington, DC: Peterson Institute for International Economics, 2017), 38.

16. Dan Breznitz, *Innovation and the State: Political Choice and Strategies for Growth in Israel, Taiwan, and Ireland* (New Haven, CT: Yale University Press, 2007), 148, 151; Carl Levin and John McCain, *Offshore Profit Shifting and the U.S. Tax*

Code—Part 2 (Apple Inc.), memorandum prepared for the Permanent Subcommittee on Investigations, of the US Senate Homeland Security and Government Affairs Committee, 113th Cong., 1st sess., 2013 (Washington, DC: Government Printing Office), 28–29; OECD, "Table II.1. Statutory Corporate Income Tax Rate," OECD. Stat, accessed January 31, 2020.

17. Levin and McCain, *Offshore Profit Shifting*, 4, 20.

18. It is worth noting that Singapore's Global Trading Program allows commodity-trading companies to avail themselves of substantially lower corporate tax rates. Levin and McCain, *Offshore Profit Shifting*, 18–19, 27–28.

19. Levin and McCain, *Offshore Profit Shifting*, 20–21, 23, 28; Simon Bowers, "Apple's Cash Mountain, How It Avoids Tax, and the Irish Link," *Irish Times*, November 6, 2017; William Lazonick, Mariana Mazzucato, and Öner Tulum, "Apple's Changing Business Model: What Should the World's Richest Company Do with All Those Profits?," *Accounting Forum* 37, no. 4 (2013): 264; Thomas R. Tørsløv, Ludvig S. Wier, and Gabriel Zucman, "The Missing Profits of Nations," NBER Working Paper no. 24701 (Cambridge, MA: National Bureau of Economic Research, 2018): 19–22.

20. Alex Barker, Vincent Boland, and Vanessa Houlder, "Brussels in Crackdown on 'Double Irish' Tax Loophole," *Financial Times*, October 9, 2014; Mary Cosgrove, "Ireland: Finance Bill 2017 Restricts IP Capital Allowance, Addresses MLI," MNE Tax, October 23, 2017, https://mnetax.com/ireland-finance-bill-2017-restricts-ip-capital-allowance-addresses-mli-24129; Jesse Drucker and Simon Bowers, "After a Tax Crackdown, Apple Found a New Shelter for Its Profits," *New York Times*, November 6, 2017; Stephen C. Loomis, "The Double Irish Sandwich: Reforming Overseas Tax Haven," *St.Mary's Law Journal* 43, no. 4 (2012): 836–839; European Commission, "State Aid: Irish Tax Treatment of Apple is Illegal," press release, August 29, 2016.

21. CPB Netherlands Bureau for Economic Policy Analysis, "Study on R&D Tax Incentives," *Taxation Papers* 52 (2015): 43–46; Annette Alstadsæter, Salvador Barrios, Gaëtan Nicodème, Agnieszka Maria Skonieczna, and Antonio Vezzani, "Patent Boxes Design, Patents Location, and Local R&D," *Economic Policy* 33, no. 93 (2018): 133–134, 141–144; Gary Guenther, *Patent Boxes: A Primer*, Congressional Research Service, 2017, 2, 5–6.

22. Ash Kelly, "Is B.C. an International Financial Hub or Corporate Tax Haven?," CBC News, May 4, 2017.

23. OECD (Organisation for Economic Cooperation and Development), "Background Brief—Inclusive Framework on BEPS" (Paris: OECD, 2017), 6–7; Rafael Sanz Gomez, "The OECD's Nexus Approach to IP Boxes: A European Union Law Perspective," WU International Taxation Research Paper Series 2015-12 (Vienna University of Economics and Business, 2015), 6; OECD, *Countering Harmful Tax Practices More Effectively, Taking into Account Transparency and Substance, Action 5-2015 Final Report*, OECD/G20 Base Erosion and Profit Shifting Project (Paris: OECD Publishing, 2015), 28–30.

24. "Artificial Intelligence (AI) in Canada," *Canadian Encyclopedia*, April 11, 2019; Vector Institute, "New Artificial Intelligence Research Institute Launched in Toronto to Anchor Canada as a Global Economic Supercluster," (Toronto: Vector Institute,

March 30, 2017); James Mcleod, "Innovation Nation: Montreal's AI Supercluster Is All about the Little Guy," *Financial Post*, February 20, 2019; Peter Cowan and Jim Hinton, "Artificial Intelligence Is Creating a Seismic Shift in the Way That People Interact with Technology. Research Institutions and For-Profit Companies Are Moving to Patent the Commercial Aspects of This New Area in a Land Grab Which Could See Rights Holders Reap Future Benefits," *IAM-Media*, 2018; Joe Castaldo, "Why Does Canada Give Away Its Best Ideas in AI?," *Macleans*, April 13, 2017, https://www.macleans.ca/politics/ottawa/why-does-canada-give-away-its-best-ideas-in-ai/.

25. Gallini and Hollis, "To Sell or Scale Up," 19–22, 25; James Hinton and Peter Cowan, "Canada Needs an Innovative Intellectual Property Strategy," *Globe and Mail*, May 19, 2017.

26. Warren Clarke, "A Worthwhile Intervention? The Potential Role for a Sovereign Patent Fund in Canada," in *New Thinking on Innovation, Special Report* (Waterloo: Centre for International Governance Innovation, 2017); Warren Clarke and J. W. Hinton, *Mobilizing National Innovation Assets: Understanding the Role of Sovereign Patent Funds*, (Toronto: DEEP Centre for Digital Entrepreneurship and Economic Performance, 2016): 2–3.

27. Murphree, Michael, and Dan Breznitz. "Standards, Patents and National Competitiveness." CIGI Paper, September 30, 2016: 2–3, 4. https://www.cigionline.org/publications/standards-patents-and-national-competitiveness. .

28. Michael Murphree and Dan Breznitz, "Indigenous Digital Technology Standards for Development: The Case of China," *Journal of International Business Policy* 1, no. 2 (2018): 234–252.

The desire to offer standards at the highest level of current technology necessarily means that *standards have to be based upon proprietary technology*. Two terms are relevant to this discussion: *embedded patents* and *essential patents*. Embedded patents are all those listed in the protocols of a technology standard. They are those submitted by actors involved in the drafting of a standard as quanta of technology for the development and completion of the standard. Such patents may be considered either essential or non-essential. Essential patents are those that must be used (infringed) if a firm or user adopts or creates a standard-compatible product. Thus, anyone who uses the standard must license them. To give a simple example, imagine a boutique steel firm develops a new alloy for an ultra-strong but lightweight steel. In the interests of building safety and cost-effectiveness, a construction standard is developed that mandates the use of steel with the capabilities matching those of the proprietary steel, and the firm's patents are, therefore, embedded in the standard. By definition, making a standards-compliant structure will have to use steel based on the proprietary technology. This is thus an essential IP. Firms seeking to comply with the standard are legally obliged to license the steel technology from the IP-holder, or else "invent around" the IP. However—given that any new steel would need to be certified as standards-compliant—licensing is far more time- and cost-effective.

29. Murphree and Breznitz, "Standards, Patents and National Competitiveness," 7–8.

30. Yin Pingping and Yuan Quan, "Young Minds Focused on IP Education," *China Daily*, November 1, 2019; Shen Changyu, "China—on Course to Become an IP

Powerhouse," *WIPO Magazine*, November 2016, 4–5; Yuan Quan and Yin Pingping, "Feature: IP Education Focuses China's Young Minds," *Xinhuanet*, September 24, 2019; Sean O'Connor, *How Chinese Companies Facilitate Technology Transfer from the United States*, U.S.-China Economic and Security Review Commission: Staff Research Report, 2019, 3; Bloomberg News, "Forced or Not? Why U.S. Says China Steals Technology," *Washington Post*, October 30, 2019.

31. Federal Trade Commission, "Patent Assertion Entity Activity: An FTC Study," United States of America Federal Trade Commission, 2016, 100–101; President's Council of Economic Advisers, the National Economic Council, and the Office of Science & Technology Policy, "Patent Assertion and U.S. Innovation," Executive Office of the President, 2013, 1, 4.

32. See for example, the USPTO 2012 initiative: "Third-Party Preissuance Submissions," Initiatives, United States Patent Office, accessed 21 January 2020,

Chapter 10

1. Alan O. Ebenstein, *Hayek's Journey: The Mind of Friedrich Hayek* (Basingstoke, UK: Palgrave Macmillan, 2003), 140; "The Sveriges Riksbank Prize in Economic Sciences in Memory of Alfred Nobel 1974," NobelPrize.org, accessed 21 January 2020.

   Nobel himself never thought there should be a prize for the "science of economics." However, for political reasons, the Bank of Sweden established a prize in memory of Alfred Nobel to celebrate the bank's 300th anniversary. The official name of the prize is "The Sveriges Riksbank Prize in Economic Science in the Memory of Alfred Nobel," which was first awarded in 1969 and quickly became known as "The Nobel Prize in Economics." The move has been highly successful in both raising the prestige of economics as a science and, even more importantly from the point of the view of the Swedish economists behind the move, changing the views in economics as to what is "good" economic inquiry (aka worthy of the prize) and what is not. A highly amusing endeavor by cynical economists is to count how many economists from the University of Chicago have won the prize versus all other economists in the rest of the world put together. In his acceptance speech, Hayek himself argued against giving such a prize to economists, specifically because of the elevated public status it grants to the awardee.

2. Friedrich A. von Hayek, "Individualism: True and False," in *Individualism and Economic Order*, Midway Reprint (Chicago: University of Chicago Press, 1980), 1–32; Friedrich A. von Hayek, "Economics and Knowledge," in *Individualism and Economic Order*, Midway Reprint (Chicago: University of Chicago Press, 1980), 33–56; Friedrich A. von Hayek, "The Meaning of Competition," in *Individualism and Economic Order*, Midway Reprint (Chicago: University of Chicago Press, 1980), 92–106.

3. Friedrich A. von Hayek, "The Meaning of Competition (1948)," in *The Market and Other Orders*, ed. Bruce Caldwell, vol. 15, The Collected Works of F.A. Hayek (London: Routledge, 2014), 105–116.

4. Eugene F. Fama, "Random Walks in Stock Market Prices," *Financial Analysts Journal* 51, no. 1 (1995): 76, 78; Eugene F. Fama, "Efficient Capital Markets: A Review of Theory and Empirical Work," *Journal of Finance* 25, no. 2 (1970): 384; Nathanaël Colin-Jaeger and Thomas Delcey, "When Efficient Market Hypothesis Meets Hayek on Information: Beyond a Methodological Reading," *Journal of Economic Methodology* 27, no. 2 (2020): , 106-107, 110-112 .

5. Owen A. Lamont and Richard H. Thaler, "Anomalies: The Law of One Price in Financial Markets," *Journal of Economic Perspectives* 17, no. 4 (2003): 191–202; Hyman Minsky, Irwin Friend, and Victor L. Andrews, "Financial Crisis, Financial Systems, and the Performance of the Economy," *Hyman P. Minsky Archive* 232 (1960): 175–177; Hyman Minsky, "The Financial-Instability Hypothesis: Capitalist Processes and the Behavior of the Economy," in *Financial Crises: Theory, History, and Policy*, ed. Charles P. Kindleberger and Jean-Pierre Laffargue (Cambridge: Cambridge University Press, 1982), 24–26, 30–33; Hyman Minsky, "A Theory of Systemic Fragility," *Hyman P. Minsky Archive* 231 (1977):12; Robert J. Shiller, *Narrative Economics: How Stories Go Viral and Drive Major Economic Events* (Princeton, NJ: Princeton University Press, 2019), 114–135, 228–238; Robert J. Shiller, "Speculative Asset Prices," *American Economic Review* 104, no. 6 (2014): 1492–1494.

6. Douglas O. Cook, Laurie Krigman, and J. Chris Leach, "An Analysis of SEC Guidelines for Executing Open Market Repurchases," *Journal of Business* 76, no. 2 (2003): 293–294; Amy K. Dittmar, "Why Do Firms Repurchase Stock," *Journal of Business* 73, no. 3 (2000): 334, 346, 347, 349.

7. William Lazonick and Mary O'Sullivan, "Maximizing Shareholder Value: A New Ideology for Corporate Governance," *Economy and Society* 29, no. 1 (2000): 13–35; William Lazonick, "Profits without Prosperity," *Harvard Business Review*, September 1, 2014; Adam Samson, "US Boards to Authorise $1tn in Stock Buybacks in 2018—Goldman," *Financial Times*, August 6, 2018, sec. Markets; Bob Pisani, "Stock Buybacks Hit a Record $1.1 Trillion, and the Year's Not Over," CNBC, December 18, 2018; David Rogers, "Senate Passes $787 Billion Stimulus Bill," *Politico*, February 13, 2009.

8. The literature on financialization is immense, big enough to fill several libraries. For those interested, two points of departure are from socioeconomics, which tried to analyze how companies came to view themselves as financial assets and how that changed the background of management from engineers, to marketeers, to financiers. A good book to begin with is Niel Fligstein's *The Transformation of Corporate Control*. For a more economic approach, a good first dive, delving deeply into the accounts and financial transaction of companies, is the work of William Lazonick; see William Lazonick, *Sustainable Prosperity in the New Economy?* (Kalamazoo, MI: W.E. Upjohn Institute, 2009); William Lazonick, "Innovative Business Models and Varieties of Capitalism: Financialization of the U.S. Corporation," *Business History Review* 84, no. 4 (2010): 675–702; William Lazonick, "The Financialization of the U.S. Corporation: What Has Been Lost, and How It Can Be Regained," *Seattle University Law Review* 36, no. 2 (2013): 857–910.

9. Jeff Sommer, "Are Markets Efficient? Even the Supreme Court Is Weighing In," *New York Times*, June 28, 2014, sec. Your Money.

10. Suzanne Berger, *Making in America: From Innovation to Market* (Cambridge, MA: MIT Press, 2013), 17–19, 31–33, 39–44, 47–49; Richard M. Locke and Rachel L. Wellhausen, *Production in the Innovation Economy* (Cambridge, MA: MIT Press, 2014), 4–5.

11. Berger, *Making in America*, 189, 190–193.

12. Berger, *Making in America*, 47.

13. Suzanne Berger, "How Finance Gutted Manufacturing," *Boston Review*, March 1, 2014.

14. J. M. Keynes, "The Pure Theory of Money: A Reply to Dr. Hayek," *Economica* 34 (1931): 394.

15. Shlomo Breznitz, "The Seven Kinds of Denial," in *The Denial of Stress*, ed. Shlomo Breznitz (New York: International Universities Press, 1983), 269, 278.

16. Berger, "How Finance Gutted Manufacturing.".

17. Shoshanna Solomon, "Israel to Provide Loan Guarantees for Startups, Tech Chief Says," *Times of Israel*, February 28, 2018.

18. Chau-Jung Kuo, Chin-Ming Chen, and Chao-Hsien Sung, "Evaluating Guarantee Fees for Loans to Small and Medium-Sized Enterprises," *Small Business Economics* 37, no. 2 (September 1, 2011): 206; Yeong-Jia Goo and An-Yu Shih, "Impact of Credit Guarantee on the Survival of SMEs and Default Prediction for SMEs: Empirical Evidence from Taiwan," in *ICSB World Conference Proceedings, Washington* (Washington, DC: International Council for Small Business, 2015), 2–4.

19. As an aside, using debt financing means that the companies taking debt have to develop a cash flow (that is, actually finding customers who are willing to pay for the services and products they offer), preferably reaching a positive one. This is something I view as healthy if your ultimate wish is economic growth, but many of my (vastly richer) finance friends think is old-fashioned and completely unnecessary. Companies after all, in their view, are just another financial asset to be bought and sold, not organizations aiming to grow and reach profitability.

20. Bronwyn H. Hall and Josh Lerner, "The Financing of R&D and Innovation," in *Handbook of the Economics of Innovation*, vol. 1 (Amsterdam: North-Holland, 2010), 616–617; Kee H. Chung and Peter Wright, "Corporate Policy and Market Value: A q-Theory Approach," *Review of Quantitative Finance and Accounting* 11, no. 3 (November 1, 1998): 291–293, 301.

21. Dan Breznitz, "Industrial R&D as a National Policy: Horizontal Technology Policies and Industry-State Co-evolution in the Growth of the Israeli Software Industry," *Research Policy* 36, no. 9 (November 1, 2007): 1471; "R&D Fund," Programs, Israel Innovation Authority (website), accessed 23 January 2020.

22. Dan Breznitz, *Innovation and the State: Political Choice and Strategies for Growth in Israel, Taiwan, and Ireland* (New Haven, CT: Yale University Press, 2007), 221.

23. Robert Jay Dilger and Oscar R. Gonzales, "SBA Small Business Investment Company Program," *Journal of Current Issues in Finance, Business and Economics* 5, no. 4 (2012): 413; "Investment Capital," Funding Programs, US Small Business Administration, accessed 30 January 2020.

24. Allan L Riding and George Haines Jr., "Loan Guarantees: Costs of Default and Benefits to Small Firms," *Journal of Business Venturing* 16, no. 6 (2001): 597; Thorsten Beck, Leora F. Klapper, and Juan Carlos Mendoza, "The Typology of Partial Credit Guarantee Funds around the World," in "Partial Credit Guarantees: Experiences & Lessons Focused," special issue, *Journal of Financial Stability* 6, no. 1 (2010): 12, 15; Jacob Levitsky, "Credit Guarantee Schemes for SMEs—An International Review," *Small Enterprise Development* 8, no. 2 (June 1997): 9; Ida C. Panetta, "An Analysis of Credit Guarantee Schemes: Suggestions Provided by Literature," in *Credit Guarantee Institutions and SME Finance*, ed. Paola Leone and Gianfranco A. Vento, Palgrave Macmillan Studies in Banking and Financial Institutions (London: Palgrave Macmillan UK, 2012), 28; Paola Leone and Pasqualina Porretta, "A Comparative Analysis of Credit Guarantee Systems," in *Credit Guarantee Institutions and SME Finance*, ed. Paola Leone and Gianfranco A. Vento, Palgrave Macmillan Studies in Banking and Financial Institutions (London: Palgrave Macmillan UK, 2012), 304–305.

25. Ingrid Lunden, "Intel Buys Mobileye in $15.3B Deal, Moves Its Automotive Unit to Israel," *TechCrunch* (blog), March 13, 2017, https://techcrunch.com/2017/03/13/reports-intel-buying-mobileye-for-up-to-16b-to-expand-in-self-driving-tech/.

Chapter 11

1. Dan Breznitz, "Data and the Future of Growth: The Need for Strategic Data Policy," Data Governance in the Digital Age series (Waterloo, ON: Centre for International Governance and Innovation, 2018), 67.

2. Gary Guenther, "Patent Boxes: A Primer," Congressional Research Service, 2017, 2, 5–6; Saraiu P. Mohanty, Uma Choppali, and Elias Kougianos, "Everything You Wanted to Know about Smart Cities: The Internet of Things is the Backbone," *IEEE Consumer Electronics Magazine* 5, no. 3 (2016): 60–70.

3. Walter Isaacson, *Steve Jobs* (New York: Simon & Schuster, 2011).

4. Dan Breznitz, Michael Murphree, and Seymour Goodman, "Ubiquitous Data Collection: Rethinking Privacy Debates," *Computer* 44, no. 6 (2011): 100–102; Cathy O'Neil, *Weapons of Math Destruction: How Big Data Increases Inequality and Threatens Democracy* (New York: Random House, 2017).

5. Tim Herrera, "You're Tracked Everywhere You Go Online. Use This Guide to Fight Back," *New York Times*, November 24, 2019.

6. Arizona Commerce Authority, "How Arizona Is Leading the Autonomous Vehicle Revolution," *Harvard Business Review*, February 15, 2018, https://hbr.org/sponsored/2018/02/how-arizona-is-leading-the-autonomous-vehicle-revolution; Daisuke Wakabayashi, "Self-Driving Uber Car Kills Pedestrian in Arizona, Where Robots Roam," *New York Times*, March 19, 2018, sec. Technology.

7. Jeffrey R. Brown and Austan Goolsbee, "Does the Internet Make Markets More Competitive? Evidence from the Life Insurance Industry," *Journal of Political Economy* 110, no. 3 (2002): 482, 487–488, 503, 505; Council of Economic Advisors,

"Big Data and Differential Pricing," Office of the White House, 2015, 12; Fiona Scott Morton, P. Bouvier, A. Ezrachi, B. Jullien, R. Katz, G. Kimmelman, A. D. Melamed, and J. Morgenstern, "Committee for the Study of Digital Platforms: Market Structure and Antitrust Subcommittee-Report" (Chicago: Stigler Center for the Study of the Economy and the State, University of Chicago Booth School of Business, 2019), 34.

8. Ali M. Al-Khouri, "Data Ownership: Who Owns 'My Data,'" *International Journal of Management and Information Technology* 2, no. 1 (2012): 2; Koutroumpis Pantelis and Leiponen Aija, "Understanding the Value of (Big) Data," in *2013 IEEE International Conference on Big Data*, 2013, 39–40; Louise Matsakis, "The WIRED Guide to Your Personal Data (and Who Is Using It)," *Wired*, February 16, 2019, https://www.wired.com/story/wired-guide-personal-data-collection/.

9. George Orwell, *1984: A Novel* (New York: Signet Classic, 1977). For an interesting, and chilling, read of the economics of this, see Shoshana Zuboff, *The Age of Surveillance Capitalism: The Fight for a Human Future at the New Frontier of Power* (London: Profile Books, 2019).

10. "The World's Most Valuable Resource Is No Longer Oil, but Data," *The Economist*, May 6, 2017; Jonathan Vanian, "Why Data is the New Oil," *Fortune*, July 11, 2016; Perry Rotella, "Is Data the New Oil?," *Forbes*, April 11, 2012; "Data is the New Gold," *Forbes Africa*, July 18, 2019.

11. Breznitz, "Data and the Future of Growth," 66–67; Morton et al., "Committee for the Study of Digital Platforms, 17.

12. Morton et al., "Committee for the Study of Digital Platforms, 13–14, 21–25; D. R. Baughman and Y. A. Liu, "Fundamental and Practical Aspects of Neural Computing," in *Neural Networks in Bioprocessing and Chemical Engineering*, ed. D. R. Baughman and Y. A. Liu. (Boston: Academic Press, 1995), 30–31.

13. Breznitz, "Data and the Future of Growth," 67.

14. Paul M. Romer, "Increasing Returns and Long-Run Growth," *Journal of Political Economy* 94, no. 5 (1986): 1003–1004; Paul M. Romer, "Endogenous Technological Change," *Journal of Political Economy* 98, no. 5 (1990): S75, S83–85, S89; Carlota Perez, "Technological Revolutions and Techno-Economic Paradigms," *Cambridge Journal of Economics* 34, no. 1 (2010): 187–188; Paul Stoneman and Giuliana Battisti, "The Diffusion of New Technology," in *Handbook of the Economics of Innovation*, ed. Bronwyn H. Hall and Nathan Rosenberg, vol. 2 (Amsterdam: North-Holland, 2010), 743–744.

15. Taking this insight further, my friend Gernot Grabher, together with his coauthor Jonas König, have remarked that data, which is coded life, should be considered as the fourth addition to the three Polanyian false commodities of capital, land, and labor; see Gernot Grabher and Jonas König, "Embedding Disruption: A Polanyian Perspective on the Platform Economy," *Environment and Planning A: Economy and Space* (forthcoming); Karl Polanyi, *The Great Transformation: The Political and Economic Origins of Our Time* (Boston: Beacon Press, 2001), 71–80.

16. Breznitz, "Data and the Future of Growth," 67–68.

17. Breznitz, "Data and the Future of Growth," 69; John Zysman, Martin Kenney, and Laura Tyson, "Beyond Hype and Despair: Developing Healthy Communities in the

Era of Intelligent Tools," Innovation Policy Lab White Paper (Toronto: Munk School of Global Affairs and Public Policy, 2019): 4–5; Dafna Bearson, Martin Kenney, and John Zysman, "Labor in the Platform Economy: New Work Created, Old Work Reorganized, and Value Creation Reconfigured," BRIE Working Paper (Berkeley, CA: Berkeley Roundtable on the International Economy, 2019), 2–3.

18. Innar Liiv, "Welcome to E-Estonia, the Tiny Nation That's Leading Europe in Digital Innovation," *The Conversation*, April 14, 2017, https://theconversation.com/welcome-to-e-estonia-the-tiny-nation-thats-leading-europe-in-digital-innovation-74446; Jaan Priisalu and Rain Ottis, "Personal Control of Privacy and Data: Estonian Experience," *Health and Technology* 7, no. 4 (December 1, 2017): 444.

19. Breznitz, "Data and the Future of Growth," 69–70.

20. Breznitz, "Data and the Future of Growth," 69; Shiri Breznitz, "The Geography of Industrial Districts: Why does the Biotechnology Industry in Massachusetts Cluster in Cambridge?" (MA diss., University of Massachusetts, Lowell, 2000), 31–32.

21. "Directive 2009/136/EC of the European Parliament and of the Council of 25 November 2009 Amending Directive 2002/22/EC on Universal Service and Users' Rights Relating to Electronic Communications Networks and Services, Directive 2002/58/EC Concerning the Processing of Personal Data and the Protection of Privacy in the Electronic Communications Sector and Regulation (EC) No 2006/2004 on Cooperation between National Authorities Responsible for the Enforcement of Consumer Protection Laws (Text with EEA Relevance)," Pub. L. No. 32009L0136, OJ L 337 (2009), 7.

22. Breznitz, "Data and the Future of Growth," 69–70.

23. Priisalu and Ottis, "Personal Control of Privacy and Data," 443–444.

24. My sincere hope is that at by the time you read this book, at least several systems to manage individual property rights will already be offered in the market. Currently, there are two interesting and different solutions. The first is openPDS (Personal Data Storage), which envisions a central reservoir of an individual's data to which applications send queries. The second is SOLID (Social Linked Data), which envisions using the core infrastructure of the Internet to allow for a decentralized data reservoir of an individual's data. For detailed descriptions of both, see Yves-Alexandre De Montjoye, Erez Shmueli, Samuel S. Wang, and Alex Sandy Pentland, "openPDS: Protecting the Privacy of Metadata through SafeAnswers," *PloS ONE* 9, no. 7 (2014): e98790, https://journals.plos.org/plosone/article?id=10.1371/journal.pone.0098790; Andrei Sambra, Essam Mansour, Sandro Hawke, Maged Zereba, Nicola Greco, Abdurrahman Ghanem, Dmitri Zagidulin, Ashraf Aboulnaga, and Tim Berners-Lee, *Solid: A Platform for Decentralized Social Applications Based on Linked Data*, Technical Report (Cambridge, MA: MIT CSAIL, 2016); Christian Bizer, Tom Heath, and Tim Berners-Lee, "Linked Data—The Story So Far," *International Journal on Semantic Web and Information Systems* 5, no. 3 (2009): 1–22.

25. This literature is fast expanding; for example, see Charles I. Jones and Christopher Tonetti, "Nonrivalry and the Economics of Data," NBER Working Paper no. w26260 (Cambridge, MA: National Bureau of Economic Research, 2019); Wilfried San-Zantman and Anastasios Dosis, "The Ownership of Data," Toulouse School

of Economics Working Paper no. 19-1025 (2019); Maryam Farboodi, Roxana Mihet, Thomas Philippon, and Laura Veldkamp, "Big Data and Firm Dynamics," NBER Working Paper no.25515 (Cambridge, MA: National Bureau of Economic Research, 2019); Daron Acemoglu, Ali Makhdoumi, Azarakhsh Malekian, and Asuman Ozdaglar, "Too Much Data: Prices and Inefficiencies in Data Markets," NBER Working Paper no. w26296 (Cambridge, MA: National Bureau of Economic Research, 2019); Dirk Bergemann, Alessandro Bonatti, and Alex Smolin, "The Design and Price of Information," *American Economic Review* 108, no. 1 (2018): 1–48; Dirk Bergemann, Alessandro Bonatti, and Tan Gan, "The Economics of Social Data," Cowles Foundation Discussion Paper no. 2203 (2019); Ajay Agrawal, Joshua Gans, and Avi Goldfarb, eds. *The Economics of Artificial Intelligence: An Agenda*, NBER Conference Report (Chicago: University of Chicago Press, 2019).

Bibliography

Acemoglu, Daron. 2002. "Technical Change, Inequality, and the Labor Market." *Journal of Economic Literature* 40 (1): 7–72.

Acemoglu, Daron, Ali Makhdoumi, Azarakhsh Malekian, and Asuman Ozdaglar. 2019. "Too Much Data: Prices and Inefficiencies in Data Markets." Working Paper 26296. Cambridge, MA: National Bureau of Economic Research.

Al-Khouri, Ali M. 2012. "Data Ownership: Who Owns 'My Data'?" *International Journal of Management & Information Technology* 2 (1): 1–8.

"Al Qaeda Forces in Standoff With Pakistanis; Iraq One Year Later." 2004. CNN WOLF BLITZER REPORTS. CNN, March 19, 2004. http://www.cnn.com/TRANSCRIPTS/0403/19/wbr.00.html.

Alstadsæter, Annette, Salvador Barrios, Gaetan Nicodeme, Agnieszka Maria Skonieczna, and Antonio Vezzani. 2018. "Patent Boxes Design, Patents Location, and Local R&D." *Economic Policy* 33 (93): 131–177.

Amabile, Teresa, Colin M. Fisher, and Julianna Pillemer. 2014. "IDEO's Culture of Helping." *Harvard Business Review* January 1, 2014.

Ambos, Tina C., Björn Ambos, and Bodo B. Schlegelmilch. 2006. "Learning from Foreign Subsidiaries: An Empirical Investigation of Headquarters' Benefits from Reverse Knowledge Transfers." *International Business Review* 15 (3): 294–312.

Amighini, Alessia, and Roberta Rabellotti. 2006. "How Do Italian Footwear Industrial Districts Face Globalization?" *European Planning Studies* 14 (4): 485–502.

Amin, Ash, and Daminan Thomas. 1996. "The Negotiated Economy: State and Civic Institutions in Denmark." *Economy and Society* 25 (2): 255–281.

Angel, D. P. 1991. "High-Technology Agglomeration and the Labor Market: The Case of Silicon Valley." *Environment and Planning A: Economy and Space* 23 (10): 1501–1516.

Angelelli, Pablo, Luna Facundo, and Claudia Suaznábar. 2017. "Agencias Latinoamericanas de Fomento de La Innovación y El Emprendimiento: Características y Retos Futuros." Washington, DC: Inter-American Development Bank.

"Appcelerator Secures $4.1 Million in Series A Venture Funding." 2008. *Venture Capital Reporter* (blog), December 9, 2008.

Armstrong, Ben (Ben David). 2019. "Brass Cities : Innovation Policy and Local Economic Transformation." PhD diss., Massachusetts Institute of Technology.

Arora, Ashish, Andrea Fosfuri, and Alfonso Gambardella. 2001. *Markets for Technology: The Economics of Innovation and Corporate Strategy*. Cambridge, MA: MIT Press.

Arrow, Kenneth J. 1962. "Economic Welfare and the Allocation of Resources for Invention." In *The Rate and Direction of Inventive Activity*, edited by National Bureau of Economic Research, 609–626. Economic and Social Factors. Princeton, NJ: Princeton University Press.

Arthur, Charles, and Technology Editor. 2010. "Apple Sues HTC over IPhone Patents." *Guardian*, March 2, 2010, sec. Technology.

Arthur, W. Brian, Steven N. Durlauf, David A. Lane, and SFI Economics Program, eds. 1997. *The Economy as an Evolving Complex System II*. Proceedings Volume, Santa Fe Institute Studies in the Sciences of Complexity, vol. 27. Reading, MA: Addison-Wesley.

"Artificial Intelligence (AI) in Canada." In *The Canadian Encyclopedia*. Accessed December 29, 2019.

Athreye, Suma S. 2005. "The Indian Software Industry." In *From Underdogs to Tigers: The Rise and Growth of the Software Industry in Brazil, China, India, Ireland, and Israel*, edited by Ashish Arora and Alfonso Gambardella, 7–40. Oxford: Oxford University Press.

Atlanta Business Chronicle. 2006. "Scientific-Atlanta Now Part of Cisco." February 27, 2006.

———. 2008. "Atlanta's Tech Industry Boom Began in 1970s." April 14, 2008.

Avnimelech, Gil, and Morris Teubal. 2004. "Strength of Market Forces and the Successful Emergence of Israel's Venture Capital Industry: Insights from a Policy-Led Case of Structural Change." *Revue Économique* 55 (6): 1265–1300.

———. 2004. "Venture Capital Start-Up Co-evolution and the Emergence & Development of Israel's New High Tech Cluster." *Economics of Innovation and New Technology* 13 (1): 33–60.

Avnimelech, Gil, Dafna Schwartz, and Raphael Bar-El. 2007. "Entrepreneurial High-Tech Cluster Development: Israel's Experience with Venture Capital and Technological Incubators." *European Planning Studies* 15 (9): 1181–1198.

Bahrami, Homa, and Stuart Evans. 1995. "Flexible Re-cycling and High-Technology Entrepreneurship." *California Management Review* 37 (3): 62–89.

Bandinelli, Romeo, and Sergio Terzi. 2013. "An Exploratory Study on Product Lifecycle Management in the Fashion Chain: Evidences from the Italian Leather Luxury Industry." In *Industrial Engineering: Concepts, Methodologies, Tools, and Applications*, edited by Information Resources Management Association, 1402–1417. Hershey, PA: Engineering Science Reference.

Baron, Justus, and Tim Pohlmann. 2018. "Mapping Standards to Patents Using Declarations of Standard-Essential Patents." *Journal of Economics & Management Strategy* 27 (3): 504–534.

Barrows, Howard S. 1996. "Problem-Based Learning in Medicine and Beyond: A Brief Overview." *New Directions for Teaching and Learning* 1996 (68): 3–12.

Barrows, Howard S., and Robyn M. Tamblyn. 1980. *Problem-Based Learning: An Approach to Medical Education*. Springer Series on Medical Education 1. New York: Springer.

Bartlett, Donald L., and James B. Steele. 2011. "Apple's American Job Disaster." *Philadelphia Inquirer*, November 20, 2011, sec. Opinion.

Bathelt, Harald, Francesca Golfetto, and Diego Rinallo. 2014. *Trade Shows in the Globalizing Knowledge Economy*. Oxford: Oxford University Press.

Bathelt, Harald, Anders Malmberg, and Peter Maskell. 2004. "Clusters and Knowledge: Local Buzz, Global Pipelines and the Process of Knowledge Creation." *Progress in Human Geography* 28 (1): 31–56.

Baughman, D. R., and Y. A. Liu. 1995. "Fundamental and Practical Aspects of Neural Computing." In *Neural Networks in Bioprocessing and Chemical Engineering*, edited by D. R. Baughman and Y. A. Liu, 21–109. Boston: Academic Press.

Baumol, William J. 2002. *The Free-Market Innovation Machine: Analyzing the Growth Miracle of Capitalism*. Princeton, NJ: Princeton University Press.

Bearson, Dafna, Martin Kenney, and John Zysman. 2019. "Labor in the Platform Economy: New Work Created, Old Work Reorganized, and Value Creation Reconfigured." BRIE Working Paper 3363003. Berkeley, CA: Berkeley Roundtable on the International Economy.

Beck, Thorsten, Leora F. Klapper, and Juan Carlos Mendoza. 2010. "The Typology of Partial Credit Guarantee Funds around the World." In "Partial Credit Guarantees: Experiences & Lessons," special issue, *Journal of Financial Stability* 6 (1): 10–25.

Beijing Hua tong ren shi chang xin xi you xian ze ren gong si, and University of Michigan, eds. n.d. *China Data Online = Zhongguo Shu Ju Zai Xian*. China: All China Marketing Research Co.

Bergemann, Dirk, and Alesandro Bonatti. 2019. "The Economics of Social Data." Cowles Foundation Discussion Paper 2171. New Haven, CT: Cowles Foundation for Research in Economics, Yale University.

Berger, Suzanne. 2013. *Making in America: From Innovation to Market*. Cambridge, MA: MIT Press.

Berkow, Jameson. 2010. "FP Tech Desk: Shopify Raises $7-Million in New Funding." *Financial Post*, December 13, 2010, sec. Technology.

Bessen, James, Jennifer Ford, and Michael J. Meurer. 2011. "The Private and Social Costs of Patent Trolls Property." *Regulation* 34 (4): 26–35.

Bijker, Wiebe E. 1995. *Of Bicycles, Bakelites, and Bulbs: Toward a Theory of Sociotechnical Change*. Inside Technology. Cambridge, MA: MIT Press.

Bilton, Nick. 2010. "Apple Sues Phone Maker HTC Over Patents." *Bits Blog* (blog), March 2, 2010.

Bizer, Christian, Tom Heath, and Tim Berners-Lee. 2009. "Linked Data—The Story So Far." *International Journal on Semantic Web and Information Systems* 5 (3): 1–22.

Block, Fred. 2008. "Swimming against the Current: The Rise of a Hidden Developmental State in the United States." *Politics & Society* 36 (2): 169–206.

Block, Fred L., and Matthew R. Keller, eds. 2015. *State of Innovation: The U.S. Government's Role in Technology Development*. London: Routledge.

Bloomberg. 2019. "9921:Taiwan Stock Quote—Giant Manufacturing Co Ltd." Bloomberg. com. Accessed November 25, 2019.

Bloomberg News. 2019. "Forced or Not? Why U.S. Says China Steals Technology." June 15, 2019.

Bohacz, Ray T. 2005. "The River Runs through It." *Hemmings Motor News*, 2005.

Bonvillian, William B. 2017. "Advanced Manufacturing: A New Policy Challenge." *Annals of Science and Technology Policy* 1 (1): 1–131.

Bonvillian, William B., and Richard Van Atta. 2011. "ARPA-E and DARPA: Applying the DARPA Model to Energy Innovation." *Journal of Technology Transfer* 36 (5): 469.

Bresnahan, Timothy F., and M. Trajtenberg. 1995. "General Purpose Technologies 'Engines of Growth'?" *Journal of Econometrics* 65 (1): 83–108.

Breznitz, Dan. 2005. "Collaborative Public Space in a National Innovation System: A Case Study of the Israeli Military's Impact on the Software Industry." *Industry and Innovation* 12 (1): 31–64.

———. 2005. "Development, Flexibility and R&D Performance in the Taiwanese IT Industry: Capability Creation and the Effects of State–Industry Coevolution." *Industrial and Corporate Change* 14 (1): 153–187.

———. 2006. "Innovation-Based Industrial Policy in Emerging Economies? The Case of Israel's IT Industry." *Business and Politics* 8 (3): 1–35.

———. 2007. "Industrial R&D as a National Policy: Horizontal Technology Policies and Industry-State Co-evolution in the Growth of the Israeli Software Industry." *Research Policy* 36 (9): 1465–1482.

———. 2007. *Innovation and the State: Political Choice and Strategies for Growth in Israel, Taiwan, and Ireland.* New Haven, CT: Yale University Press.

———. 2014. "Why Germany Dominates the U.S. in Innovation." *Harvard Business Review,* May 27, 2014.

———. 2018. *Data and the Future of Growth.* Data Series Special Report. Waterloo, ON: Center for International Governance Innovation.

Breznitz, Dan, and Peter Cowhey. 2012. "America's Two Systems of Innovation: Innovation for Production in Fostering U.S. Growth." *Innovations: Technology, Governance, Globalization* 7 (3): 127–154.

Breznitz, Dan, Chris Forman, and Wen Wen. 2018. "The Role of Venture Capital in the Formation of a New Technological Ecosystem: Evidence from the Cloud." *MIS Quarterly* 42 (4): 1143–1169.

Breznitz, Dan, and Michael Murphree. 2011. *Run of the Red Queen: Government, Innovation, Globalization, and Economic Growth in China.* New Haven, CT: Yale University Press.

———. 2013. "China's Run—Economic Growth, Policy, Interdependences, and Implications for Diverse Innovation Policies in a World of Fragmented Production." In *The Third Globalization: Can Wealthy Nations Stay Rich in the Twenty-First Century,* edited by John Zysman and Dan Breznitz, 35–56. Oxford: Oxford University Press.

Breznitz, Dan, and Darius Ornston. 2013. "The Revolutionary Power of Peripheral Agencies: Explaining Radical Policy Innovation in Finland and Israel." *Comparative Political Studies* 46 (10): 1219–1245.

———. 2014. "Scaling Up and Sustaining Experimental Innovation Policies with Limited Resources: Peripheral Schumpeterian Development Agencies." In *Making Innovation Policy Work: Learning from Experimentation,* edited by Mark A. Dutz, Yevgeny Kuznetsov, Esperanza Lasagabaster, and Dirk Pilat, 247–284. Paris: OECD.

———. 2018. "The Politics of Partial Success: Fostering Innovation in Innovation Policy in an Era of Heightened Public Scrutiny." *Socio-Economic Review* 16 (4): 721–741.

Breznitz, Dan, Darius Ornston, and Steven Samford. 2018. "Mission Critical: The Ends, Means, and Design of Innovation Agencies." *Industrial and Corporate Change* 27 (5): 883–896.

Breznitz, Dan, and Vincenzo Palermo. 2018. "Privacy, Innovation and Regulation: Examining the Impact of the European 'Cookie Law' on Technological Trajectories." SSRN Scholarly Paper 3136789. Rochester, NY: Social Science Research Network.

Breznitz, Dan, and Steven Samford. 2017. "Innovation Agency Case Study: Canada's Industrial Research Assistance Program (NRC-IRAP)." Washington, DC: Inter-American Development, Bank Division of Competitiveness, Technology, and Innovation.

Breznitz, Dan, and Mollie Taylor. 2014. "The Communal Roots of Entrepreneurial-Technological Growth—Social Fragmentation and Stagnation: Reflection on Atlanta's Technology Cluster." *Entrepreneurship & Regional Development* 26 (3–4): 375–396.

Breznitz, Dan, and Amos Zehavi. 2010. "The Limits of Capital: Transcending the Public Financer–Private Producer Split in Industrial R&D." *Research Policy* 39 (2): 301–312.

Breznitz, Dan, and John Zysman. 2013. "Conclusion: A Third Globalization, Lessons for Sustained Growth?" In *The Third Globalization: Can Wealthy Nations Stay Rich in the Twenty-First Century?*, edited by Dan Breznitz and John Zysman, 373–396. Oxford: Oxford: Oxford University Press.

Breznitz, Shiri M. 2014. *The Fountain of Knowledge: The Role of Universities in Economic Development.* Innovation and Technology in the World Economy. Stanford, CA: Stanford Business Books.

Breznitz, Shlomo. 1983. "The Seven Kinds of Denial." In *The Denial of Stress*, edited by Shlomo Breznitz, 257–280. New York: International Universities Press.

Brown, Jeffrey R., and Austan Goolsbee. 2002. "Does the Internet Make Markets More Competitive? Evidence from the Life Insurance Industry." *Journal of Political Economy* 110 (3): 481–507.

Brown, Tim. 2008. "Design Thinking." *Harvard Business Review*, June 1, 2008.

Brun, Alessandro, Federico Caniato, Maria Caridi, Cecilia Castelli, Giovanni Miragliotta, Stefano Ronchi, Andrea Sianesi, and Gianluca Spina. 2008. "Logistics and Supply Chain Management in Luxury Fashion Retail: Empirical Investigation of Italian Firms." In "Logistics Management in Fashion Retail Supply Chains," special section, *International Journal of Production Economics* 114 (2): 554–570.

Bruno, Michael. 1989. "Israel's Crisis and Economic Reform: A Historical Perspective." NBER Working Paper 3075. Cambridge, MA: National Bureau of Economic Research.

Brynjolfsson, Erik, and Tom Mitchell. 2017. "What Can Machine Learning Do? Workforce Implications." *Science* 358 (6370): 1530–1534.

Buciuni, Giulio, and Dan Breznitz. 2015. "Keeping Up in an Era of Global Specialization: Semi-Public Goods and the Competitiveness of Integrated Manufacturing Districts." In *The Oxford Handbook of Local Competitiveness*, edited by David B. Audretsch, Albert N. Link, and Mary Walshok, 102–125. Oxford: Oxford University Press.

Buciuni, Giulio, Giancarlo Coro', and Stefano Micelli. 2014. "Rethinking the Role of Manufacturing in Global Value Chains: An International Comparative Study in the Furniture Industry." *Industrial and Corporate Change* 23 (4): 967–996.

Buciuni, Giulio, and Vladi Finotto. 2016. "Innovation in Global Value Chains: Co-Location of Production and Development in Italian Low-Tech Industries." *Regional Studies* 50 (12): 2010–2023.

Buciuni, Giulio, and Gary Paul Pisano. 2015. "Can Marshall's Clusters Survive Globalization?" Harvard Business School Working Paper Series # 15-088. Cambridge, MA: Harvard Business School.

———. 2018. "Knowledge Integrators and the Survival of Manufacturing Clusters." *Journal of Economic Geography* 18 (5): 1069–1089.

Burkett, Scott. 2008. "Standing at the Crossroads in the ATL." Scott Burkett's Pothole on the Infobahn (blog), August 2, 2008. http://www.scottburkett.com/atlanta-business-scene/standing-at-the-crossroads-in-the-atl-794.html.

Business Wire. 2007. "HTC Touch™ Delivers New Touch Screen Experience." Businesswire.com, June 5, 2007.

Cai, Fang, and Yang Du. 2011. "Wage Increases, Wage Convergence, and the Lewis Turning Point in China." In "Sustainable Natural Resource Use in Rural China," special issue, *China Economic Review* 22 (4): 601–610.

Cairns, John A., Michael Gent, Joel Singer, Keith J. Finnie, Gordon M. Froggatt, Douglas A. Holder, George Jablonsky, et al. 1985. "Aspirin, Sulfinpyrazone, or Both in Unstable Angina." *New England Journal of Medicine* 313 (22): 1369–1375.

Case Western Reserve University. 2018. "Cleveland Tomorrow." In *Encyclopedia of Cleveland History.* Accessed July 2, 2019.

———. 2018. "Default." In *Encyclopedia of Cleveland History.* Accessed July 2, 2019.

———. 2018. "Economy." In *Encyclopedia of Cleveland History.* Accessed July 2, 2019.

Casper, Steven. 2007. "How Do Technology Clusters Emerge and Become Sustainable?: Social Network Formation and Inter-firm Mobility within the San Diego Biotechnology Cluster." In "Biotechnology: Its Origins, Organization, and Outputs," special issue, *Research Policy* 36 (4): 438–455.

Castaldo, Joe. 2017. "Why Does Canada Give Away Its Best Ideas in AI?" *Macleans*, April 13, 2017.

Cecere, Grazia, Nicoletta Corrocher, and Riccardo David Battaglia. 2015. "Innovation and Competition in the Smartphone Industry: Is There a Dominant Design?" In "New Empirical Approaches to Telecommunications Economics: Opportunities and Challenges," special issue, *Telecommunications Policy* 39 (3): 162–175.

Centre for Probe Development and Commercialization. "Partners." Accessed January 21, 2020.

Champion, David, and Nicholas G. Carr. 2000. "Starting Up in High Gear." *Harvard Business Review*, July 1, 2000.

Chang, Pao-Long, Chiung-Wen Hsu, and Chien-Tzu Tsai. 1999. "A Stage Approach for Industrial Technology Development and Implementation—the Case of Taiwan's Computer Industry." *Technovation* 19 (4): 233–241.

Changyu, Shen. 2016. "China—on Course to Become an IP Powerhouse." *WIPO Magazine*, 2016.

Chemical Institute of Canada. 2016. "Probing Genomes to Unearth New Uses for Old Drugs." Ottawa: Chemical Institute of Canada, March 1, 2016.

Christensen, Clayton M. 1997. *The Innovator's Dilemma: When New Technologies Cause Great Firms to Fail.* Management of Innovation and Change Series. Boston, MA: Harvard Business School Press.

Chung, Kee H., and Peter Wright. 1998. "Corporate Policy and Market Value: A q-Theory Approach." *Review of Quantitative Finance and Accounting* 11 (3): 293–310.

Clarke, Warren. 2017. "A Worthwhile Intervention? The Potential Role for a Sovereign Patent Fund in Canada." In *New Thinking on Innovation*, 127–132. Waterloo, ON: Centre for International Governance Innovation.

Clarke, Warren, and James W. Hinton. 2016. "Mobilizing National Innovation Assets: Understanding the Role of Sovereign Patent Funds." Waterloo, ON: Centre for Digital Entrepreneurship and Economic Performance.

"Cleveland, Ohio Population History, 1840–2017." BiggestUSCities.com. Accessed December 13, 2019.

Coase, R. H. 1937. "The Nature of the Firm." *Economica* 4 (16): 386–405.

———. 2013. "The Problem of Social Cost." *Journal of Law & Economics* 56 (4): 837–877.

Coe, Neil M., Peter Dicken, and Martin Hess. 2008. "Global Production Networks: Realizing the Potential." *Journal of Economic Geography* 8 (3): 271–295.

Cohen Goldner, Sarit, Zvi Eckstein, and Yoram Weiss. 2012. *Immigration and Labor Market Mobility in Israel, 1990–2009.* Cambridge, MA: MIT Press.

Cohen, Norma. 2012. "'Efficient Markets Hypothesis' Inefficient." *Financial Times*, January 24, 2012.

Colin-Jaeger, Nathanaël, and Thomas Delcey. 2020. "When Efficient Market Hypothesis Meets Hayek on Information: Beyond a Methodological Reading." *Journal of Economic Methodology* 27 (2): 97–116.

Cook, Douglas O., Laurie Krigman, and J. Chris Leach. 2003. "An Analysis of SEC Guidelines for Executing Open Market Repurchases." *Journal of Business* 76 (2): 289–315.

Coppola, Gabrielle, Ryan Beene, and Dana Hull. 2018. "Arizona Became Self-Driving Proving Ground before Uber's Deadly Crash." Bloomberg.com, March 20, 2018.

Cosgrove, Mary. 2017. "Ireland: Finance Bill 2017 Restricts IP Capital Allowance, Addresses MLI." *MNE Tax* (blog), October 23, 2017.

Council of Economic Advisors. 2015. "Big Data and Differential Pricing." Washington, DC: Executive Office of the President.

Cowan, Peter, and Jim Hinton. 2018. "Intellectual Property and Artificial Intelligence: What Does the Future Hold?" *IAM-Media*, February 1, 2018.

Cozzens, Susan E., Kamau Bobb, Kendall Deas, Sonia Gatchair, Albert George, and Gonzalo Ordonez. 2005. "Distributional Effects of Science and Technology-Based Economic Development Strategies at State Level in the United States." *Science and Public Policy* 32 (1): 29–38.

Culpan, Tim, and Hugo Miller. 2011. "HTC Takes Lead in U.S. Smartphone Market as Apple, RIM Decline." Bloomberg.com, November 2, 2011.

Daly, Angela. 2011. "Recent Issues for Competition Law on the Internet." San Domenico di Fiesole, Italy: European University Institute.

Dann, Larry Y. 1981. "Common Stock Repurchases: An Analysis of Returns to Bondholders and Stockholders." *Journal of Financial Economics* 9 (2): 113–138.

"Data Explorer." 2020. Eurostat, January 31, 2020.

"Data Is the New Gold." 2019. *Forbes Africa* (blog), July 18, 2019.

Dear, M. J., J. J. Drake, and Lloyd George Reeds, eds. 1987. *Steel City: Hamilton and Region*. Toronto: University of Toronto Press.

Dedrick, Jason, Kenneth L. Kraemer, and Greg Linden. 2010. "Who Profits from Innovation in Global Value Chains?: A Study of the IPod and Notebook PCs." *Industrial and Corporate Change* 19 (1): 81–116.

Diatto. "Chronology of Automobiles." Turin, Italy: Diatto. http://diatto.com/EN/pagine/chronology.html. Accessed July 6, 2019.

Dilger, Robert Jay, and Oscar R. Gonzales. 2012. "SBA Small Business Investment Company Program." *Journal of Current Issues in Finance, Business and Economics; Hauppauge* 5 (4): 407–435.

Directive 2009/136/EC of the European Parliament and of the Council of 25 November 2009 Amending Directive 2002/22/EC on Universal Service and Users' Rights Relating to Electronic Communications Networks and Services, Directive 2002/58/EC Concerning the Processing of Personal Data and the Protection of Privacy in the Electronic Communications Sector and Regulation (EC) No 2006/2004 on Cooperation between National Authorities Responsible for the Enforcement of Consumer Protection Laws (Text with EEA Relevance). 2009. 337. Vol. OJ L.

Dittmar, Amy K. 2000. "Why Do Firms Repurchase Stock." *Journal of Business* 73 (3): 331–355.

Dobson, Wendy, Julia Tory, and Daniel Trefler. 2017. "NAFTA Modernization: A Canadian Perspective." In *A Path Forward for NAFTA*, edited by Fred Bergsten and Monica de Bolle, 14. Washington, DC: Peterson Institute for International Economics.

D'Orazio, Dante. 2015. "Valve's VR Headset Is Called the Vive and It's Made by HTC." *The Verge*, March 1, 2015.

Dosis, Anastasios, and Wilfried Sand-Zantman. 2019. "The Ownership of Data." SSRN Scholarly Paper 1025. Toulouse: Toulouse School of Economics.

Drucker, Jesse, and Simon Bowers. 2017. "After a Tax Crackdown, Apple Found a New Shelter for Its Profits." *New York Times*, November 6, 2017, sec. World.

Drury, Horace Bookwalter. 1915. *Scientific Management: A History and Criticism*. Studies in History, Economics and Public Law, edited by the Faculty of Political Science of Columbia University, vol. 65, no. 2; no. 157. New York: Columbia University.

Duhigg, Charles, and Keith Bradsher. 2012. "Apple, America and a Squeezed Middle Class." *New York Times*, January 21, 2012, sec. Business Day.

Dutz, Mark Andrew, Yevgeny Kuznetsov, Esperanza Lasagabaster, Dirk Pilat, Organisation for Economic Co-operation and Development, World Bank Group, and Banco Nacional de Desenvolvimento Econômico e Social (Brazil), eds. 2014. *Making Innovation Policy Work: Learning from Experimentation*. Paris: OECD.

Ebenstein, Alan O. 2003. *Hayek's Journey: The Mind of Friedrich Hayek*. Basingstoke, UK: Palgrave Macmillan.

Economics, E. G. P. A. 2001. "The Operational Achievements of the Israeli Technology Incubators Program." *Report for the Technology Incubators Administration, the Office of the Chief Scientist in the Ministry of Trade and Industry*, Israel.

Economist. 2014. "Startups Are a Great Start, but Not the Goal." April 4, 2014.

———. 2017. "The World's Most Valuable Resource Is No Longer Oil, but Data." May 6, 2017.

Egan, Edward J., and David J. Teece. 2015. "Untangling the Patent Thicket Literature." Working paper. Houston: James A. Baker III Institute for Public Policy of Rice University.

European Commission. "State Aid: Irish Tax Treatment of Apple Is Illegal." Press Corner. Brussels: European Commission. Accessed December 29, 2019.

Fama, Eugene F. 1970. "Efficient Capital Markets: A Review of Theory and Empirical Work." *Journal of Finance* 25 (2): 383–417.

———. 1995. "Random Walks in Stock Market Prices." *Financial Analysts Journal* 51 (1): 75–80.

Farboodi, Maryam, Roxana Mihet, Thomas Philippon, and Laura Veldkamp. 2019. "Big Data and Firm Dynamics." Working Paper 25515. Cambridge, MA: National Bureau of Economic Research.

Feldman, Mark, and Michal Abouganem. 2002. "Development of the High-Tech Industry in Israel, 1995–1999: Labour Force and Wages." Working Paper Series 1. Jerusalem: Central Bureau of Statistics.

Felsenstein, Daniel. 1997. "The Making of a High Technology Node: Foreign-Owned Companies in Israeli High Technology." *Regional Studies* 31 (4): 367–380.

Financial Services Authority. 2009. *The Turner Review: A Regulatory Response to the Global Banking Crisis*. London: Financial Services Authority. http://www.actuaries. org/CTTEES_TFRISKCRISIS/Documents/turner_review.pdf.

Fischer, Stanley, Ratna Sahay, and Carlos A. Végh. 2002. "Modern Hyper- and High Inflations." *Journal of Economic Literature* 40 (3): 837–880.

Florida, Richard L. *The Rise of the Creative Class: And How It's Transforming Work, Leisure, Community and Everyday Life*. New York: Basic Books, 2002.

Florida, Richard L., and Martin Kenney. 1988. "Venture Capital-Financed Innovation and Technological Change in the USA." *Research Policy* 17 (3): 119–137.

Flügge, Eva. 1929. "Possibilities and Problems of Integration in the Automobile Industry." *Journal of Political Economy* 37: 150–174.

Fogarty, Michael S., Gasper S. Garofalo, David C. Hammack, and Hiram C. Haydn. 2002. "Cleveland from Startup to the Present: Innovation and Entrepreneurship in the 19th and Early 20th Century." Cleveland: Center for Regional Economic Issues, Weatherhead School of Management, Case Western University.

Folsom, Burton W. 1988. "Charles Schwab and the Steel Industry." Atlanta: Foundation for Economic Education, September 1, 1988.

Friedman, Milton, and Rose D. Friedman. 1982. *Capitalism and Freedom*. Chicago: University of Chicago Press.

Fuchs, Erica R. H. 2009. "Cloning DARPA Successfully." *Issues in Science and Technology* 26 (1): 651–677.

———. 2010. "Rethinking the Role of the State in Technology Development: DARPA and the Case for Embedded Network Governance." *Research Policy* 39 (9): 1133–1147.

Fujita, Masahisa, and Jacques-François Thisse. 1996. "Economics of Agglomeration." *Journal of the Japanese and International Economies* 10 (4): 339–378.

Fuller, Douglas, Akintunde Akinwande, and Charles Sodini. 2003. "Leading, Following or Cooked Goose? Innovation Successes and Failures in Taiwan's Electronics Industry." *Industry and Innovation* 10 (2): 179–196.

Furukawa, Yuichi. 2007. "The Protection of Intellectual Property Rights and Endogenous Growth: Is Stronger Always Better?" *Journal of Economic Dynamics and Control* 31 (11): 3644–3670.

———. 2010. "Intellectual Property Protection and Innovation: An Inverted-U Relationship." *Economics Letters* 109 (2): 99–101.

Fusion Pharma. 2020. "Targeted Alpha Therapeutics, Technology." Hamilton, ON: Fusion Pharma. Accessed January 31, 2020.

Galasso, Alberto, and Mark Schankerman. 2010. "Patent Thickets, Courts, and the Market for Innovation." *RAND Journal of Economics* 41 (3): 472–503.

Gallini, Nancy, and Aidan Hollis. 2019. "To Sell or Scale Up: Canada's Patent Strategy in a Knowledge Economy." IRPP Study 72. Montreal: Institute for Research on Public Policy (IRPP).

Gannes, Liz. 2013. "The Backstory on Google's Investment in Google Glass Micro-Display Supplier Himax." *All Things D* (blog), July 22, 2013. http://allthingsd.com/20130722/the-backstory-on-googles-investment-in-google-glass-microdisplay-supplier-himax/.

Ge, Wei. 1999. *Special Economic Zones and the Economic Transition in China*. Economic Ideas Leading to the 21st Century, vol. 5. Singapore: World Scientific.

Gereffi, Gary. 1996. "Global Commodity Chains: New Forms of Coordination and Control among Nations and Firms in International Industries." *Competition & Change* 1 (4): 427–439.

Gereffi, Gary, John Humphrey, and Timothy Sturgeon. 2005. "The Governance of Global Value Chains." *Review of International Political Economy* 12 (1): 78–104.

Gergils, Håkan. 2005. *Dynamic Innovation Systems in the Nordic Countries: A Summary Analysis and Assessment*. Stockholm: SNS Förlag.

Gertler, Meric S., and David A. Wolfe, eds. 2016. *Growing Urban Economies: Innovation, Creativity, and Governance in Canadian City-Regions.* Toronto: University of Toronto Press.

Giachetti, Claudio, and Gianluca Marchi. 2010. "Evolution of Firms' Product Strategy over the Life Cycle of Technology-Based Industries: A Case Study of the Global Mobile Phone Industry, 1980–2009." *Business History* 52 (7): 1123–1150.

Glass, Ira, Alex Blumberg, and Laura Sydell. 2011. "When Patents Attack!" Mp3. *This American Life*, July 22, 2011.

Goldfarb, Avi, Ajay Agrawal, and Joshua Gans, eds. 2019. *The Economics of Artificial Intelligence: An Agenda.* National Bureau of Economic Research Conference Report. Chicago: University of Chicago Press.

Gomes, Mark. 2013. "Google Glass Coming Early—Shares Of Himax Are Poised to Triple." Seeking Alpha, March 5, 2013. https://seekingalpha.com/article/1246121-google-glass-coming-early-shares-of-himax-are-poised-to-triple.

Gompers, Paul, and Josh Lerner. 1998. "Venture Capital Distributions: Short-Run and Long-Run Reactions." *Journal of Finance* 53 (6): 2161–2183.

———. 1999. *The Venture Capital Cycle.* Cambridge MA: MIT Press.

Goo, Yeong-Jia, and An-Yu Shih. 2015. "Impact of Credit Guarantee on the Survival of SMEs and Default Prediction for SMEs: Empirical Evidence from Taiwan." In *ICSB World Conference Proceedings; Washington*, 1–20. Washington, DC: International Council for Small Business (ICSB).

Gornall, Will, and Ilya A. Strebulaev. 2020. "Squaring Venture Capital Valuations with Reality." *Journal of Financial Economics* 135 (1): 120–143.

Grabher, Gernot, and Jonas König. forthcoming "Embedding Disruption: A Polanyian Perspective on the Platform Economy." *Environment and Planning A: Economy and Space* (forthcoming).

Granovetter, Mark S. 1973. "The Strength of Weak Ties." *American Journal of Sociology* 78 (6): 1360–1380.

———. 2005. "The Impact of Social Structure on Economic Outcomes." *Journal of Economic Perspectives* 19 (1): 33–50.

Grossman, Gene M., and Elhanan Helpman. 1993. *Innovation and Growth in the Global Economy.* Cambridge, MA: MIT Press.

Guenther, Gary. 2017. "Patent Boxes: A Primer." CRS Report for Congress. Washington, DC: Congressional Research Service.

Guyatt, Gordon, John Cairns, David Churchill, Deborah Cook, Brian Haynes, Jack Hirsh, Jan Irvine, et al. 1992. "Evidence-Based Medicine: A New Approach to Teaching the Practice of Medicine." *JAMA* 268 (17): 2420–2425.

———. 1997. "Evidence-Based Medicine." In "Fatal and Neonatal Hematology for the 21st Century," special issue, *Seminars in Perinatology* 21 (1): 3–5.

Haines, Michael R., and Inter-university Consortium For Political and Social Research. 2005. "Historical, Demographic, Economic, and Social Data: The United States, 1790–2002: Version 3." Ann Arbor, MI: Inter-university Consortium for Political and Social Research.

Hall, Bronwyn H., Adam B. Jaffe, and Manuel Trajtenberg. 2001. "The NBER Patent Citation Data File: Lessons, Insights and Methodological Tools." Working Paper 8498. Cambridge, MA: National Bureau of Economic Research.

Hall, Bronwyn H., and Josh Lerner. 2010. "The Financing of R&D and Innovation." In *Handbook of the Economics of Innovation.* Vol. 1. Amsterdam: North-Holland.

Hargadon, Andrew B., and Martin Kenney. 2012. "Misguided Policy? Following Venture Capital into Clean Technology." *California Management Review* 54 (2): 118–139.

Hartley, Matt. 2011. "Shopify Rings up US$15-Million Funding Round." *Financial Post*, October 17, 2011, sec. FP Startups.

Hatfield, Henry Rand. 1900. "The Taylor White Process for Tool Steel." *Journal of Political Economy* 8 (4): 538–539.

Hayek, Friedrich A. von. 1980. *Individualism and Economic Order*. Midway Reprint. Chicago: University of Chicago Press.

———. 2014. "The Meaning of Competition (1948)." In *The Market and Other Orders*, edited by Bruce Caldwell, 105–116. Vol. 3 of the Collected Works of F.A. Hayek. London: Routledge.

Heiskala, Risto, and Timo J. Hämäläinen. 2007. "Social Innovation or Hegemonic Change? Rapid Paradigm Change in Finland in the 1980s and 1990s." In *Social Innovations, Institutional Change, and Economic Performance: Making Sense of Structural Adjustment Processes in Industrial Sectors, Regions, and Societies*, edited by Timo J. Hämäläinen and Risto Heiskala, 11–51. Cheltenham, UK: Edward Elgar.

Helpman, Elhanan, and Manuel Trajtenberg. 1996. "Diffusion of General Purpose Technologies." Working Paper 5773. Cambridge, MA: National Bureau of Economic Research.

Hemphill, Thomas A. 2014. "Policy Debate: The US Advanced Manufacturing Initiative: Will It Be Implemented as an Innovation—or Industrial—Policy?" *Innovation* 16 (1): 67–70.

Herrera, Tim. 2019. "You're Tracked Everywhere You Go Online. Use This Guide to Fight Back." *New York Times*, November 24, 2019, sec. Smarter Living.

Hessen, Robert. 1972. "The Transformation of Bethlehem Steel, 1904–1909." *Business History Review* 46 (3): 339–360.

Hinton, James, and Peter Cowan. 2017. "Canada Needs an Innovative Intellectual Property Strategy." *Globe and Mail*, May 19, 2017, sec. Opinion.

Hippel, Eric von. 1976. "The Dominant Role of Users in the Scientific Instrument Innovation Process." *Research Policy* 5 (3): 212–239.

———. 1986. "Lead Users: A Source of Novel Product Concepts." *Management Science* 32 (7): 791–805.

———. 2005. *Democratizing Innovation*. Cambridge, MA: MIT Press.

———. 2017. *Free Innovation*. Cambridge, MA: MIT Press.

Hogue, Tom. 2019. "The Forge and Innovation Factory: Innovation and Incubation Work Well Together in Hamilton." *Hamilton Spectator*, November 7, 2019, sec. News-Business.

Hong, Sung Gul. 1997. *The Political Economy of Industrial Policy in East Asia: The Semiconductor Industry in Taiwan and South Korea*. Cheltenham, UK: Edward Elgar.

Houlder, Vanessa, Vincent Boland, and Alex Barker. 2014. "Brussels in Crackdown on 'Double Irish' Tax Loophole." *Financial Times*, October 9, 2014.

Hounshell, David A. 1985. *From the American System to Mass Production, 1800–1932: The Development of Manufacturing Technology in the United States*. Studies in Industry and Society 4. Baltimore: Johns Hopkins University Press.

HTC. 2016. "HTC 2015 Annual Report."

———. 2019. "HTC 2018 Annual Report."

Hu, Mei-Chih, and Ching-Yan Wu. 2014. "Giant Bicycle and King Liu." In *Handbook of East Asian Entrepreneurship*, edited by Fu-Lai Tony Yu and Ho-Don Yan, 289–299. London: Routledge Handbooks Online.

Huberty, Mark. 2013. *Energy Systems Transformation: State Choices at the Intersection of Sustainability and Growth*. Oxford: Oxford University Press.

Hurtarte, Jeorge S., Evert A. Wolsheimer, and Lisa M. Tafoya. 2007. *Understanding Fabless IC Technology*. Communications Engineering Series. Amsterdam: Elsevier/Newnes.

Hussain, Daanish, Travis Southin, and Christopher Villegas-Cho. 2016. "From Exit Nation to Startup Nation." White paper. Toronto: Munk School of Global Affairs and Public Policy.

Hwang, Y. Dolly. 1991. *The Rise of a New World Economic Power: Postwar Taiwan*. Contributions in Economics and Economic History, no. 121. New York: Greenwood.

IDEO. 2020. "Creating the First Usable Mouse." Palo Alto, CA: IDEO. Accessed January 31, 2020.

Illumacell. n.d. "Photodynamic Therapy: How Does It Work?". Hamilton, ON: Illumacell Inc. Accessed January 21, 2020.

Improvement in fastening pocket-openings. 1873. United States US139121A, issued May 20, 1873.

Innovation Policy Lab Database. 2019. Toronto: Innovation Policy Lab, Munk School of Global Affairs and Public Policy.

innovationisrael.org. 2019. "Investing NIS 15 Million to Promote Investment in Israeli Hi-Tech amongst Israel's Institutional Investors," November 13, 2019. https://innovationisrael.org.il/en/news/investing-nis-15-million-promote-investment-israeli-hi-tech-amongst-israels-institutional.

Isenberg, Daniel. 2012. "Focus Entrepreneurship Policy on Scale-Up, Not Start-Up." *Harvard Business Review*, November 30, 2012.

Isenberg, Daniel, and Vincent Onyemah. 2016. "Fostering Scaleup Ecosystems for Regional Economic Growth (Innovations Case Narrative: Manizales-Mas and Scale Up Milwaukee)." *Innovations* 11 (1–2): 60.

———. 2017. "Midsize Cities Are Entrepreneurship's Real Test." *Harvard Business Review*, January 24, 2017.

———. 2017. "Start-Ups Won't Save the Economy. But 'Scale Ups' Could." Cologny, Switzerland: World Economic Forum. https://www.weforum.org/agenda/2017/03/start-ups-entrepreneurship-scale-ups-latin-america/.

Israel Innovation. 2020. "R&D Fund, Programs," https://innovationisrael.org.il/en/program/rd-fund. Accessed January 23, 2020.

Israel Ministry of Economy. 2015. "Government Approves National Authority for Technology and Innovation." Israel Ministry of Foreign Affairs, June 21, 2015.

ISS. 2007. "Company Timeline." Web.Archive. https://web.archive.org/web/20070420103923/http://www.iss.net/about/timeline/index.html.

Jaffe, Adam B., and Joshua Lerner. 2004. *Innovation and Its Discontents: How Our Broken Patent System Is Endangering Innovation and Progress, and What to Do about It*. Princeton, NJ: Princeton University Press.

Janeway, William H. 2018. *Doing Capitalism in the Innovation Economy: Reconfiguring the Three-Player Game between Markets, Speculators and the State*. 2nd ed. Cambridge: Cambridge University Press.

Jing, Fu. 2008. "Shenzhen Zen: Fishing Village Turned Boomtown." *China Daily*, August 4, 2008.

Johnson, Chalmers. 1984. "Introduction: The Idea of Industrial Policy." In *The Industrial Policy Debate*, edited by Chalmers Johnson, 3–16. San Francisco: ICS Press.

Jones, Charles I., and Christopher Tonetti. 2019. "Nonrivalry and the Economics of Data." Working Paper 26260. Cambridge, MA: National Bureau of Economic Research.

Karo, Erkki, and Rainer Kattel. 2016. "How to Organize for Innovation: Entrepreneurial State and Organizational Variety." Working Papers in Technology Governance and Economic Dymanics 39. Tallinn, Estonia: Tallinn University of Technology.

Keating, W. Dennis, Norman Krumholz, and David C. Perry, eds. 1995. *Cleveland: A Metropolitan Reader*. Kent, OH: Kent State University Press.

Kelley, Tom, and Jonathan Littman. 2001. *The Art of Innovation: Lessons in Creativity from IDEO, America's Leading Design Firm*. New York: Currency/Doubleday.

Kelly, Ash. 2017. "Is B.C. an International Financial Hub or Corporate Tax Haven?" CBC News, May 4, 2017. https://www.cbc.ca/news/canada/british-columbia/is-b-c-an-international-financial-hub-or-corporate-tax-haven-1.4098667.

Kenney, Martin, Dan Breznitz, and Michael Murphree. 2013. "Coming Back Home after the Sun Rises: Returnee Entrepreneurs and Growth of High Tech Industries." *Research Policy* 42 (2): 391–407.

Kenney, Martin, and Andrew Hargadon. 2014. "Venture Capital and Clean Technology." In *Can Green Sustain Growth?: From the Religion to the Reality of Sustainable Prosperity*, edited by John Zysman and Mark Huberty, 59–76. Stanford, CA: Stanford University Press.

Kenney, Martin, and John Zysman. 2019. "Unicorns, Cheshire Cats, and the New Dilemmas of Entrepreneurial Finance." *Venture Capital* 21 (1): 35–50.

Kindleberger, Charles P., and Jean Pierre Laffargue, eds. 1982. *Financial Crises: Theory, History, and Policy*. Cambridge: Cambridge University Press.

Kitch, Edmund W. 1977. "The Nature and Function of the Patent System." *Journal of Law and Economics* 20 (2): 265–290.

Klingler-Vidra, Robyn. 2018. *The Venture Capital State: The Silicon Valley Model in East Asia*. The Venture Capital State. Ithaca, NY: Cornell University Press. http://www.degruyter.com/cornellup/view/title/543896.

Koh, Winston T. H., and Poh Kam Wong. 2005. "The Venture Capital Industry in Singapore: A Comparative Study with Taiwan and Israel on the Government's Role." SMU Edge Conference: Bridging The Gap - Entrepreneurship in Theory and Practice, November 7, 2005.

Krugman, Paul. 1991. "Increasing Returns and Economic Geography." *Journal of Political Economy* 99 (3): 483–499.

———. 2018. "Paul Krugman Explains Trade and Tariffs." *New York Times*, March 15, 2018, sec. Opinion.

Kuo, Chau-Jung, Chin-Ming Chen, and Chao-Hsien Sung. 2011. "Evaluating Guarantee Fees for Loans to Small and Medium-Sized Enterprises." *Small Business Economics* 37 (2): 205–218.

Kushida, Kenji E., and John Zysman. 2009. "The Services Transformation and Network Policy: The New Logic of Value Creation." *Review of Policy Research* 26 (1–2): 173–194.

Lai, Hsien-che, Yi-chia Chiu, and Horng-der Leu. 2005. "Innovation Capacity Comparison of China's Information Technology Industrial Clusters: The Case of Shanghai, Kunshan, Shenzhen and Dongguan." *Technology Analysis & Strategic Management* 17 (3): 293–316.

Lam, W. Raphael, Xiaoguang Liu, and Alfred Schipke. 2015. "China's Labor Market in the 'New Normal.'" IMF Working Papers. Washington, DC: International Monetary Fund, July 2015.

Lamkin, Paul. 2016. "HTC Vive VR Headset Sales Revealed." *Forbes*, October 21, 2016.

Lamont, Owen A., and Richard H. Thaler. 2003. "Anomalies: The Law of One Price in Financial Markets." *Journal of Economic Perspectives* 17 (4): 191–202.

Lamoreaux, Naomi R., and Kenneth Lee Sokoloff. 2007. "Financing Invention during the Second Industrial Revolution: Cleveland, Ohio, 1870–1920." In *Financing Innovation in the United States, 1870 to the Present*, edited by Naomi R. Lamoreaux and Kenneth Lee Sokoloff, 39–84. Cambridge, MA: MIT Press.

Lamoreaux, Naomi R., Margaret Levenstein, and Kenneth L. Sokoloff. 2006. "Mobilizing Venture Capital during the Second Industrial Revolution: Cleveland, Ohio, 1870–1920." *Capitalism and Society* 1 (3).

Langlois, Richard N. 1992. "Transaction-Cost Economics in Real Time." *Industrial and Corporate Change* 1 (1): 99–127.

Langlois, Richard N., and Paul L. Robertson. 1992. "Networks and Innovation in a Modular System: Lessons from the Microcomputer and Stereo Component Industries." *Research Policy* 21 (4): 297–313.

Lazonick, William. 2009. *Sustainable Prosperity in the New Economy?* Kalamazoo, MI: W.E. Upjohn Institute.

———. 2010. "Innovative Business Models and Varieties of Capitalism: Financialization of the U.S. Corporation." *Business History Review* 84 (4): 675–702.

———. 2012. "The Financialization of the U.S. Corporation: What Has Been Lost, and How It Can Be Regained." *Seattle University Law Review* 36 (2): 857–910.

———. 2014. "Profits without Prosperity." *Harvard Business Review*, September 1, 2014.

Lazonick, William, Mariana Mazzucato, and Öner Tulum. 2013. "Apple's Changing Business Model: What Should the World's Richest Company Do with All Those Profits?" *Accounting Forum* 37 (4): 249–267.

Lee, Chong-Moon, ed. 2000. *The Silicon Valley Edge: A Habitat for Innovation and Entrepreneurship*. Stanford, CA: Stanford University Press.

Lee, Wen-Hsiung, and Wei-Tzen Yang. 2000. "The Cradle of Taiwan High Technology Industry Development—Hsinchu Science Park (HSP)." *Technovation* 20 (1): 55–59.

Lerner, Joshua. 1994. "Venture Capitalists and the Decision to Go Public." *Journal of Financial Economics* 35 (3): 293–316.

———. 2001. "The Venture Capital Revolution." *Journal of Economic Perspectives* 15 (2): 145–168.

———. 2009. *Boulevard of Broken Dreams: Why Public Efforts to Boost Entrepreneurship and Venture Capital Have Failed and What to Do about It*. Kauffman Foundation Series on Innovation and Entrepreneurship. Princeton, NJ: Princeton University Press.

Li, Hongbin, Lei Li, Binzhen Wu, and Yanyan Xiong. 2012. "The End of Cheap Chinese Labor." *Journal of Economic Perspectives* 26 (4): 57–74.

Lichtman, Moshie, and Adrian Filut. 2011. "'Build Smaller Apartments, Fines for Empty Homes.'" *Jerusalem Post*, September 25, 2011, sec. Business.

Lieberman, Marvin B., and David B. Montgomery. 1988. "First-Mover Advantages." *Strategic Management Journal* 9 (S1): 41–58.

Liiv, Innar. 2017. "Welcome to E-Estonia, the Tiny Nation That's Leading Europe in Digital Innovation." *The Conversation*, April 4, 2017.

Lin, Otto Chui Chao. 2018. *Innovation and Entrepreneurship: Choice and Challenge.* Singapore: World Scientific.

Livingstone, David. 2011. "Melting the Core Steel Workforce: 1981–2003." In *Manufacturing Meltdown: Reshaping Steel Work*, edited by David Livingstone, Dorothy Smith, and Warren E. Smith, 9–71. Halifax, Nova Scotia: Fernwood.

Locke, Richard M., and Rachel L. Wellhausen. 2014. *Production in the Innovation Economy.* Cambridge, MA: MIT Press.

Loomis, Stephen C. 2011. "The Double Irish Sandwich: Reforming Overseas Tax Havens Recent Development." *St. Mary's Law Journal* 43 (4): 825–854.

Luna, Facundo. 2017. "Ana´ Lisis de Agencias de Innovacio´n: Estudio de Caso: Corporacio´n de Fomento" [Analysis of innovation agencies: Case study: Growth Corporation of Chile]. Washington, DC: Inter-American Development Bank.

Lundberg, Shelly. 2018. "The 2018 Report of the Committee on the Status of Women in the Economics Profession." Nashville, TN: American Economic Association.

Lunden, Ingrid. 2013. "Google Takes 6.3% Stake In Google Glass Tech Supplier Himax Display as It Preps to Ramp Up Production." *TechCrunch* (blog), July 22, 2013.

———. 2017. "Intel Buys Mobileye in $15.3B Deal, Moves Its Automotive Unit to Israel." *TechCrunch* (blog), March 13, 2017.

Luukkonen, Terttu. 2006. "Venture Capital Industry in Finland: Country Report for the Venture Fun Project." ETLA Discussion Paper. Helsinki: ETLA.

Markusen, Ann. 1996. "Sticky Places in Slippery Space: A Typology of Industrial Districts." *Economic Geography* 72 (3): 293–313.

Martin, Ron, and Peter Sunley. 2015. "On the Notion of Regional Economic Resilience: Conceptualization and Explanation." *Journal of Economic Geography* 15 (1): 1–42.

Martin, Ron, Peter Sunley, Ben Gardiner, and Peter Tyler. 2016. "How Regions React to Recessions: Resilience and the Role of Economic Structure." *Regional Studies* 50 (4): 561–585.

Marx, Matt, and Lee Fleming. 2012. "Non-compete Agreements: Barriers to Entry . . . and Exit?" *Innovation Policy and the Economy* 12 (January): 39–64.

Marx, Matt, Jasjit Singh, and Lee Fleming. 2015. "Regional Disadvantage? Employee Non-compete Agreements and Brain Drain." *Research Policy* 44 (2): 394–404.

Maskell, Peter, and Anders Malmberg. 2007. "Myopia, Knowledge Development and Cluster Evolution." *Journal of Economic Geography* 7 (5): 603–618.

Mastakis, Louise. 2019. "The WIRED Guide to Your Personal Data (and Who Is Using It)." *Wired*, February 15, 2019. https://www.wired.com/story/wired-guide-personal-data-collection/.

Mathews, John A. 2002. "The Origins and Dynamics of Taiwan's R&D Consortia." *Research Policy* 31 (4): 633–651.

Mathews, John A., and Tong-sŏng Cho. 2000. *Tiger Technology: The Creation of a Semiconductor Industry in East Asia.* Cambridge Asia-Pacific Studies. Cambridge: Cambridge University Press.

Mazzucato, Mariana. 2013. *The Entrepreneurial State: Debunking Public vs. Private Sector Myths.* London: Anthem Press.

Mcleod, James. 2019. "Innovation Nation: Montreal's AI Supercluster Is All about the Little Guy." *Financial Post*, February 20, 2019, sec. Technology.

"McMaster Opens $33M Biomedical Engineering and Advanced Manufacturing Research Centre." 2018. *Brighter World* (blog), McMaster University, March 7, 2018. https://

brighterworld.mcmaster.ca/articles/mcmaster-opens-33m-biomedical-engineering-and-advanced-manufacturing-research-centre/.

"McMaster-Based Company Nabs over $140M in Financing for Cancer Research." 2019. CBC, April 3, 2019.

Meaney, Constance. 2015. "State Policy and the Development of Taiwan's Semiconductor Industry." In *The Role of the State in Taiwan's Development*, edited by Joel D. Aberdach, 170–92. London: Routledge.

Medhora, Rohinton P., Karima Bawa, Benjamin Bergen, Joël Blit, Dan Ciuriak, Warren Clarke, Neil Desai, et al. 2017. "New Thinking on Innovation." Waterloo, ON: Centre for International Governance Innovation, November.

"Medical Milestones." 2020. *The BMJ*. https://www.bmj.com/content/medical-milestones. Accessed January 10, 2020.

Min, Chia Yin. 2015. "Over $380 Million Invested in R&D, 19 Labs Set Up: A*Star." *The Straits Times*, March 19, 2015.

"Minimum Wage—Guangdong." 2020. WageIndicator.Org. Accessed February 6, 2020.

Minsky, Hyman. 1977. "A Theory of Systemic Fragility." In *Financial Crises: Institutions and Markets in a Fragile Environment*, edited by E. D. Altman and A. W. Sametz, 138–152. New York: John Wiley & Sons.

———. 2008. "The Financial-Instability Hypothesis: Capitalist Processes and the Behavior of the Economy." In *Financial Crises: Theory, History, and Policy*, edited by Charles P. Kindleberger and Jean Pierre Laffargue, 13–39. Cambridge: Cambridge University Press.

Minsky, Hyman, Irwin Friend, and Victor Andrews. 1960. "Financial Crisis, Financial Systems, and the Performance of the Economy." Private Capital Markets; A Series of Research Studies Prepared for the Commission On Money And Credit. Washington, DC: Commission On Money And Credit, July.

Mohanty, Saraju P., Uma Choppali, and Elias Kougianos. 2016. "Everything You Wanted to Know about Smart Cities: The Internet of Things Is the Backbone." *IEEE Consumer Electronics Magazine* 5 (3): 60–70.

Moore, G. E. 1998. "Cramming More Components Onto Integrated Circuits." *Proceedings of the IEEE* 86 (1): 82–85.

Moorhead, Patrick. 2019. "Who Are Apple's IPhone Contract Manufacturers?" *Forbes*, April 13, 2019.

Morton, Fiona Scott, Pascal Bouvier, Ariel Ezrachi, Bruno Jullien, Roberta Katz, Gene Kimmelman, A. Douglas Melamed, and Jamie Morgenstern. 2019. "Committee for the Study of Digital Platforms: Market Structure and Antitrust Subcommittee-Report." Chicago: Stigler Center for the Study of the Economy and the State, University of Chicago Booth School of Business.

Mulcahy, Diane. 2014. "Venture Capitalists Get Paid Well to Lose Money." *Harvard Business Review*, August 5, 2014.

Murphree, Michael, and Dan Breznitz. 2016. "Standards, Patents and National Competitiveness." CIGI Paper 40. Waterloo, ON: Centre for International Governance Innovation.

———. 2018. "Indigenous Digital Technology Standards for Development: The Case of China." *Journal of International Business Policy* 1 (3): 234–252.

———. 2020. "Collaborative Public Spaces and Upgrading through Global Value Chains: The Case of Dongguan." *Global Strategy Journal* 10 (3): 556–584.

Murphree, Michael, Li Tang, and Dan Breznitz. 2016. "Tacit Local Alliance and SME Innovation in China." *International Journal of Innovation and Regional Development* 7 (3): 184–202.

National Economic Council (US). 2016. "Revitalizing American Manufacturing: The Obama Administration's Progress in Establishing a Foundation for Manufacturing Leadership." Washington, DC: The White House, National Economic Council.

Nelson, Richard R. 1959. "The Simple Economics of Basic Scientific Research." *Journal of Political Economy* 67 (3): 297–306.

Networks of Centres of Excellence of Canada, Communications. 2016. "Centre for Probe Development and Commercialization—CPDC, Funded Networks and Centres." Ottawa: Networks of Centres of Excellence of Canada, June 28, 2016.

Neufeld, V. R., and H. S. Barrows. 1974. "The 'McMaster Philosophy': An Approach to Medical Education." *Academic Medicine* 49 (11): 1040.

New York Times. 1991. "Apple Will Buy Colorado Plant." *New York Times*, March 21, 1991, sec. Business Day.

Nicas, Jack. 2019. "A Tiny Screw Shows Why IPhones Won't Be 'Assembled in U.S.A.'" *New York Times*, January 28, 2019, sec. Technology.

Noble, Gregory W. 1998. *Collective Action in East Asia: How Ruling Parties Shape Industrial Policy*. Cornell Studies in Political Economy. Ithaca, NY: Cornell University Press.

O'Connor, Sean. 2019. *How Chinese Companies Facilitate Technology Transfer from the United States*. U.S.-China Economic and Security Review Commission: Staff Research Report. Washington, DC: U.S.-China Economic and Security Review Commission.

O'Neil, Cathy. 2017. *Weapons of Math Destruction: How Big Data Increases Inequality and Threatens Democracy*. First paperback edition. New York: Broadway Books.

OECD (Organisation for Economic Co-operation and Development). n.d. "Table II.1. Statutory Corporate Income Tax Rate." OECD.Stat. Paris: OECD. Accessed January 31, 2020.

———. 2007. *OECD Reviews of Innovation Policy: Chile 2007*. Paris: OECD.

———. 2014. *OECD Science, Technology and Industry Outlook 2014*. Paris: OECD.

———. 2018. *Education Policy Outlook 2018: Putting Student Learning at the Centre*. Paris: OECD Publishing.

———. 2018. *OECD Economic Surveys: Israel 2018*. Paris: OECD.

Oricchio, Gianluca. 2012. "The Efficient-Market Hypothesis (EMH) and Financial Crisis." In *Corporate Management in a Knowledge-Based Economy*, edited by Gianfranco Zanda, 155–168. London: Palgrave Macmillan UK.

Ornston, Darius. 2012. *When Small States Make Big Leaps: Institutional Innovation and High-Tech Competition in Western Europe*. Cornell Studies in Political Economy. Ithaca, NY: Cornell University Press.

———. 2017. "Networks, Brokerage, and State-Led Technology Diffusion in Small Industry." *American Journal of Sociology* 122 (5): 1339–1370.

———. 2018. *Good Governance Gone Bad: How Nordic Adaptability Leads to Excess*. Ithaca, NY: Cornell University Press.

Orwell, George. 1977. *1984: A Novel*. New York: New American Library.

Osawa, Juro, and Paul Mozur. 2014. "The Rise of China's Innovation Machine." *Wall Street Journal*, January 16, 2014, sec. Tech.

Oxman, Andrew D., David L. Sackett, Gordon H. Guyatt, George Browman, Deborah Cook, Hertzel Gerstein, Brian Haynes, et al. 1993. "Users' Guides to the Medical Literature: I. How to Get Started." *JAMA* 270 (17): 2093–2095.

Pantelis, Koutroumpis, and Leiponen Aija. 2013. "Understanding the Value of (Big) Data." In *2013 IEEE International Conference on Big Data*, 38–42.

"Patents." 2015. *Last Week Tonight with John Oliver*. Avalon Television.

Perez, Carlota. 2010. "Technological Revolutions and Techno-Economic Paradigms." *Cambridge Journal of Economics* 34 (1): 185–202.

Perez-Aleman, Paola. 2005. "Cluster Formation, Institutions and Learning: The Emergence of Clusters and Development in Chile." *Industrial and Corporate Change* 14 (4): 651–677.

Perry, Martin K. 1989. "Vertical Integration: Determinants and Effects." In *Handbook of Industrial Organization*. Vol. 1, 183–255. Amsterdam: Elsevier.

Piore, Michael J. 2011. "Beyond Markets: Sociology, Street-Level Bureaucracy, and the Management of the Public Sector." *Regulation & Governance* 5 (1): 145–164.

Piore, Michael J., Phech Colatat, and Elisabeth Beck. 2020. "NSF and DARPA as Models for Research Funding: An Institutional Analysis." In *The DARPA Model for Transformative Technologies: Perspectives on the U.S. Defense Advanced Research Projects Agency*, edited by William Boone Bonvillian, Richard Van Atta, and Patrick Windham, 45–76. Cambridge, UK: Open Book Publishers.

Piore, Michael J., and Andrew Schrank. 2018. *Root-Cause Regulation: Protecting Work and Workers in the Twenty-First Century*. Cambridge, MA: Harvard University Press.

Pisani, Bob. 2018. "Stock Buybacks Hit a Record $1.1 Trillion, and the Year's Not Over." Trader Talk. CNBC, December 18, 2018. https://www.cnbc.com/2018/12/18/stock-buybacks-hit-a-record-1point1-trillion-and-the-years-not-over.html.

Pisano, Gary P., and Willy C. Shih. 2009. "Restoring American Competitiveness." *Harvard Business Review*, July 1, 2009.

———. 2012. *Producing Prosperity: Why America Needs a Manufacturing Renaissance*. Boston, MA: Harvard Business Review Press.

Png, I. P. L. 2015. "Law and Innovation: Evidence from State Trade Secrets Laws." *Review of Economics and Statistics* 99 (1): 167–179.

Polanyi, Karl. 2001. *The Great Transformation: The Political and Economic Origins of Our Time*. 2nd Beacon Paperback ed. Boston, MA: Beacon Press.

Porter, Michael E. 1998. "Clusters and the New Economics of Competition." *Harvard Business Review*, November 1, 1998.

———. 1998. *The Competitive Advantage of Nations: With a New Introduction*. New York: Free Press.

PricewaterhouseCoopers. 2019. "PwC/CB Insights MoneyTree Explorer." https://www.pwc.com/us/en/industries/technology/moneytree/explorer.html#/. Accessed November 24, 2019.

Priisalu, Jaan, and Rain Ottis. 2017. "Personal Control of Privacy and Data: Estonian Experience." *Health and Technology* 7 (4): 441–451.

Prince, Marcelo, and Willa Plank. 2012. "A Short History of Apple's Manufacturing in the U.S." *Wall Street Journal*, December 6, 2012.

Prud'homme, Dan, and Max Von Zedtwitz. 2018. "The Changing Face of Innovation in China." *MIT Sloan Management Review* 59 (4): 24–32.

Quan, Yuan, and Yin Pingping. 2019. "Feature: IP Education Focuses China's Young Minds." *Xinhua*, September 24, 2019.

———. 2019. "Young Minds Focused on IP Education." *China Daily*, November 1, 2019, Hong Kong edition, sec. Technology.

Rabellotti, Roberta. 2004. "How Globalization Affects Italian Industrial Districts: The Case of Brenta." In *Local Enterprises in the Global Economy: Issues of Governance and Upgrading*, edited by Hubert Schmitz, 140–173. Cheltenham, UK: Edward Elgar.

Ramirez, Edith, Maureen K. Ohlhausen, and Terrell Mcsweeny. 2016. "Patent Assertion Entity Activity: An FTC Study." Washington, DC: Federal Trade Commission.

Rehn, Olli. 1996. "Corporatism and Industrial Competitiveness in Small European States: Austria, Finland and Sweden, 1945–95." PhD diss., University of Oxford.

Reid, T. R. 1986. "'Crosstalk' Gets Caught in Crossfire of Competition." *Washington Post*, April 14, 1986, sec. Business.

Reuters. 2001. "Company News; Via Technologies Is Sued for Patent Infringement." *New York Times*, September 8, 2001, sec. Business.

———. 2012. "Rialto in Jeans, as Venice Finds Cash for Repair." December 14, 2012.

———. 2018. "U.S. Lifts Ban on Suppliers Selling to China's ZTE." July 13, 2018.

———. 2018. "Arizona Says Not Time to Rein in Self-Driving Cars after Uber Fatality." March 21, 2018.

Ribao, Nanfang. 2007. "Xiao Qi Lian Yin Ji Huo Chan Ye Chuang Xin Ji Yin" [School-business marriage enlivens industry innovation gene]. *Nanfang Ribao*, June 28, 2007.

Rin, Marco Da, Thomas Hellmann, and Manju Puri. 2013. "A Survey of Venture Capital Research." In *Handbook of the Economics of Finance*. Vol. 2, edited by George M. Constantinides, Milton Harris, and Rene M. Stulz, 573–648. Amsterdam: Elsevier.

Rivas, Gonzalo. 2012. "La experiencia de CORFO y la transformación productiva de Chile. Evolución, aprendizaje y lecciones de desarrollo." Serie Políticas Públicas y Transformación Productiva. Caracas: CAF.

Rogers, David. 2009. "Senate Passes $787 Billion Stimulus Bill." *Politico*, February 13, 2009.

Romer, Paul M. 1986. "Increasing Returns and Long-Run Growth." *Journal of Political Economy* 94 (5): 1002–1037.

———. 1990. "Endogenous Technological Change." *Journal of Political Economy* 98 (5): S71–102.

Rosenberg, Nathan. 1975. "Problems in the Economist's Conceptualization of Technological Innovation." *History of Political Economy* 7 (4): 456–481.

———. 1983. *Inside the Black Box: Technology and Economics*. Cambridge: Cambridge University Press.

———. 1994. *Exploring the Black Box: Technology, Economics, and History*. Cambridge: Cambridge University Press.

Rosenberg, Nathan, and L. E. Birdzell. 1986. *How the West Grew Rich: The Economic Transformation of the Industrial World*. New York: Basic Books.

Rosenberg, Nathan, and W. Edward Steinmueller. 1988. "Why Are Americans Such Poor Imitators?" *American Economic Review* 78 (2): 229–234.

Rosenthal, Stuart S., and William C. Strange. 2001. "The Determinants of Agglomeration." *Journal of Urban Economics* 50 (2): 191–229.

Rotella, Perry. 2012. "Is Data the New Oil?" *Forbes*, April 2, 2012.

Roth, Erik, Jeongmin Seong, and Jonathan Woetzel. 2015. *Gauging the Strength of Chinese Innovation*. Washington, DC: McKinsey Global Institute.

Rubin, Tzameret H., Tor Helge Aas, and Andrew Stead. 2015. "Knowledge Flow in Technological Business Incubators: Evidence from Australia and Israel." *Technovation* 41–42 (July): 11–24.

Russell, Joseph A. 1942. "Fordlandia and Belterra, Rubber Plantations on the Tapajos River, Brazil." *Economic Geography* 18 (2): 125.

Sabel, Charles, and Anna Lee Saxenian. 2008. "A Fugitive Success." Sitra Reports. Helsinki: Sitra.

Sackett, David L. 1981. "How to Read Clinical Journals: I. Why to Read Them and How to Start Reading Them Critically." *Canadian Medical Association Journal* 124 (5): 555–558.
———. 1991. *Clinical Epidemiology: A Basic Science for Clinical Medicine.* 2nd ed. Boston: Little, Brown.

Sahlman, William A. 1990. "The Structure and Governance of Venture-Capital Organizations." *Journal of Financial Economics* 27 (2): 473–521.

Samford, Steven. 2015. "Innovation and Public Space: The Developmental Possibilities of Regulation in the Global South." *Regulation & Governance* 9 (3): 294–308.

Samson, Adam. 2018. "US Boards to Authorise $1tn in Stock Buybacks in 2018— Goldman." *Financial Times,* August 6, 2018, sec. Markets.

Sanz-Gomez, Rafael. 2015. "The OECD's Nexus Approach to IP Boxes: A European Union Law Perspective." WU International Taxation Research Paper Series no. 2015-12. *SSRN Electronic Journal.* http://dx.doi.org/10.2139/ssrn.2589065.

Sargent, John F., Jr. 2012. "The Obama Administration's Proposal to Establish a National Network for Manufacturing Innovation." CRS Report for Congress. Congressional Research Service.

Satariano, Adam, and Jack Nicas. 2018. "E.U. Fines Google $5.1 Billion in Android Antitrust Case." *New York Times,* July 18, 2018, sec. Technology.

Saxenian, AnnaLee. 1994. *Regional Advantage: Culture and Competition in Silicon Valley and Route 128.* Cambridge, MA: Harvard University Press.

Schumpeter, Joseph A. 2013. *Capitalism, Socialism and Democracy.* London: Routledge.

S.C. Williams Library. 2007. "Patents." F.W. Taylor Collection, Special Collections. November 12, 2007.

Segal, Adam. 2003. *Digital Dragon: High-Technology Enterprises in China.* Cornell Studies in Political Economy. Ithaca, NY: Cornell University Press.

Senor, Dan, and Saul Singer. 2011. *Start-Up Nation: The Story of Israel's Economic Miracle.* Toronto: McClelland & Stewart.

Shapiro, Carl. 2000. "Navigating the Patent Thicket: Cross Licenses, Patent Pools, and Standard Setting." *Innovation Policy and the Economy* 1 (January): 119–150.

Shefer, Daniel, and Amnon Frenkel. 2002. "For the Support of Entrepreneurship." Israeli Financing Instruments for the Support of Entrepreneurship. Haifa, Israel: Samuel Neaman Institute.

Sherwood, Harriet. 2011. "Israeli Protests: 430,000 Take to Streets to Demand Social Justice." *Guardian,* September 4, 2011, sec. World News.

Shiller, Robert J. 2014. "Speculative Asset Prices." *American Economic Review* 104 (6): 1486–1517.
———. 2019. *Narrative Economics: How Stories Go Viral and Drive Major Economic Events.* Princeton, NJ: Princeton University Press.

Shimokawa, Koichi. 1994. "From the Ford System to the Just-in-Time Production System." *Japanese Yearbook on Business History* 10: 83–105.

Shiraz, Muhammad, Md. Whaiduzzaman, and Abdullah Gani. 2013. "A Study on Anatomy of Smartphone." *Computer Communication & Collaboration* 1.1: 24–31.

Shopify Inc. 2015. "Form F-1 Registration Statement." Washington, DC: Securities and Exchange Commission.

Simmie, James, and Ron Martin. 2010. "The Economic Resilience of Regions: Towards an Evolutionary Approach." *Cambridge Journal of Regions, Economy and Society* 3 (1): 27–43.

Sisson, William. 1992. "A Revolution in Steel: Mass Production in Pennsylvania, 1867–1901." *IA: The Journal of the Society for Industrial Archeology* 18 (1–2): 79–93.

Smith, Yves. 2018. "Fake 'Unicorns' Are Running Roughshod over the Venture Capital Industry." Intelligencer. *New York Magazine*, November 14, 2018.

Solomon, Shoshanna. 2018. "Israel to Provide Loan Guarantees for Startups, Tech Chief Says." *Times of Israel*, February 28, 2018.

Sommer, Jeff. 2014. "Are Markets Efficient? Even the Supreme Court Is Weighing In." *New York Times*, June 28, 2014, sec. Your Money.

Souther, Jonathan Mark. 2017. *Believing in Cleveland: Managing Decline in "The Best Location in the Nation."* Urban Life, Landscape, and Policy. Philadelphia: Temple University Press.

Spiller, Pablo T., and Morris Teubal. 1977. "Analysis of R&D Failure." *Research Policy* 6 (3): 254–275.

Steinbock, Dan. 2001. *The Nokia Revolution: The Story of an Extraordinary Company That Transformed an Industry.* New York: AMACOM.

Stone, Brad. 2010. "Apple Sues Nexus One Maker HTC." *New York Times*, March 2, 2010, sec. Technology.

Stoneman, Paul, and Giuliana Battisti. 2010. "The Diffusion of New Technology." In *Handbook of the Economics of Innovation*, edited by Bronwyn H. Hall and Nathan Rosenberg. Vol. 2, 733–760. Amsterdam: North-Holland.

Stradling, D., and R. Stradling. 2008. "Perceptions of the Burning River: Deindustrialization and Cleveland's Cuyahoga River." *Environmental History* 13 (3): 515–535.

Sturgeon, Timothy J. 2002. "Modular Production Networks: A New American Model of Industrial Organization." *Industrial and Corporate Change* 11 (3): 451–496.

Sturgeon, Timothy, Johannes Van Biesebroeck, and Gary Gereffi. 2008. "Value Chains, Networks and Clusters: Reframing the Global Automotive Industry." *Journal of Economic Geography* 8 (3): 297–321.

Subcommittee on Advanced Manufacturing. 2018. "Strategy for American Leadership in Advanced Manufacturing." Washington, DC: Executive Office of the President of the United States.

Sur, Roger L., and Philipp Dahm. 2011. "History of Evidence-Based Medicine." *Indian Journal of Urology* 27 (4): 487–489.

"The Sveriges Riksbank Prize in Economic Sciences in Memory of Alfred Nobel 1974." n.d. NobelPrize.org. Accessed January 21, 2020.

Sweeny, Alastair. 2009. *BlackBerry Planet: The Story of Research in Motion and the Little Device That Took the World by Storm.* Mississauga, ON: John Wiley & Sons Canada.

Takeishi, Akira, and Yaichi Aoshima. 2006. "Case Study Shimano: Market Creation through Component Integration." In *Management of Technology and Innovation in Japan*, edited by Cornelius Herstatt, Christoph Stockstrom, Hugo Tschirky, and Akio Nagahira, 29–48. Berlin: Springer.

Tang, Li, Michael Murphree, and Dan Breznitz. 2016. "Structured Uncertainty: A Pilot Study on Innovation in China's Mobile Phone Handset Industry." *Journal of Technology Transfer* 41 (5): 1168–1194.

Taylor, Phil. 2019. "Adapsyn Signs $162M Microbe-Mining Deal with Pfizer." *FierceBiotech*, August 7, 2019.

Teubal, Morris. 1982. "The R&D Performance through Time of Young, High-Technology Firms: Methodology and an Illustration." *Research Policy* 11 (6): 333–346.

————. 1997. "A Catalytic and Evolutionary Approach to Horizontal Technology Policies (HTPs)." *Research Policy* 25 (8): 1161–1188.

Thiel, Peter A., and Blake Masters. 2014. *Zero to One: Notes on Startups, or How to Build the Future*. New York: Crown Business.

Thomson Reuters and Clarivate Analytics, eds. 2020. *InCites*. New York: Thomson Reuters. Accessed February 6, 2020.

Times Higher Education. 2018. "World University Rankings." September 26, 2018.

Torres, Cristian. 2015. "Gobierno define los siete sectores estratégicos para el desarrollo de clústers en el país." *Redbionova*, February 6, 2015.

Trajtenberg, Manuel. 2000. "R&D Policy in Israel: An Overview and Reassessment." Working Paper 7930. Cambridge, MA: National Bureau of Economic Research.

————. 2001. "Innovation in Israel 1968–1997: A Comparative Analysis Using Patent Data." *Research Policy* 30 (3): 363–389.

Triumvira Immunologics. 2020. "Technology & Science." Austin: Triumvira Immunologics. Accessed January 20, 2020.

Tsai, Bi-Huei, and Yiming Li. 2009. "Cluster Evolution of IC Industry from Taiwan to China." *Technological Forecasting and Social Change* 76 (8): 1092–1104.

Tsang, Amie, and Adam Satariano. 2018. "Apple to Add $1 Billion Campus in Austin, Tex., in Broad U.S. Hiring Push." *New York Times*, December 13, 2018, sec. Technology.

Upham, S. Phineas. 2006. "Innovation and the Interrelatedness of Core Competencies: How Taiwan's Giant Bicycles Broke into the US Bicycle Market." *Managing Global Transitions* 4 (1): 41–62.

US Patent Office. 2020. "Third-Party Preissuance Submissions." Accessed February 1, 2020.

US Small Business Administration. n.d. "Investment Capital." Funding Programs. Washington, DC: US Small Business Administration. Accessed January 30, 2020.

Utterback, James M., and William J. Abernathy. 1975. "A Dynamic Model of Process and Product Innovation." *Omega* 3 (6): 639–656.

Varian, Hal R. 2010. *Intermediate Microeconomics: A Modern Approach*. 8th ed. New York: W. W. Norton.

Vermaelen, Theo. 1981. "Common Stock Repurchases and Market Signalling: An Empirical Study." *Journal of Financial Economics* 9 (2): 139–183.

VIA Technologies, Inc. and Subsidiaries. 2002. "Consolidated Financial Statements for the Years Ended December 31, 2001 and 2000 and Independent Auditors' Report." Fremont, CA: VIA Technologies.

————. 2018. "Consolidated Financial Statements for the Years Ended December 31, 2017 and 2016 and Independent Auditors' Report." Fremont, CA: VIA Technologies.

Vidra, Robyn Klingler, Martin Kenney, and Dan Breznitz. 2016. "Policies for Financing Entrepreneurship through Venture Capital: Learning from the Successes of Israel and Taiwan." *International Journal of Innovation and Regional Development* 7 (3): 203.

Wade, Robert. 2004. *Governing the Market: Economic Theory and the Role of Government in East Asian Industrialization*. 2nd paperback ed., with a new introduction by the author. Princeton, NJ: Princeton University Press.

Wang, Lee-Rong. 1995. "Taiwan's Venture Capital." *Journal of Industry Studies* 2, no. 1 (August 1, 1995): 83–94.

Wakabayashi, Daisuke. 2017. "Google Is Buying HTC's Smartphone Expertise for $1.1 Billion." *New York Times*, September 20, 2017, sec. Technology.

——. 2018. "Self-Driving Uber Car Kills Pedestrian in Arizona, Where Robots Roam." *New York Times*, March 19, 2018, sec. Technology.

Wang, Jici, and John H. Bradbury. 1986. "The Changing Industrial Geography of the Chinese Special Economic Zones." *Economic Geography* 62 (4): 307–320.

Warrian, Peter. 2016. "Biotech and Lunch Buckets: The Curious Knowledge Networks of Steel Town." *Innovations Systems Research Network (ISRN) Working Paper*. Toronto, ON: University of Toronto.

Warrian, Peter, and Allison Bramwell. 2016. "Innovation in an Industrial City: Economic Transformation in Hamilton." In *Growing Urban Economies: Innovation, Creativity, and Governance in Canadian City-Regions*, edited by David A. Wolfe and Meric S. Gertler, 181–210. Toronto: University of Toronto Press.

Warrian, Peter. 2020. *Canadian Metallurgy, Its Benefits and Contribution to the Economy and Society*. Ottawa, ON: Ingentium.

Williams, Heidi L. 2013. "Intellectual Property Rights and Innovation: Evidence from the Human Genome." *Journal of Political Economy* 121 (1): 1–27.

——. 2017. "How Do Patents Affect Research Investments?" *Annual Review of Economics* 9 (1): 441–469.

Williamson, Oliver E. 1971. "Managerial Discretion, Organization Form, and the Multi-Division Hypothesis." In *The Corporate Economy: Growth, Competition, and Innovative Potential*, edited by Robin Marris and Adrian Wood, 343–386. London: Palgrave Macmillan UK.

Wilson, Mark. 2008. "T-Mobile G1: Full Details of the HTC Dream Android Phone." *Gizmodo*, September 23, 2008.

WIPO (World Intellectual Property Organization). 2019. "WIPO Statistics Database." Geneva: WIPO.

Wong, Joseph. 2011. *Betting on Biotech: Innovation and the Limits of Asia's Developmental State*. Ithaca, NY: Cornell University Press.

Wu, Wei-Li, and Yi-Chih Lee. 2014. "From OEM Supplier to a Global Leading Company." *Journal of Business Case Studies (Online)* 10 (3): 225.

Yan, Sophia. 2017. "'Made in China' Isn't So Cheap Anymore, and That Could Spell Headache for Beijing." *CNBC (Online)*, February 27, 2017.

Yan, Yu. 2016. "China's Labor Market: Shrinking Workforce, Rising Wages." *China Daily*, November 21, 2016.

Yang, Chun, and Haifeng Liao. 2010. "Backward Linkages of Cross-Border Production Networks of Taiwanese PC Investment in the Pearl River Delta, China." *Tijdschrift Voor Economische En Sociale Geografie* 101 (2): 199–217.

Yoffie, David B., and Renee Kim. 2009. "HTC Corp. in 2009." HBS Case Collection. Cambridge, MA: Harvard Business School, June.

Yoffie, David B., Juan Alcacer, and Renee Kim. 2012. "HTC Corp. in 2012." HBS Case Collection. Cambridge, MA: Harvard Business School, May.

Yu, Fu-Lai Tony. 2012. "Giants: Taiwan's World Brand Bicycle." In *Entrepreneurship and Taiwan's Economic Dynamics*, edited by Fu-Lai Tony Yu, 89–100. Berlin: Springer.

Yuan, Yiming, Hongyi Guo, Wieqi Li, Hongfei Wu, Weiqi Li, Shanshan Luo, Haiqing Lin, and Yuan. 2010. "China's First Special Economic Zone: The Case of Shenzhen." In *Building Engines for Growth and Competitiveness in China: Experience with Special Economic Zones and Industrial Clusters*, edited by Douglas Zhihua Zeng, 55–85. Washington, DC: World Bank.

Zehavi, Amos, and Dan Breznitz. 2017. "Distribution Sensitive Innovation Policies: Conceptualization and Empirical Examples." *Research Policy* 46 (1): 327–336.

Zheng, Douglas Zhihua. 2010. "How Do Special Economic Zones and Industrial Clusters Drive China's Rapid Development." In *Building Engines for Growth and Competitiveness in China: Experience with Special Economic Zones and Industrial Clusters*, edited by Douglas Zhihua Zheng, 1–53. Washington, DC: World Bank.

Zider, Bob. 1998. "How Venture Capital Works." *Harvard Business Review*, November 1, 1998.

Zuboff, Shoshana. 2019. *The Age of Surveillance Capitalism: The Fight for a Human Future at the New Frontier of Power.* New York: PublicAffairs.

Zysman, John. 1983. *Governments, Markets, and Growth: Financial Systems and the Politics of Industrial Change.* Cornell Studies in Political Economy. Ithaca, NY: Cornell University Press.

———. 1994. "How Institutions Create Historically Rooted Trajectories of Growth." *Industrial and Corporate Change* 3 (1): 243–283.

Zysman, John, and Dan Breznitz. 2012. "Double Bind: Governing the Economy in an ICT Era." *Governance* 25 (1): 129–150.

Zysman, John, Stuart Feldman, Kenji E. Kushida, Jonathan Murray, and Niels Christian Nielsen. 2013. *Services with Everything: The ICT-Enabled Digital Transformation of Services.* Oxford: Oxford University Press.

Zysman, John, Martin Kenney, and Laura D'Andrea Tyson. 2019. "Beyond Hype and Despair: Developing Healthy Communities in the Era of Intelligent Tools." Innovation Policy White Paper 3414691. Toronto: Munk School of Global Affairs and Public Policy.

Index

For the benefit of digital users, indexed terms that span two pages (e.g., 52–53) may, on occasion, appear on only one of those pages.

Figures are indicated by an italic *f* following the page number.